JOURNAL FOR THE STUDY OF THE OLD TESTAMENT SUPPLEMENT SERIES
211

Sheffield Academic Press

Retribution and Eschatology in Chronicles

Brian E. Kelly

Journal for the Study of the Old Testament
Supplement Series 211

Published by
Sheffield Academic Press Ltd
Mansion House
19 Kingfield Road
Sheffield, S11 9AS
England

Typeset by Sheffield Academic Press
and
Printed on acid-free paper in Great Britain
by Bookcraft
Midsomer Norton, Somerset

British Library Cataloguing in Publication Data

A catalogue record for this book is available
from the British Library

ISBN 1-85075-579-5

CONTENTS

Contents

ACKNOWLEDGMENTS

This study is a slight revision of a dissertation submitted to the University of Bristol in July 1993, which has been updated to take account of works on Chronicles which have since appeared, especially Sara Japhet's magisterial commentary (1993). All translations are my own, unless otherwise stated. I wish to express my warmest thanks to my supervisors Dr J.J. Bimson of Trinity College, Bristol, Dr M.J. Selman of Spurgeon's College, London, and Professor H.G.M. Williamson of Oxford University for their encouragement and generous help, and not least for the benefits of their own very considerable scholarship. Naturally the customary disclaimers apply!

Funding for my study was provided by the British Academy, with further generous financial help from the Tyndale House Council, Cambridge. I am also grateful to Tyndale House for the use of its superb library facilities on several occasions, and to Miss Su Brown, Assistant Librarian at Trinity College, Bristol, for patiently tracking down obscure bibliographical items. I wish to thank Professor David Clines and the editors of the Sheffield Academic Press for accepting and preparing this work for publication.

My greatest debt of gratitude is to my wife Anne, who sacrificed much to make this study possible. I dedicate this work to her with love.

Scarborough, December 1995.

ABBREVIATIONS

AB	Anchor Bible
ABR	*Australian Biblical Review*
AnBib	Analecta Biblica
ATD	Das Alte Testament Deutsch
AUR	*Aberdeen University Review*
BA	*Biblical Archaeologist*
BASOR	*Bulletin of the American Schools of Oriental Research*
BEATAJ	Beiträge zur Erforschung des Alten Testaments und des Antiken Judentums
Bib	*Biblica*
BKAT	Biblische Kommentar: Altes Testament
BTB	*Biblical Theology Bulletin*
BWANT	Beiträge zur Wissenschaft vom Alten und Neuen Testament
BZ	*Biblische Zeitschrift*
CBC	Cambridge Biblical Commentaries
CBQ	*Catholic Biblical Quarterly*
ConBOT	Coniectanea biblica, Old Testament
CTM	*Concordia Theological Monthly*
EvT	*Evangelische Theologie*
ETL	*Ephemerides Theologicae Lovaniensiae*
FOTL	Forms of the Old Testament Literature
FRLANT	Forschungen zur Religion und Literatur des Alten und Neuen Testaments
HAT	Handbuch zum Alten Testament
HBT	*Horizons in Biblical Theology*
HSAT	Die Heilige Schrift des Alten Testaments
HSM	Harvard Semitic Monograph
HTR	*Harvard Theological Review*
ICC	International Critical Commentary
IEJ	*Israel Exploration Journal*
Int	*Interpretation*
JAOS	*Journal of the American Oriental Society*
JBL	*Journal of Biblical Literature*
JETS	*Journal of the Evangelical Theological Society*
JJS	*Journal of Jewish Studies*
JPOS	*Journal of the Palestine Oriental Society*

JSNTSup	*Journal for the Study of the New Testament*, Supplement Series
JSOT	*Journal for the Study of the Old Testament*
JSOTSup	*Journal for the Study of the Old Testament*, Supplement Series
JSS	*Journal of Semitic Studies*
JTS	*Journal of Theological Studies*
KAT	Kommentar zum Alten Testament
NCB	New Century Bible
OLP	*Orientalia Lovaniensia Periodica*
OTL	Old Testament Library
OTS	*Oudtestamentische Studiën*
PEGLMBS	*Proceedings, Eastern Great Lakes and Midwest Biblical Societies*
PEQ	*Palestinian Exploration Quarterly*
RB	*Revue Biblique*
RTP	*Revue de théologie et de philosophie*
SBLSP	*Society of Biblical Literature Seminar Papers*
SBT	Studies in Biblical Theology
SEÅ	*Svensk exegetisk årsbok*
THAT	E. Jenni and C. Westermann (eds.), *Theologisches Handwörterbuch zum Alten Testament*
TynBul	*Tyndale Bulletin*
TDOT	G.J. Botterweck and H.H. Ringgren (eds.), *Theological Dictionary of the Old Testament*
TOTC	Tyndale Old Testament Commentaries
TQ	*Theologische Quartalschrift*
TZ	*Theologische Zeitschrift*
VT	*Vetus Testamentum*
VTSup	*Vetus Testamentum*, Supplements
WBC	World Biblical Commentary
WTJ	*Westminster Theological Journal*
ZAW	*Zeitschrift für die alttestamentliche Wissenschaft*
ZDPV	*Zietschrift des deutschen Palästina-Vereins*
ZTK	*Zeitschrift für Theologie und Kirche*

Chapter 1

THE SCOPE OF THIS STUDY

1. *Introduction*

'Retribution' and 'eschatology' refer to two of the principal concerns of theological investigation of the books of Chronicles: how the author conceived of divine reward and punishment, and the hope or expectation which he entertained for his community.[1] Both themes are by any reckoning of the first importance for the interpretation of the work. They are regularly discussed in reviews of the Chronicler's theology,[2] where it is typically argued that the writer develops these themes in ways that diverge significantly from the general Old Testament tradition. There is broad scholarly agreement on the nature and significance of the Chronicler's 'retributive' thought, but no consensus about his 'eschatological' outlook.

The present study undertakes a fresh examination of these questions. It goes beyond previous investigations in arguing that these researches have, in large measure, misconstrued the nature and significance of retribution in Chronicles, and it offers a new and more positive appraisal of the phenomenon. Similarly, the 'eschatology' of the work (its outlook

1. The singular is used without prejudice to the question whether the work should be attributed to an individual or a circle, but the consensus opinion, which I consider likely, is that an individual author is responsible for the great majority of the work (albeit that he was handling traditional materials), and has expressed himself throughout with a distinctive personal style.

2. Among commentaries, summarizing reviews of the Chronicler's theology usually take the form of a number of discrete topics: cf. Rothstein and Hänel 1927: ix-xliv; Rudolph 1955: xiii-xxiv; Myers 1966: lxiv-lxxxv; Williamson 1982: 24-33; Braun 1986: xxix-xli. Similar treatment can be found in book (Noth 1967; Japhet 1989) and article form (North 1963; Braun 1979). A different, integrative approach which looks for a 'centre' or 'thematizing idea' is represented by Mosis in his 1973 monograph (Chronicles as an extended typological treatment of the theme of exile and restoration) and Johnstone in his programmatic essay on מעל (1986).

on the future) is examined from several perspectives which together provide a wider base for determining the shape of the writer's theological outlook than earlier studies concentrating largely on the Chronistic portrayal of David have allowed. Besides contributing to a more balanced assessment of the theological outlook of the book, a careful interpretation of these central concerns may, it is hoped, cast some light on the *Sitz im Leben* and purpose of the work.

The form of this study is as follows. This introductory chapter discusses questions of the unity, provenance and dating of the Chronicler's work, as a preliminary step to delineating his theology. The following chapter reviews and criticizes the prevailing understandings of the Chronicler's doctrine of retribution, for which Chapters 3–5 proposes a fresh interpretation. The approach here is based mainly on a synoptic comparison of Chronicles with its *Vorlage* (taking into account especially the writer's additions and interpretative comments), but the likely traditio-historical background to the writer's thought and the narrative structure of his presentation are also examined.[3] Chapters 6–8 examine the eschatological question in a similar way. Chapter 9 reviews both themes in relation to the Deuteronomistic History, while Chapter 10 presents the conclusions and some implications for further investigation.

Our study must begin by considering two closely related matters: the boundaries of the Chronicler's work, and its provenance and unity. Although it is becoming increasingly common in modern biblical interpretation to concentrate on the 'final' or 'canonical' form of a given work, it remains a necessary task to determine the original extent of a discrete text. This is still a problematic matter where Chronicles is concerned, not least because it is frequently maintained that the work has been significantly supplemented by other hands at different historical periods.[4]

2. The Extent of the Chronicler's Work

The principal question here is the literary relationship of Chronicles to Ezra–Nehemiah: should these books be considered as separate works

---

3.   Some of the historical problems raised by the Chronicler's additional material, most of which is used to illustrate his retributive doctrine, are discussed in Chapter 5.

4.   It may be added that the validity of literary approaches to the biblical text depends upon historically delimiting that text or the stages of its growth.

(presumably by different authors[5]) or do they belong together (in part at least) as a continuous composition, the 'Chronicler's History Work' ('chronistisches Geschichtswerk', *ChrG*)? A decision made at this level has immediate bearing on how the writer's theology and purpose should be assessed, since it defines how much and what kind of material can be properly termed 'Chronistic'. Also related to this question, and discussed below, are the dating of the work and whether the genealogies of 1 Chronicles 1–9 were originally part of the composition. At present there is no overall scholarly agreement on any of these matters, so it remains a necessary (if only preliminary) task to set out and justify a working position.

The previous consensus, which held that Chronicles, Ezra and Nehemiah originally belonged together as a single continuous composition, was due first to a brief but seminal discussion by Zunz (1966),[6] who proposed four basic arguments for that conclusion. These were as follows:

1. The parallel between Ezra 1.1-3a and 2 Chron. 36.22-23.
2. The evidence of 1 Esdras.
3. Linguistic similarities between the books.
4. Similarity in outlook, interests and theology.

Subsequent work mainly elaborated or modified these points. Only a small number of scholars rejected this consensus,[7] which prevailed without substantial challenge until 1968 when Japhet re-opened the question with an investigation of the linguistic evidence. Williamson (1977a: 5-82) extended this challenge with an examination not only of the vocabulary of Chronicles and Ezra–Nehemiah, but also the evidence of the Greek versions, Josephus and 1 Esdras, and the ideology reflected in the respective works. Both Japhet and Williamson have concluded decisively that Chronicles and Ezra–Nehemiah could not be the work of the same author. Each of their arguments has in turn been disputed, but the current tendency is to support distinguishing authorship.[8] The following

5. Willi's suggestion (1972: 181) that Chronicles and Ezra–Nehemiah are independent works of the same compiler has found little favour; cf. Ackroyd 1991: 329 n. 2.

6. Zunz 1966: 21-32. His work was originally published in 1832.

7. See Williamson 1977a: 5 n. 3 for details.

8. Recent studies which now distinguish authorship include: Newsome 1975, Braun 1979, Johnstone 1986, Throntveit 1987, De Vries 1989, Strübind 1991, Riley 1993, Selman 1994a; 1994b. The new arguments are rejected (or at least considered

discussion surveys and evaluates the debate since 1968. It supports Japhet's and Williamson's conclusion, although it interprets some of the evidence in different ways.

1. *The Parallel of Ezra 1.1-3a and 2 Chronicles 36.22-23*

The parallel between these passages is close but not exact: there are slight differences in usage and Chronicles appears to end rather abruptly, in mid-sentence (ויעל). This sudden and unexpected conclusion suggests that it has been abbreviated from the fuller form in Ezra. The secondary version in Chronicles is sometimes attributed to a later hand by proponents of separate authorship.[9] However, as I will argue in Chapter 8, it was in keeping with the purpose of the Chronicler to conclude his work on a note that resumes but also modifies the opening words of Ezra.

The overlap has been explained as reflecting the history of the canonization process. According to Curtis and Madsen (1910: 3), the contents of Ezra–Nehemiah were considered as more important and so were accepted into the canon first. The overlap was then presumably intended to signal the original unity of the work when Chronicles was admitted into the canon. However, Willi (1972: 176-84) and Williamson (1977a: 10-11) argue that such a view is without any historical foundation and misrepresents the process of canonization. More recently, Haran (1985: 1-11; 1986: 18-20) has maintained that the 'Chronistic work' (1 and 2 Chronicles and Ezra–Nehemiah) was too long to be contained on one scroll (according to the prevailing custom of assigning a single scroll to each sacred work), so Ezra 1.1-3 was added as a catchline to facilitate the reader's transition from the scroll containing Chronicles to the one containing its continuation, Ezra–Nehemiah. Williamson (1987b: 56-59) rejects this claim, pointing out that neither the Pentateuch nor the Deuteronomistic History has catchlines, although both corpora are divided over several scrolls. To the objection that there is a thematic break between Chronicles and Ezra–Nehemiah (the caesura of the exile), it should be noted that there are also decisive thematic breaks between portions of the Pentateuch and the Deuteronomistic History, and yet no catchlines are inserted to keep the narrative flowing without interruption.

---

inconclusive) by Gunneweg 1981: 146-61; McKenzie 1985: 17-25; Becker 1988; Blenkinsopp 1989: 47-54; Oeming 1990: 41-47; Mason 1990: 7-11; see below for further comment.

9. Cf. Williamson 1982: 415; De Vries 1989: 11.

Williamson (1983) considers Ezra 1–6 to be a later composition than Chronicles, and suggests that 2 Chron. 36.22-23 was subsequently added with a 'liturgical' motive of ending the book on a positive note (1977a: 7-10; 1982: 419). Japhet (1991: 310 n. 47) remarks that this argument is not otherwise attested:

> It may be based on the technique by which the Massoretes provide a 'positive' conclusion for all biblical books which have a negative ending; cf. the Massorah conclusions of Isaiah, Malachi, Ecclesiastes, and Lamentations. In all these cases, however, the appended verse is taken from the same passage, as near as possible to the end.

Since it is the Chronicler's practice to make free use of the earlier scriptures of his community (and other possible citations from Ezra–Nehemiah are noted below), I consider it more likely that the writer himself adopted these verses from Ezra and assimilated them to his own style.[10] There is, of course, no versional evidence that the verses were not once part of the original composition. In any case, even proponents of the unity of Chronicles with Ezra–Nehemiah recognize that this doublet provides no evidence of the original extent of the Chronicler's work.[11]

2. The Evidence of 1 Esdras

This apocryphal work represents a Greek version of the last two chapters of Chronicles, Ezra and Neh. 8.1-13 in a continuous narrative. It also includes portions without parallel in the Hebrew Bible (1 Esd. 1.21-22; 3.1–5.6) and presents Ezra 1–4 in a different order from the MT.[12] 1 Esdras can be seen either as a fragment of an original *ChrG* or as a compilation from Chronicles and Ezra–Nehemiah (which is itself fragmentary).[13] Recently it has been proposed that the extant form of 1 Esdras is itself a complete work as it was written, or at least that the present beginning is original. There are some persuasive features to this suggestion. If it is correct, 1 Esdras is clearly a derivative work and cannot be adduced as evidence for the original form of the Chronicler's work.

10. So also Japhet 1993: 1062.
11. Cf. McKenzie 1985: 17.
12. Cf. Pohlmann 1970: 14 for a tabulation of the approximate relationship between the books.
13. Cf. Pohlmann 1970: 15-26 for a review of opinions on this question up to 1955.

The 'fragment hypothesis' has been defended in the greatest detail by Pohlmann (1970). He considers the present beginning (καὶ ἤγαγεν) too abrupt and unusual to be original, and takes a similar view of the ending (9.55, καὶ ἐπισυνήχθησαν). Pohlmann argues that 1 Esd. 1.1 (= 2 Chron. 35.1, the account of Josiah's passover) presupposes a *Vorlage* which began at least at 2 Chronicles 34, with Josiah's accession and reforms. However, he then immediately suggests that the work originally contained the whole of Chronicles (p. 33). He also considers that the evidence of Josephus (*Ant.* 11.1-183) shows that he used 1 Esdras and did not know Ezra–Nehemiah in its present form (pp. 114-26).

The 'compilation hypothesis' is defended by Williamson in a detailed response to Pohlmann (1977a: 14-36). Williamson concurs with Pohlmann that the present beginning and ending of 1 Esdras are not original. He concedes that the work may have begun with the equivalent of 2 Chronicles 34. The witness of Josephus is equivocal, but the additional material in 1 Esd. 1.21-22 (on which Pohlmann fails to comment) is a clear indication that 1 Esdras is a secondary work and not simply a fragment of the Chronicler's original composition. These verses state that Josiah acted uprightly (καὶ ὠρθώθη τὰ ἔργα 'Ιωσίου[14]) toward his Lord, but then notes that the people of that time were sinning against the Lord 'more than every people and kingdom...so that the words of the Lord rose up against Israel'. Williamson considers 1 Esd. 1.22 to be a repudiation of the Chronicler's doctrine of retribution (which presumably absolved previous generations from their share of guilt in the exile) and finds instead a veiled reference to Manasseh: 'The words echo precisely the judgment on Manasseh's reign already mentioned in both 2 Kgs 21.9 and 2 Chron. 33.9, and the reference—*en tois emprosthen chronois*—makes it clear that the reader is expected to appreciate this' (1977a: 19).

The text is not easy to interpret, but it appears from 1 Esd. 1.22 (κατ' αὐτόν) that Josiah's reign is in view and that the conduct of that time is being described.[15] Van der Kooij[16] points out that the distinction in

14. ὀρθόομαι can mean 'to succeed', but the emphasis in 1 Esd. 1.21 is not on the success of Josiah's deeds but on their piety (ἐν καρδίᾳ πλήρει εὐσεβείας).

15. *Pace* Williamson 1977a: 19 n. 1, χρόνοις is better taken as 'times' rather than as 'written records' (the parallel with 1 Esd. 1.40 is not exact).

16. Van der Kooij 1991a. It may also be noted here that the verse need not be taken as a repudiation of the Chronicler's doctrine of retribution: as I argue in Chapter 4, this is more complex than is generally allowed, and already in 2 Chron. 28

vv. 21-22 is between the pious king and 'those who sinned', a contrast that corresponds exactly with Huldah's oracle, where Josiah is commended but Judah's doom is pronounced because of the people's disobedience (2 Kgs 22.15-20 = 2 Chron. 34.23-28). The oracle also speaks of the 'words (pl.) which you have heard' (cf. 1 Esd. 1.22, λογοὶ). An allusion to this passage implies instead that 2 Chronicles 34 was not part of the *Vorlage* of 1 Esdras. Van der Kooij adduces other evidence from this verse and elsewhere which indicates the originality of the present beginning of 1 Esdras (1991a: 249-51). Although its form (καὶ + verb of action) is 'abrupt' and striking (Pohlmann, Mowinckel), this could reflect the translation style of the work, and has analogies in Lev. 1.1 and Num. 1.1. A closer analogy is found in Chronicles itself, in 1 Chron. 10.1-2, which abruptly begins the narrative without identifying Saul (although his genealogy is given in 1 Chron. 9.35-36) or the circumstances of the battle. Van der Kooij finds a further point of comparison in the form of these chapters:

> Just as in 1 Chron. 10, the author of 1 Esdr. 1 does not offer his remarks about King Josiah until later in the text, viz. at the end of v. 20 (cf. 1 Chron. 10: at the end of the chapter). 1.20 gave him the first opportunity to formulate in the text his general remarks, in the sense of a judgment of the king and the people. (1991a: 251)[17]

This approach is complemented by Eskenazi's recent suggestion (1986: 39-61) that 1 Esdras is a distinct composition by the Chronicler himself. She argues that the principal ideological characteristics of the two works are similar, and notes that both end apparently in mid-sentence with a verb (ויעל, contrast Ezra 1.3; καὶ ἐπισυνήχθησαν, contrast Neh. 8.13). Eskenazi comments (1986: 57): 'Each of these [concluding] verbs can be construed as a keynote or as a pointer to the communal task for the immediate future.' The argument that the present ending of 1 Esdras is original and not mutilated has found little support from commentators[18]

the Chronicler has signalled the coming exile as the *inevitable* outcome of the people's disobedience (a view reiterated in 2 Chron. 34.25).

17. 'Wie in I Chr 10 bietet der Autor von I Esr 1 seine Bemerkungen zum König Josia erst später im Text, nämlich im Anschluß an V. 20 (vgl. I Chr 10: am Ende des Kapitels). 1,20 bot ihm die erste Gelegenheit im Text, seine allgemeinen Bemerkungen, im Sinne einer Beurteilung des Königs und des Volkes, zu formulieren.'

18. Williamson 1977a: 21-22. See also Coggins and Knibb 1979: 74 for a brief discussion of the possibility that the present ending is original.

but it may account more easily for the fact that Josephus's use of this work apparently breaks off at this point.[19] A further study by van der Kooij (1991b) makes just this point and argues that the last two words (καὶ ἐπισυνήχθησαν) should be understood not as a short and independent phrase (which would be very unusual) but as part of the ὅτι-clause of v. 55. As a result, the last pericope of the work, 9.37-55, would not end abruptly but finish with a clause giving the reasons for the festivity and joy, a feature which would be comparable to the description in 7.10-15. On this basis, the present ending of 1 Esdras would be original.

3. *Linguistic Similarities between the Books*

The lexical and syntactical features of Chronicles have been the subject of detailed investigation. It is agreed that these works have a great deal in common linguistically: this is apparent from the extensive lists of 'peculiarities of style and vocabulary' drawn up by Driver (1913: 535-40), and Curtis and Madsen (1910: 27-36), and more recently, from Polzin's study (1976) of the syntax and lexicography of Late Biblical Hebrew (LBH).

Appeals to linguistic evidence are necessarily limited in what they can

---

19. Not all of Eskenazi's arguments are convincing. Her description of the Chronicler's doctrine of retribution (1986: 51-53) is inaccurate, while the story of the three guardsmen (1 Esd. 3.1-5.6; cf. pp. 46-47), upon which she lays some emphasis, is almost certainly an interpolation, and thus has no bearing in a comparison of the works. Nevertheless, Eskenazi rightly notes the emphasis in 1 Esdras on the Davidide Zerubbabel (an emphasis absent from Ezra–Nehemiah). McKenzie (1985: 18-25) has defended a modified form of the 'fragment hypothesis' against Williamson. His position depends on Cross's argument (1975) that the first edition of Chronicles was equivalent to 1 Chron. 10–2 Chron. 34 + 1 Esd. 1.1–5.65 (= Ezra 3.13). This in turn reflects in part R. Klein's contention that 1 Esdras preserves an older text type of Ezra than Ezra MT (1966; 1969: 99-107). However, Klein's interpretation of the data may be questioned (cf. Eskenazi 1986: 60 n. 63), while McKenzie's (and Cross's) reconstruction of the prehistory of the text is challenged by the likelihood that Ezra 2 (= 1 Esd. 5.7-46) is dependent on Neh. 7.1-72a, a passage which is not paralleled in 1 Esdras (cf. Williamson 1985: 29-31). McKenzie's explanation for the absence of 1 Esd. 1.21-22 from Chronicles (1985: 163-64, 177-78) is unconvincing and lacking in methodological control. Finally, we should note the early and separate translation of Chronicles and Ezra–Nehemiah in the LXX (the LXX of Chronicles originating probably in Alexandria in the third century BCE; cf. Allen 1974: 21-23), which is an important early witness against any original unity of the works.

establish. Apart from the difficulties of distinguishing sources and determining the right comparative methods, by themselves such approaches can affirm at best only the *likelihood* of common authorship, a conclusion which must be corroborated by other means. Talshir (1988: 167) admits as much:

> [I]n order to prove that two works are by separate authors it is sufficient to prove that clear-cut oppositions in language and style exist between them. In contrast, there is no simple way to prove the opposite; for affinity in language between two literary works is no proof of authorship.

Japhet's ground-breaking article (1968) set out to provide just such evidence of 'opposition in language' between Chronicles and Ezra–Nehemiah. She argued for thirty-six distinctions between these works in three areas: linguistic opposition in the formation of the imperfect consecutive and the form of theophoric names ending in יָ or יְהוּ; technical terms dealing with the cult; and stylistic peculiarities. Her work has been challenged, but in my view not decisively.[20]

---

20. Cf. Welten 1973: 4 n. 18; Cross 1975: 14; Gunneweg 1981: 147. Three recent substantial discussions of the language of LBH should be mentioned here. (1) Polzin (1976: 54-55) questions Japhet's conclusions, although his challenge is really only at the level of how Japhet understands the relationship of the Hebrew of Chronicles to the 'standard' practice of LBH. Polzin is concerned with a different question than authorship, that of establishing the form(s) of LBH prose. To this end he demonstrates the considerable degree of syntactic and grammatical similarity between Chronicles and Ezra–Nehemiah (excluding the Nehemiah Memoir). His illustrative discussion of the 'lexicographic features of the Chronicler' (pp. 124-50) is not intended to demonstrate unity of authorship, nor is it restricted to Chronicles or Ezra–Nehemiah. Polzin confirms instead that Chronicles and Ezra–Nehemiah (excluding NM) belong to the same stage of development of LBH (p. 71). (2) Rooker (1990) is positive about Polzin's contribution but finds some difficulties and inconsistencies in his methodology (pp. 31, 38). Polzin maintains that grammatical-syntactical distinctions provide more objective criteria than lexicographical features in discussions of linguistic typology (*contra* Hurvitz), but Rooker (pp. 58-59) considers this unfounded. Like Polzin's, Rooker's own work is concerned with a different question from that being considered here, but he examines a wider range of literature than Polzin and his concluding tables (pp. 182-83) contain a number of interesting *obiter dicta* which show both similarities and differences between Chronicles and Ezra–Nehemiah. (3) Talshir (1988) attempts to overturn Japhet's results and return the burden of proof to the advocates of separate authorship. His discussion has some methodological problems and omissions which make its conclusions less than convincing. Talshir distinguishes the components of Ezra–Nehemiah but does not separate the synoptic and non-synoptic parts of Chronicles

Williamson (1977a: 37-59) advanced Japhet's argument considerably by concentrating not on alleged cases of linguistic opposition between the works but on their supposed similarities. To this end he examined afresh the lists of Driver, and Curtis and Madsen, which have been frequently cited as evidence of common authorship.[21] He proposed a number of criteria for defining stylistic peculiarities, which were then applied to the 140 examples in the lists. From these Williamson deduced only six examples that satisfied the criteria (1977a: 58-59).

Throntveit (1982) next applied Williamson's criteria (which were confined to vocabulary) to Polzin's list of grammatical-syntactical features of LBH. He concluded that the similarities in these respects between Chronicles and Ezra–Nehemiah were also reflected in other post-exilic writings and that linguistic analysis alone could not decide the question of authorship. This view reflects the judgment of most commentators. It is also worth bearing in mind the limited amount of data available for comparison. As Selman (1994a: 68) reminds us, 'the non-synoptic material in Chronicles comprises by far the largest literary unit in Late Biblical Hebrew. The evidence therefore for assessing whether Chronicles and Ezra–Nehemiah might be attributed to a single author is actually quite restricted'.

4. *Similarity in Outlook, Interests and Theology*
The decisive case for difference in authorship is made above all, and most persuasively, with reference to the outlook and theological perspectives of the works, and among those who have examined the question in detail (Williamson 1977a: 60-70; 1982: 9-11; Braun 1979; Strübind 1991: 27-35), such a consensus has developed.[22] Chronicles

---

for comparative purposes (unlike Polzin). He interprets differently the significance of the contrast between Chronicles and Ezra-Nehemiah over the formation of the 1 c.s. imperfect waw-consecutive. (Japhet [1968: 334-35] found full forms here in Chronicles with short forms used everywhere else.) Talshir attributes the absence of the ואקטלה form from Chronicles (contrast its frequency in Ezra) to a different scribal tradition (pp. 172-75). Polzin (p. 55) made a similar suggestion and excluded this feature (A.10 in his designation) from his summary of the syntax of LBH syntax (p. 75). Talshir does not engage with most of Japhet's list of technical terms or stylistic peculiarities (Japhet 1968: 348-71).

21. However, as Williamson (1977a: 38) points out, the original purpose of these lists was not to prove common authorship (which was accepted on other grounds) but simply to illustrate the Chronicler's 'peculiarities of style'.

22. Of recent studies, only Blenkinsopp (1988), Oeming (1990) and Mason

and Ezra–Nehemiah certainly have many interests in common, as previous commentators have noted (cf. Curtis and Madsen 1910: 4-5;
Eissfeldt 1965: 530-32) but they also differ significantly in their treatment of these questions. Three important subjects may illustrate these
differences.

(i) *David and the Davidic covenant.* The presentation of Chronicles is
dominated by David and the covenant with him, through which the
dynasty is established and the temple is built. In Ezra–Nehemiah, by
contrast, David is much more a peripheral figure, and no mention at all
is made of the 'eternal covenant'.[23] Williamson (1982: 10) remarks that
the silence of Ezra–Nehemiah about the covenant is not explained
merely on the grounds that such a subject would have been inappropriate in a work describing the post-exilic restoration, but that the silence
reflects instead a substantial difference in outlook compared with
Chronicles: the redactor of Ezra–Nehemiah retained a vital sense of the
importance of the Sinai covenant and the promises to the patriarchs,
whereas the Chronicler handled the theme of the Davidic covenant in a
way that reflects 'a fundamental development in the covenantal basis of
God's relationship with Israel'. Williamson goes on to speak of this
development 'result[ing] in a shift away from the emphasis of the
Deuteronomic historian on the Exodus and Sinai'. It would perhaps be
more accurate to describe the Chronicler's outlook as *subsuming* the
Sinaitic (and patriarchal) traditions into the Davidic covenant, rather than
neglecting them.[24] Nevertheless, Williamson's basic point stands, and I
will return (in Chapter 9) to consider the significance of this thematic difference between Chronicles and Ezra–Nehemiah. 'Deuteronomistic'
thought and the importance of the Sinaitic covenant are evident especially in the confessions and prayers of Ezra 9 and Nehemiah 1 and 9,
but no appeal is made there to the Davidic covenant as a basis for hope
or restoration.

(1990) have argued for the same outlook in both works (e.g. an anti-Samaritan
Tendenz or hostility to mixed marriages); see below.

23. Cf. 1 Chron. 17.12; 2 Chron. 7.18; 13.5; 21.7; 23.3; contrast Ezra 3.10 and
Neh. 12.24, which refer only to David's role in the institution of sacred song.

24. It is evident that the Mosaic Law has foundational significance for the
Chronicler, while David is presented as a second Moses in his receipt of the תבנית for
the temple (1 Chron. 28.11, 12, 18-19; cf. Exod. 25.9, 40). Allusions to the
Abrahamic covenant are found with reference to the promise of the land (cf. 1 Chron.
16.16; 2 Chron. 20.7).

As for the actual description of the Judean restoration and the temple rebuilding, it seems likely that if the author/editor of Ezra–Nehemiah had shared the same outlook on the Davidic covenant as we find in Chronicles, he would surely have mentioned the Davidic lineage of Zerubbabel (cf. 1 Chron. 3.19; Hag. 2.23, in allusion to Jer. 22.24). But he makes no mention of this fact, nor does he place any emphasis on Zerubbabel as an individual. Instead, the redactor links him constantly with Jeshua and the other leaders of the post-exilic community. The book of Ezra is also silent or unclear about Zerubbabel's status as governor (cf. Hag. 2.21) and his role as temple builder (cf. Zech. 4.6-10), details which would hardly have escaped the Chronicler. Japhet attributes these facts to a distinctly different religio-historical outlook held by the editor of Ezra–Nehemiah.[25]

(ii) *Aspects of the cult and religious practice.* A concern with the temple and right religious practice is common to most of the post-exilic writings. This fact is hardly surprising, given the nature of that society. Chronicles and Ezra–Nehemiah reflect the same social reality, yet there are differences in their presentation which would be difficult to attribute to a common author. The Levites play a more important and extensive role in Chronicles (cf. Williamson 1977a: 69), while Ezra–Nehemiah mentions other cultic personnel, the Nethinim and the 'sons of Solomon's servants', who are absent from Chronicles (other than a bare mention of the Nethinim in 1 Chron. 9.2, which is dependent on Neh. 11.3; cf. Japhet 1968: 351-54). There also appear to be differences between the works on the relation between the Levites and the orders of gatekeepers and singers (cf. 1 Chron. 9.17-18, 33-34; 2 Chron. 5.12; Ezra 7.24; Neh. 11.15-16; 13.10). Writing at a time when the unity of Chronicles with Ezra–Nehemiah was not questioned, von Rad (1930: 82-85, 102) observed these differences but attributed them to the sources used by the compiler.

Williamson (1977a: 60-61) has emphasized the different attitudes apparently taken over mixed marriages. While these are condemned in Ezra–Nehemiah, the Chronicler appears to condone them, mentioning numerous examples in the genealogies and elsewhere (cf. 1 Chron. 2.3,

---

25. Cf. Japhet 1982: 76: 'The House of David, as a vehicle of aspirations to national unity and as a symbol "par excellence" of salvific hopes, has no place in this world view [sc. of Ezra–Nehemiah] and therefore is conspicuously absent from the book.'

17, 34; 3.1; 4.17; 2 Chron. 2.13; 8.11), and failing to condemn Solomon on this point (contrast Neh. 13.26).

(iii) *The concept of Israel*. There is a growing consensus that the Chronicler has an inclusive view of Israel's identity, which appears to differ in some respects from the understanding reflected in Ezra–Nehemiah. Until recently the prevailing opinion maintained that the Chronicler's concept of 'Israel' was exclusivist and confined to Judah and Benjamin. Japhet (1989: ch. 3) has challenged this view with a broad base of evidence, while Williamson (1977a: 87-131) has shown from a close study of the use of ישראל in the work and the Chronicler's portrayal of Hezekiah (2 Chron. 29–32) that the survivors of the northern tribes retain their status as legitimate members of Israel. Both studies point out the difficulties that may arise in this area by projecting the outlook of Ezra–Nehemiah onto Chronicles (Williamson 1977a: 1-4; Japhet 1989: 269), and it will be shown in this study that this applies to other areas of the Chronicler's theology. Japhet's and Williamson's conclusion here is supported by Braun's observations (1977; 1979: 57) on the Chronicler's positive attitude toward the north.

The viewpoint expressed in the various literary layers of Ezra–Nehemiah is more difficult to determine. An 'inclusivist' attitude is reflected in Ezra 6.21 toward those native Israelites who 'had joined [the returned exiles] and separated themselves from the pollutions of the peoples of the land', as Pohlmann (1991) emphasizes. However, Ezra–Nehemiah does take a hostile attitude toward 'the peoples of the lands' (Ezra 3.3) and those Yahwists of mixed origin who sought to participate in the temple building (Ezra 4.1-5). A more positive attitude toward aliens is reflected in Chronicles, and indeed, 2 Chron. 30.25 notes that inclusion was actually achieved in the religious assembly at Hezekiah's Passover.

The list of ideological differences between the works could be extended to include the centrality of Jacob or the function of prophecy in Chronicles, but the above examples provide sufficient illustration of this point. To summarize: the linguistic arguments advanced in the past to support unity of authorship point in fact in the opposite direction, while the points of substantive ideological difference are decisive for treating Chronicles and Ezra–Nehemiah as works as separate authorship. That position is accordingly adopted in this study as a basis for

examining the Chronicler's theology and the relationship of his work to
Ezra–Nehemiah.[26]

3. *The Unity, Provenance and Dating of the Chronicler's Work*

The remaining questions of introduction may be discussed more briefly.
A wide diversity of views have been expressed on these matters, which
also affect interpretation, but as Selman (1994a: 65-75) notes, this range
of opinion often reflects the different starting points of scholars.

On the present form of the Chronicler's work, most discussion centres
on the originality of the extensive genealogical material in 1 Chronicles
1–9, 23–27. Although these sections have often been seen as
secondary[27] or the subject of extensive reworking,[28] a new appreciation
of the function and form of these chapters has strengthened the case for
accepting them, largely as they are, as integral and original parts of the
composition.[29] The most comprehensive study of 1 Chronicles 1–9 is by
Oeming (1990), who argues against Noth for the basic coherence of
1 Chronicles 1–9 and the integral, 'kerygmatic' connection of this unit
with the narrative. As we will see below, the recurrent themes of the
narrative are indeed reflected in the lists and narrative notes of
1 Chronicles 1–9, which thus contribute to the total message of the
work. It is generally believed that the author of Chronicles belonged to
Levitical circles. This remains the most likely hypothesis, even if Noth
(1967: 114-22) is correct in seeing the Levitical lists in the work
(e.g. 1 Chron. 15.4-10) as secondary insertions.

The dating of the work is necessarily related to judgments made about

26. Blenkinsopp (1989: 41-54) disputes Williamson's contention (1983b) that
Ezra 2 is dependent on Neh. 7, and argues for a number of formal and ideological
parallels between the works. On the first point (p. 43) Blenkinsopp's literary arguments are not very convincing, while his discussion of vocabulary and ideology
(pp. 47-54) does not pay sufficient attention to the particular nuances of the
Chronicler's presentation. Williamson (1987a) uses his understanding of the relationship between Ezra 2 and Neh. 9 in a criticism of McKenzie's (1985) attempt to reassert the 1 Esdras hypothesis. Neither Mason nor Oeming contributes new arguments
in support of a unified 'Chronicler's History'.

27. Cf. Welch 1935; Noth 1967 (on 1 Chron. 23–27); Cross 1975; Braun 1986
(on 1 Chron. 23–27); Throntveit 1987.

28. Cf. Rudolph 1955; Kartveit 1989 (on 1 Chron. 1–9).

29. Cf. Johnson 1969; Johnstone 1986; Wright 1990 (on 1 Chron. 23–27); Willi
1991.

its original form. If the above arguments are correct, that Chronicles is to be distinguished as a literary entity from Ezra–Nehemiah and that 1 Chronicles 1–9 is integral to the work, then a date at some point in the fourth century BCE, perhaps the earlier half, would seem to agree with most of the available data.[30] The two passages in particular which may help fix a *terminus a quo* for the work are the list of David's descendants in 1 Chron. 3.17-24, which takes us at least five generations after Zerubbabel, and 1 Chron. 9.2-34, the list of those who repopulated Jerusalem. Verses 2-17 of this passage are apparently dependent on Neh. 11.3-19; the small increase in the numbers in the Chronicler's version suggests the passage of a few years.[31] As well as this section, and the overlap in 2 Chron. 36.22-23, the following smaller details indicate that the Chronicler knew and made use of Ezra–Nehemiah:

1. The description in 1 Chron. 22.2-4 and 2 Chron. 2.7-15 (E 8-16) of the temple preparations, bracketing the Sidonians and the Tyrians, and detailing the payment in barley, wine and oil, and the shipment of logs by sea to Joppa, has several verbal parallels with the account of the construction of the second temple in Ezra 3.7, and may be taken to be a conscious allusion to that description.[32]

---

30. For discussions the dating of Chronicles, cf. Welten 1973: 199-200; Williamson 1977a: 83-86; 1982: 15-17; Throntveit 1987: 97-107. Welten's late dating (c. 200 BCE) rests on the evidence he sees reflected in the work of the author's acquaintance with Hellenistic armies and catapults (cf. 2 Chron. 26.15); these points are fairly answered by Williamson (1982: 338). Throntveit favours an original work c. 527–515 BCE, which he thinks was subsequently redacted to include 1 Chron. 1–9, 23–27 and parts of 29.1-19 (to account for the Persian loan-word *birah* and the reference to 'darics' in v. 7, part of Williamson's evidence for the *terminus a quo* of the work). In Throntveit's view the 'original' work reflected the dyarchic view of king and high priest found in Zech. 1–8 and so should be linked with early Restorationist hopes supposedly associated with Zerubbabel. However, a closer reading of the Chronicler's depiction of the office of high priest cannot support this interpretation (cf. Chapter 8 below). Throntveit's view is clearly influenced by Cross's and Freedman's understanding of the original form and purpose of Chronicles, but it involves an arbitrary severing of 1 Chron. 1–9 from the work, and some special pleading.

31. Williamson (1985: 348-49) suggests that both passages could be 'free editorial adaptations' of an original list.

32. Williamson (1985: 47; cf. below) argues that the relationship is the other way round, but it seems more likely that the Chronicler (deviating from his *Vorlage* in this

2.   2 Chron. 3.2 places special emphasis on the fact that Solomon 'began to build in the second month' of the fourth year of his reign (ויחל לבנות בחדש השני). While this agrees with the details of 1 Kgs 6.1, the language suggests that a further typological allusion is intended to the commencement of rebuilding works in Ezra 3.8 (בחדש השני החלו).

3.   The Chronicler's additional information about Joash's assassins (2 Chron. 24.26) has been seen as an adaptation of data taken from Ezra 9–10.[33]

If the above interpretation correctly reflects the relationship of the books, it suggests that Ezra–Nehemiah and Chronicles are discrete yet related works, with Chronicles being written not only independently but also with some degree of conscious reference to Ezra–Nehemiah. The significance of this relationship is examined further in Chapters 9 and 10.[34]

---

description) would have wished to establish a typological connection with the account of the construction of the second temple.

33.   Graham 1985.

34.   Williamson (1982) sees Chronicles as pre-dating Ezra–Nehemiah, which he argues achieved its final form c. 300 BCE (cf. Williamson 1983b). Considering only the internal evidence of that work, Japhet (1982: 89 n. 55) allows a rather earlier date ('No material in the Book of Ezra–Nehemiah obliges us [...] to date the book's composition any later than the first quarter of the fourth century BCE'), while she places Chronicles 'at the end of the Persian or, more probably, the beginning of the Hellenistic period, at the end of the fourth century BCE' (1993: 27-28). For the view that Chronicles presupposes Ezra–Nehemiah see also Johnstone 1986: 114; 1987.

Chapter 2

RETRIBUTION IN CHRONICLES:
A SURVEY AND CRITIQUE OF RESEARCH

1. *Introduction*

For most of the modern period it has been widely accepted that the
Chronicler had a pronounced interest in the question of divine retribution.[1] This theme is seen as central to the writer's theological and historical understanding, as well as playing a dominant role in the composition
of the narrative.[2] It is evident from even a cursory reading of the book,
especially 2 Chronicles 10–36, that the author does affirm a strong link
between obedience and blessing, and disobedience and punishment,
within the lifetimes of individuals and generations. In making such a

---

1.   Although 'retribution' usually denotes deserved punishment in modern par-
lance, strictly speaking it also embraces reward. The term is retained in this study for
the sake of convenience and its place in past research, and is used neutrally to signify
both divine reward and punishment (cf. German *Vergeltung*).

2.   Besides the discussions considered below, cf. also Curtis and Madsen 1910:
9 (the Chronicler treated Israel's life as 'a church with constant rewards and punishments through signal divine intervention... He made more universal the connection
between piety and prosperity and wickedness and adversity, heightening good and
bad characters, and their rewards and punishments, or creating them according to the
exigencies of the occasion'); Elmslie 1916: lv; Pfeiffer 1952: 778-89; Weiser 1961:
324 ('The dominating viewpoint of the Chronicler's presentation of history is the
idea of retribution carried through mechanically and, as regards each individual,
down to the smallest details; when history does not fit in with it, it is usually dis-
torted'); Eichrodt 1961: II, 307, 487; Bickerman 1966: 24-26; Westermann 1969:
256; Eissfeldt 1965: 535-37; Fohrer 1970: 247; Kaiser 1975: 186; Berg 1980 (the
Chronicler's doctrine is an expression of God's active ['manipulative'] control of
history which contrasts with the 'secular' view of Esther that stresses human
responsibility); Braun 1986: xxxvii-xxxix; De Vries 1989: 119-21. Alone among
modern discussions, Mosis (1973: 14-16, 201-202) denies the importance of this
theme for Chronicles.

connection, of course, the Chronicler does not differ from the general perceptions of Yahweh's actions held by other Old Testament writers,[3] but his work is certainly distinguished by the frequency of this theme and the manner of its treatment. It has long been argued that the author adhered to a rather rigid and extreme doctrine of divine reward and punishment (variously described as 'mechanical', 'individual' and 'immediate'), such that it led him to distort (or invent) the details of his historical presentation. This perception of the work is very widely maintained, even where a more sympathetic view is held of the writer's motives or historical method.

This study takes issue with this broad consensus, arguing that the writer's retributive thought is considerably more flexible and complex than is usually allowed, and that it belongs within the current of his literary and theological predecessors. The exposition of this view is presented in detail in Chapters 3 and 4. While I am concerned primarily with the theological issues raised by the work, the related historical questions are also kept in view and are discussed in Chapter 5.

As a preliminary step to my own discussion, this chapter reviews and criticizes significant ways in which the Chronicler's thought has been understood in the course of research.

2. *Retribution in Chronicles: Critical Interpretations*

The theme of reward and punishment in Chronicles has received some degree of treatment right from the beginning of modern biblical criticism, given the role of Chronicles in that pioneering work. Thus de Wette (1817), remarking that the theme belonged to 'the design of the work', argued that this concern was intended to convey the writer's conviction about the antiquity of the Mosaic Law and worship: pious kings had maintained these practices but apostates had neglected them to their ruin.[4] Graf (1866) and Vatke (1873) interpreted the

3. Koch argued in an influential essay (1955), mainly on the basis of texts from Prov. 25–29, Hosea and the Psalms, that there is no such thing as a doctrine of retribution in the Old Testament and that each person's deed instead holds the seeds of its own consequences. The validity of this view for Proverbs is firmly refuted by Boström (1990: ch. 3) while it is evidently not reflected in Chronicles. See also Chapter 9 below on the retributive doctrine in Deuteronomy and the Deuteronomistic History.

4. W.M.L. de Wette, *Lehrbuch der historisch-kritischen Einleitung in die Bibel Alten und Neuen Testaments* (Berlin, 1817), 2.135, cited in Rogerson (1992).

phenomenon as the Chronicler's didactic means of edifying and admonishing his readers. Graf, who agreed with de Wette that the writer had no proper historical sense, found instead in his narratives 'the influence and activity of the idealizing, embellishing, reforming, explaining *Sage*' which used retributive themes so as 'to bring experience into better agreement with divine judgment than it appears to happen in history'.[5]

It was, however, Wellhausen (1878; ET 1885) who first discussed the subject in detail and set it within the context of the development of Judaism, according to his understanding of that religion and its origins. Wellhausen described retribution in Chronicles as 'a divine pragmatism' that was operative in the kingdom of Judah. This is presented as an absolute law that governed the fate of the southern kingdom and its rulers, strictly in terms of their fidelity to the Mosaic Law. Moreover, the long line of prophets which the author presents existed to give expression to this outlook (1885: 203):

> [T]hey connect the deeds of men with the events of the course of the world, and utilise the sacred history as a theme for their preaching, as a collection of examples illustrative of the promptest operation of the righteousness of Jehovah... Of course their prophecies always come exactly true, and in this way is seen an astonishing harmony between inward worth and outward circumstance. Never does sin miss its punishment, and never where misfortune occurs is guilt wanting.

Wellhausen then presented a review of 2 Chronicles 10–36, in which the writer was said to find moral grounds for each misfortune that was recounted but not explained by Kings. Conversely, 'Merit is always the obverse of success' (1885: 209), and only in the cases of those pious kings of whom the Chronicler approved (including Rehoboam and Abijah, against the evidence of the *Vorlage*[6]) were the blessings of God manifested in the concrete shape of fortresses, armies and children.

Manasseh's fifty-five year reign (2 Chron. 33.1 = 2 Kgs 21.1), the longest on record, was also a 'stone of stumbling' which was removed by positing an unhistorical punishment in Babylon (1885: 207). Significantly, Wellhausen took no account of the theme of repentance in this narrative, which others have seen as the (equally) unhistorical basis for the king's restoration; instead, Manasseh was supposed to have

5. Cf. Graham 1990: 126, 132.
6. On the Chronicler's actual estimate of Rehoboam and Abijah (*contra* Wellhausen, and Welten 1973: 126), see below Chapter 4.

borne and atoned for his guilt through temporary imprisonment.

Wellhausen's own concern with Chronicles had less to do with the work itself than with the light it cast on the formation of the Pentateuch (especially as a witness to the date of the Priestly Writing). Nevertheless, building on de Wette's researches, he helped confirm the image of the work as late and historically suspect, and priestly and rigid in outlook. Chronicles reflected the general tendency of its period, 'the conviction that the Mosaic law is the starting-point of Israel's history, and that in it there is operative a play of sacred forces such as finds no other analogy; the conviction could not but lead to a complete transformation of the ancient tradition' (1885: 224). Thus, in both its theological character and historical content the book was inferior to Samuel–Kings.

Wellhausen's treatment of this theme was concise but very influential. In many respects it set the lines of later discussion of this aspect of the Chronicler's theology, both in commentaries and works of introduction, and in broader systematic studies of Old Testament theology,[7] where the tone is frequently critical or dismissive. In some specific ways, however, Wellhausen's interpretation has been corrected or modified, as the following details indicate.

First, whatever the historical basis to the account of Manasseh's captivity and repentance,[8] it is now recognized that the Chronicler draws no theological significance from the length of his reign. This is a small but important point, since this is the most frequently cited example of the way in which the writer's alleged dogmatism led him to distort the historical record.[9]

Secondly, Japhet (1989: 177-78 n. 518) points out specifically against Wellhausen that the prophets' role is not to offer an interpretation of history in the light of a retributive theory but to preach repentance. Proper appreciation of this fact should contribute to a reassessment of the writer's outlook. It will be seen that the prophets testify to Yahweh's mercy and restorative will, more so than to his judgment.

---

7. Cf. the works cited in n. 2, the majority of which reflect Wellhausen's view in some measure.

8. Cf. Williamson 1982: 389. On the historical problem, see most recently Schniedewind 1991.

9. Cf. Berg 1980; Lowery 1991: 185-89. In the following chapter the number of examples is expanded where closer attention to context and the Chronicler's express statements (as well as his silences) should lead us to a quite different interpretation of his meaning.

More generally, it should be noted that Wellhausen accepted Chronicles primarily as a work of historiography. The writer's retributive doctrine was characterized in the first instance as a (dogmatic) heuristic method for understanding and reconstructing the past. This approach has been echoed by perhaps the majority of interpreters, who have understood Chronicles primarily as a supplement (or substitute) for the Deuteronomistic History. However, if it is accepted that the writer's purpose was at least as rhetorical and paraenetic as historical, then his use of history and his attitude to the received traditions would require a more complex evaluation.[10]

The middle years of this century brought a number of studies which helped moderate attitudes to the theological and historical value of Chronicles. In von Rad's (1930) monograph the writer's retributive doctrine was interpreted essentially as an exercise in theodicy, an account of Yahweh's justice and its outworking in reward and punishment. A preoccupation with this subject was said to have marked the later stages of Israelite religion, and the approach of Chronicles was contrasted here with Job. According to von Rad, whereas Job considered the problem practically, Chronicles handled the problem of divine justice and history theoretically: 'The Chronicler proceeds from the other way round, beginning first with the dogma, and only then looking at reality' (p. 11).[11] As a result, reality is sometimes 'transformed' for the sake of the theory that God requites an individual within his life and not after it or at the end of history. Although such an insistence frequently involved the author in historical errors and inconsistencies, the Chronicler did not depict God's retribution as automatic, since the prophetic warnings testified to Yahweh's patience. The work thus treated human responsibility for sin and its consequences as a clear and rationally accounted for fact, in keeping with a comprehensive doctrine of divine justice. Moreover, this conception of history was fundamentally different

10. The view of Chronicles as primarily a work of historiography, intended to replace or supplement the Deuteronomistic History, is widely reflected also in works of introduction, Old Testament theologies and special studies (cf. von Rad 1962: 347-48; Fishbane 1985: 380-81; Japhet 1989: 505-16), although its theological and homiletical character is universally recognized. A different approach is taken in more recent German monographs, where Chronicles is seen variously as 'exegesis' of the Deuteronomistic History (Willi 1972; Strübind 1991), typologizing theology (Mosis 1973), or edifying historical fiction (Welten 1973).

11. 'Der Chronist als Theoretiker geht umgekehrt von dem primären Besitz des Dogmas aus und sieht von da erst in die Wirklichkeit.'

from the Deuteronomistic one, in limiting the effects of retribution to the individual and his generation. Whereas Kings depicted the nation's 'constantly mounting guilt' ('sich unablässig häufende Schuld') and a 'collective judgment' ('Kollektivgericht') that overtook both north and south, such concepts were foreign to the Chronicler, who attributed the destruction of Jerusalem solely to the sins of the last generation (p. 13). This is now a standard judgment in Chronicles studies, but the following chapters will show grounds for seriously questioning its accuracy.

Von Rad's later discussion of this subject (1962: 347-50) largely reproduces his earlier conclusions, though less appreciatively. He believed that, like the Deuteronomistic History, Chronicles was also concerned to point out a correspondence between guilt and punishment: 'the only difference is that it raises this correspondence to the level of complete rational proof—no disaster without guilt, no sin without punishment' (p. 348). Chronicles had 'tightened up and at the same time altered the Deuteronomist's pragmatism', and was thus very much the work of an epigone. Although this presentation was forced and unsatisfactory, a positive motive could nonetheless be discerned, for it represented the writer's contribution to the 'question of the share of the individual in Jahweh', which von Rad considered to be 'one of the hardest problems which cropped up in later Jahwism' (p. 349). Thus, the author 'never let himself on any consideration be forced from the position that Jahweh confronted each generation quite immediately and with his whole revelation' (p. 350).

Von Rad's remarks here reflect the older critical view that a greater concern for the life of the individual was a special feature of exilic and post-exilic religious thought. According to this developmentalist view,[12] this period was marked by a shift away from the strong emphasis on corporate and community responsibility of earlier Yahwism (said to be reflected, for example, in the case of Achan, or the punishment of Manasseh being visited on Zedekiah's generation) to a new recognition of individual responsibility. Ezekiel 18 was frequently cited in this context (cf. v. 20, 'The son shall not suffer for the iniquity of the father, nor the father suffer for the iniquity of the son'), and several writers (Noth, Japhet, Dillard) have in fact suggested some clear association between the (supposed) thought of that passage and the Chronicler's interest in individual responsibility.[13] It is now clear, however, that there

12. See especially Eichrodt 1961: II, 231-32; von Rad 1962: 443-44.
13. See below, Chapter 4, for a discussion of the Chronicler's actual use of the

is no simple, unilinear development in the Old Testament toward individual responsibility, and that both corporate and individual aspects of responsibility are reflected at many different points of the tradition. The attempt to see the author's retributive doctrine with its particular stress on the individual as a reflex of this alleged development must be rejected.[14]

Noth's landmark study of the Deuteronomistic History and the Chronicler's History (1967 [1943]) contained a discussion of the central theological ideas of Chronicles, in which he basically endorsed von Rad's interpretation of retribution. According to Noth, the writer set out to serve the concerns of his own period by describing (in Chronicles–Ezra–Nehemiah) the historical formation of the post-exilic community and its institutions. God had been active in this history, and the writer's doctrine of reward and punishment, strictly orientated toward the individual, was the principal expression of that conviction. The doctrine presupposed that God's will, as it was revealed in the Law, was known to Israel. The writer believed in the absolute validity of the doctrine, and therefore drew inferences about the phases of individual lives, such as Asa's illness (2 Chron. 16.1.) or Uzziah's leprosy (2 Chron. 26.16-21a).

Rudolph's commentary (1955) is in many ways the bridge to modern discussion. His treatment of retribution stands broadly in the lines of Wellhausen and von Rad (p. x), but is modified to give greater scope to the role of divine grace. While the Chronicler strove to depict the 'correspondence wrought by God between deeds and destiny in the experience of individual kings' (p. xix),[15] he did not pursue this thought to its logical extreme. In evidence of this Rudolph cited 2 Chron. 25.13 (the attack by Amaziah's mercenaries) and 2 Chron. 32.1-2 (Sennacherib's campaign). Neither incident could be traced to an actual sin, although it was certainly the general tenor of the writer's work to make such a connection. Rudolph further insisted that although the Chronicler understood divine retribution to be at work throughout Israel's history, the 'correspondence between deeds and destiny' was not a barren and unalterable principle but rested on the personal and merciful nature of Yahweh (1 Chron. 21.13; 2 Chron. 30.9) who facilitated repentance (p. xx). This point is developed in my own discussion,

motif of Ezek. 18 and the correct interpretation of 2 Chron. 27–32.

14. On the related theory of 'corporate personality', see Rogerson 1970.

15. 'Die gottgewirkte Entsprechung von Tun und Schicksal am Erleben der einzelnen Könige.'

where particular stress is laid on the fact that Yahweh forestalls punishment, and indeed enables the human response to do his will (cf. 1 Chron.
22.12; 29.18; 2 Chron. 30.12).[16]

The subject next received critical attention from North (1963) as one
of the four basic themes of the work.[17] North discerned in the author's
outlook a doctrine of 'short-range retributionism', the insistence that
God fully requited human acts within this life. This doctrine was interpreted as a reaction to developing ideas among other parts of Jewry that
were more disposed towards Persian ideas of postponed retribution or
'Greek notions of immortality' (for example, in the Alexandrian Wisdom
of Solomon). Against such trends, the Palestinian Chronicler affirmed
'the emphatic last-ditch credo of a conservative' (p. 373). The writer
held obstinately to 'the archaic Old Testament pattern of good and evil
in this life, since no one knows what Sheol may hold in store' for the
individual (p. 369). In viewing God's justice as so earth-bound, the
Chronicler was said to be clinging very literally to the early Old
Testament tradition, and his doctrine functioned principally as a kind of
moral paraenesis (p. 374).

North also argued that in the intervening post-exilic time the book of
Job had brought the validity of the old doctrine of divine justice into
question. The Chronicler responded to these more recent theological
tendencies by refusing to admit that certain questions of merit had not
been answered satisfactorily in the earlier biblical writings. Instead, he set
about correcting their data to make them conform to the more
traditional point of view.

North expressed here what is still probably the consensus view of
scholarship on the date and provenance of Old Testament reflection on
the after-life and post-mortem retribution (although this subject has lately
seen shifts of opinion and challenges[18]). However, it is very doubtful

16. The main issue, however, is the connection between the Chronicler's doctrine
of retribution and his understanding of the temple, which is examined in Chapter 4.
In a note in her recent study of the theme of peace in Chronicles, Gabriel (1990: 9
n. 28) comments in passing (with some justice) 'that the presuppositions and
implications of this rather unfortunate expression (i.e. "dogma of individual
retribution") for a theology of grace have never been reflected upon' ('daß die
gnadentheologischen Voraussetzungen und Implikationen dieser nicht eben
glücklichen Wortverbindung (i.e. "individuellen Vergeltungsdogma") nie reflektiert
werden'). Chapter 4 below attempts in part just such an exercise.

17. The other themes identified are legitimacy, cult and 'Davidism'.

18. R. Martin-Achard (1992: 680-84) argues that the roots of faith in personal

whether the writer's interest in reward and punishment should be understood in this light. Although post-mortem retribution was certainly a lively concern in the later biblical and intertestamental period,[19] the writer's views on this question are unknown and there is no indication that he was addressing it. Von Rad also hints at such an interest when he asserts that the burial notices in Chronicles were intended to signify 'the last possible point where Jahweh's activity could still reach a king [in] the granting or withholding of solemn burial'.[20] However, this is an unlikely inference of the writer's purpose. While the burial notices certainly express a judgment upon the reigns of individual kings, the writer's use is not really different from other parts of the Old Testament where this motif features.[21]

More recent study has returned to the problem of retribution in both its historiographical and theological aspects, and has considered more closely its significance for the literary structure of the work. Welten (1973) has investigated the historical status of many of the motifs of reward in the author's *Sondergut* in 2 Chronicles 10–36. He concludes that by far the great majority of this information is fictitious and was intended (in a parabolic manner) to signify approval of certain reigns, so as to encourage the embattled post-exilic community and to affirm its legitimacy over against its neighbours.[22]

Japhet (1989) provides the most extensive and stimulating discussion of the problem, in a lengthy section of her monograph (pp. 150-98).[23]

resurrection are early and originate in Yahwism, in reflection on Yahweh's justice and commitment to his own people, but clear articulation of the idea is late. L.J. Greenspoon (1981: 247-321) maintains that the belief is early and 'arose out of the larger themes associated with YHWH as Divine Warrior' (p. 319), who had power to overcome death and release those under its control. Whether or not this association is accepted, Greenspoon does present grounds for believing that the idea of bodily resurrection may be traced back to pre-exilic times.

19. Cf. 1 Enoch 22–27; Dan. 12.1-3; Jub. 23.11-31; 2 Macc. 7; Wisdom of Solomon 1–6. The dating of Isa. 24–27 (cf. 26.19) is uncertain.

20. 1962: 350.

21. Cf. 2 Kgs 9.36; Jer. 8.1-3; 16.4; Isa. 14.19.

22. See Chapter 5 for a more detailed discussion of Welten's approach to the historical value of Chronicles.

23. Because of the wider availability of this work it can be expected to play an important role in future discussion of the Chronicler's thought. The English edition has only limited engagement with scholarly work subsequent to the Hebrew edition, which is based on her 1973 thesis (although there has not been a major challenge to her views). The monograph should now be read in conjunction with the author's

The importance of her interpretation requires that it be treated at some length.

In Japhet's view, Chronicles must be understood as a work of historiography that was intended to bridge the gap inevitably created by the passage of time between the writer's present and the pre-exilic time, in order to render the formative past comprehensible and to legitimize the institutions of the present (1989: 7-10, 509-16). As a historiographical work, Chronicles does not present its ideas in a direct or systematic way (p. 7), but Japhet believes that a topical approach to its ideology (or better, its theology) is possible. Thus, her study eschews many of the conventional questions of research, in favour of interpreting the book as a self-contained entity expressing a clear and coherent system of thought. Japhet concludes, in fact, that Chronicles is unique and independent in its treatment of some fundamental themes of biblical faith, including the nature of divine justice and providence (p. 505).

Japhet's contribution to the study of retribution in Chronicles lies in two main areas. First, she enquires into the origins of the writer's particular concept and describes it quite precisely. Secondly, she provides extensive illustrations of the way she believes the narrative was reworked to express that concept. Japhet also makes important observations on the function of the Chronistic prophets, and the motif of divine testing.

Japhet asserts that the fundamental idea in the writer's 'system' is an understanding of history as a continuous expression of the relationship between God and his people, one that is unchanging and not historically constituted (pp. 116-17). God is active in the history of Israel, and the guiding principle for his action is that of reward and punishment (pp. 150-65). Such retribution is meted out constantly and consistently according to the system's rules, which are derived from the principle of 'absolute divine justice' (cf. p. 153). Biblical historiography is said to be based on the belief that history is the actualization of divine justice. Japhet holds that both Kings and Chronicles are works of theodicy which are concerned to vindicate the rightness of Yahweh's activity through the time of the monarchy. However, these works differ in their

exhaustive commentary (1993; see especially pp. 44-45), which extends her conviction that Chronicles embodies a distinctly different, even contradictory, 'historiosophy' (philosophy of history) from that of the Deuteronomistic History, at the root of which lie, *inter alia*, different understandings of divine justice. An important concern of the present study is to interact with this claim.

'starting points' and concepts of divine justice. The 'starting point' for the Deuteronomist is the challenge posed by the destruction of Judah, for which it provides a dual explanation: Manasseh's sins and the cumulative guilt of the people (pp. 158-60). However, the solution in Kings was believed to be unsatisfactory in the long run because it raised the problem of the deferral (or withholding) of punishment, allowing disobedient generations to escape scot-free, while the last generation before the exile bore an excessive load of punishment. Japhet believes that this problem was confronted in the exilic period by Ezekiel, who denied the previously accepted idea of cumulative guilt or the notion of punishing one generation for the sins of another (cf. Ezek. 18.20).

By contrast, the Chronicler's 'starting point' is within the overall religious system which the work expresses (p. 154):

> The impetus is not an immediate need to provide the believer with answers to the acute challenge posed by the destruction, but rather a general religious awareness. This awareness entails a desire to demonstrate that divine justice is at work in the world and can be discerned throughout Israelite history.

Thus, Chronicles is believed to express the same concept of strict divine justice as was customarily attributed to Ezekiel, along with the prophet's assertion of individual responsibility (pp. 161-63).[24] Japhet holds that the writer refined this further into an 'imperative of reward and punishment': 'Not only is man rewarded or punished for his deeds—each and every deed must be requited. That is the unavoidable consequence of human behaviour' (p. 163). The corollary of this claim is that there can be neither cumulative guilt nor collective retribution: the destruction must be attributed exclusively to Zedekiah and his generation, while the king and people are thought of 'as distinct "individuals", each responsible for its [*sic*] deeds' (p. 163).

Japhet next illustrates how the historical narrative of Kings has been reworked according to the principle of retribution. She argues that this takes five forms:

---

24. Japhet concedes that the actual interpretation of Ezekiel at this point and 'whether it really discusses reward and punishment as such' is a disputed question (1989: 161 n. 474), but elsewhere (p. 163 n. 482) she accepts the validity of the old notion of 'corporate personality', which she believes gave ground to a new emphasis on individual responsibility as a 'result of sociological influence on religious thought'. A connection between Chronicles and the thought of Ezekiel is re-affirmed in Japhet's commentary (1993: 45).

1.   adding appropriate punishments for transgressions in the
     Vorlage where such may be lacking;
2.   conversely, adding recompense for piety;
3.   adding a suitable sin for misfortunes, 'since every difficulty,
     affliction and defect is automatically perceived as retribution'
     (p. 167);
4.   providing a source of merit for every success; and
5.   specifying the causal link between sin and apparent punish-
     ment, where this is not stated in the *Vorlage*.[25]

Japhet thus argues that a comprehensive outlook has been applied
systematically to reinterpret 2 Kings 12–25. In all this, she is actually
quite traditional in her approach, which expressly reflects Wellhausen
(pp. 154-55). Japhet supplements this with the claim that there is a
further qualitative difference between Samuel–Kings and Chronicles
(pp. 155-56):

> The qualitative difference lies in [the Chronicler's] need to explain good
> and evil. The Deuteronomist does not account for the existence of good.
> When he describes a change for the better in Israelite history, he does not
> attribute that change to divine justice, but to God's compassion [...] In
> the case of the Chronicler, things are different.[...] he explains both good
> and evil in terms of divine justice.

The validity of this claim is examined below and in the following
chapter. According to Japhet, the writer's belief in absolute divine justice
makes all history into theodicy and gives prime importance to human
moral responsibility: 'Man becomes master of his fate; his actions are
responsible for whatever befalls him. Moreover, these actions are the
result of his free choice' (p. 175).

Within this system repentance has great importance in neutralizing the
rather rigid workings of retribution. The role of the Chronistic prophets
in warning and preaching repentance has been touched on before (by
von Rad and Noth) but Japhet gives the most thorough treatment of this

---

25. The additional material which Japhet assigns to each category is as follows:
(1) 2 Chron. 13.17-20; 16.7-9; 21.16-19; 28.17-18; 33.11; (2) 2 Chron. 14.5-7,
11-14; 15.15; 17.2-5, 10-19; 20.1-30; 24.15-16; 26.6-15; 27.3-6; 32.27-30;
(3) 2 Chron. 16.10, 12; 20.35-37; 24.17-18; 25.14-16, 27; 26.16-20; 35.22;
36.12-16; (4) 2 Chron. 11.5-23; 12.6, 7, 12; 13.10-12; 18.31; 25.7-10; 33.12-13;
(5) 1 Chron. 10.13-14; 2 Chron. 12.2, 5; 21.10; 28.19. It is clear from these
examples that Japhet treats repentance as a meritorious act (cf. 2 Chron. 12.6, 7, 12;
18.31; 33.12-13).

topic and makes an interesting connection between the Chronicler's outlook and the views on warning (התראה, אזהרה) and premeditation developed in the rabbinical period (pp. 184-87). She does, in fact, attribute the genesis of the rabbinical outlook on this question to the later biblical literature, and to Chronicles in particular.[26] Finally, Japhet concedes that several wars recounted in the book cannot be understood as punishment (pp. 193-94). She infers instead that these are examples of divinely sent tests of faith.

Japhet has without doubt presented the most comprehensive treatment of this topic. Nevertheless, her discussion cannot be said to be the last word on the subject, because it raises some critical questions about the writer's theological outlook and purpose. It must be asked first whether Chronicles does express so comprehensive a system of thought as Japhet maintains. Certainly she assumes that a systematic, abstract approach can be found within biblical thought, especially in the Deuteronomistic and later writings. Thus, in Japhet's general discussion of retribution (pp. 151-55), Yehezekel Kaufmann's views are taken as definitive, while the idea of proportionality ('measure for measure', pp. 157-58; 170) is presented as a presupposition of biblical justice. Japhet believes that the Chronicler sharpened this principle to its logical extreme (p. 214):

> The system of divine retribution demands that [Zedekiah's] generation be 'exceedingly unfaithful'; likewise, in keeping with the principle of 'measure for measure', their desecration of the temple justifies its destruction.

However, this seems too episodic a way of reading the work and, as will be argued in Chapter 4, it misses the indications of *inevitable* doom and exile which the writer gives as early as 2 Chronicles 28 and makes definitively clear in 34.28.

The doctrine of divine justice and its concomitant insistence on human freedom are also said to rule out 'ancestral merit' (pp. 157, 162-63, 165, 456 n. 32). Japhet notes two passages which appear problematic in this light: the reference to Ahijah's prophecy in 2 Chron. 10.15, where the division of the kingdom is the fulfilment of Yahweh's word to Jeroboam; and the withholding of punishment on Jehoram in 2 Chron. 21.7 because of Yahweh's 'covenant which he had made with David'.

26. This is probably the most important example of the way in which Japhet sees Chronicles as a bridge to later Judaism (cf. 1989: 505). The subject is taken up again in the conclusion to this study.

The first example is described as 'an inconsistent holdover from 1 Kgs 12.15', and the second as 'an exceptional case' (p. 162 n. 477).

Japhet argues thus in the first case because she believes the author could not conceive of punishment for Solomon's sins being visited on his descendants (pp. 156-57; cf. 1 Kgs 11.11-13). In reply to this it will be argued in Chapter 4 that the Chronicler has a more complex understanding of Solomon's obedience and the significance of his reign than Japhet's explanation allows.

The second case has nothing to do with 'ancestral merit'; its significant changes from 2 Kgs 8.19 show that it is really concerned with the Davidic covenant, which, it will be argued, is a theme of fundamental importance for understanding both the retributive doctrine and eschatological outlook of the work.[27]

These examples (which could be multiplied) point to difficulties in Japhet's attempt to derive what can only be described as a rather rationalistic system of belief from Chronicles: statements and incidents which do not conform to this pattern are taken by her as evidence of 'inconsistent editing' or a failure to systematize.[28] It would be fairer to ask whether the outlook of the work is as closed as she maintains. Japhet's tendency to over-systematize the writer's thought comes most plainly to the fore in her insistence that theodicy or divine justice is the controlling idea in the work's concern with retribution. In the following chapters it will be argued instead that a much more central theme is divine *grace*. Japhet has very little to say on this subject, orientating everything instead to the themes of divine justice and providence. Similarly, while her treatment of the defensive wars in the book as examples of divine testing has some validity (pp. 191-98), she overlooks the real kerygmatic significance of these reports as occasions of divine saving acts on Israel's behalf.[29]

27. *Contra* Japhet (1989: 497). Cf. Chapter 7 below for a discussion of this theme.

28. Three examples may be cited by way of illustration: (1) Japhet finds 'inconsistency' in the Chronicler's treatment of retribution in 2 Chron. 25.13, which 'was not reworked thoroughly' (1989: 154 n. 453). (2) Her attempt to deny the writer a real angelology or belief in supernatural beings (pp. 137-49) is forced and involves her in special pleading. (3) She concedes that some passages limit human freedom in Chronicles (2 Chron. 22.12; 29.18-19; 2 Chron. 30.12; cf. p. 175 n. 509), but does not integrate this sufficiently into her view of the anthropology of the work.

29. For a discussion of the motif of 'Yahweh war' and its eschatological/kerygmatic significance, cf. Chapter 8 below. It should be noted that Japhet discerns

More recent discussions (Braun 1979: 55-56; Williamson 1977b: 149-54; 1982: 31-33; Johnstone 1986) have recognized that retribution is more closely linked in the Chronicler's understanding with repentance. These writers have drawn attention to the writer's special theological language, as well as his stock motifs of reward and punishment. These observations are developed in the following chapter, where the significance and tradition-historical background to the language are explored. Braun (1979: 55-56) and Williamson (1977a: 67-68) have also argued that the Chronicler's particular concept of retribution and the terms related to it are absent from Ezra–Nehemiah (including the prayers of Ezra 9 and Nehemiah 9), or are used in a quite different way. It is thus taken as a criterion for distinguishing authorship of the different works.

Probably the most emphatic use of the idea of 'immediate retribution' is to be found in Dillard's commentary (1987). Dillard sees the doctrine as fundamental to the structure of the narrative in 2 Chronicles 10–36, especially to its time scheme. Following Rudolph (1952), he holds that the narrative has been strictly periodized into times of faithfulness and unfaithfulness (within which some events may have been dis-chronologized) to give expression to the doctrine. Virtually all the *Sondergut* is seen to be 'in the service of retribution theology' and Dillard believes that Ezekiel or some similar source stimulated the author to offer 'a counterpoise' to the retributive doctrine found in Kings (1987: 80-81).[30]

3. *Summary and Conclusion*

The history of research into this problem has revealed a basic consistency of approach, which has been modified at different points, but not radically so.

---

in Chronicles a very positive conviction about the human capacity to know and do God's will; see below.

30. Dillard (1987: 77) rightly lays great store by the Chronistic insertion of 2 Chron. 7.13-15, but one-sidedly refers to it as 'spell[ing] out the key concepts and vocabulary of retribution theology'; see Chapter 4 for an analysis of these verses. Other recent writers (Begg 1982; Duke 1990) have stressed the paraenetic or hortatory significance of retributive thought, rather than its supposed purpose as a comprehensive theory of history. However, these discussions, while they doubtless pick up an element of truth in their interpretations, tend to oversimplify the Chronicler's message (either into rather wooden moralizing or an extended summons to support the cult in the pursuit of blessing).

First, beginning with Wellhausen's remark about a 'divine pragmatism' perceived by the Chronicler to be at work in the history of
Israel, most writers have accepted that the writer was primarily a historian who had set about reformulating the traditions of Samuel–Kings
according to certain dogmatic presuppositions. Contrary to the evidence
of Samuel–Kings, the Chronicler assumed that the Priestly Law had
always been in force and had been faithfully obeyed in the kingdom of
David and Solomon, but with much less consistency and zeal in post-
schism Judah. The Chronicler accepted the absolute validity of the Law
(indeed, as part of that institution he could scarcely imagine things
otherwise), which he demonstrated by filling out the gaps or puzzling
inconsistencies in the earlier traditions. Everywhere he strove to remove
ambiguity from his received historical picture. Not infrequently, this
resulted in a narrative which was contrived or historically unreliable.
Japhet's belief that the Chronicler depicts a world controlled by a strict
theodicy is essentially a variant on this idea.

Secondly, the Chronicler is believed to have defined the older biblical
doctrine of retribution much more sharply. Notions of collective judgment or the deferment of punishment to a later generation were rejected
in favour of a divine recompense strictly merited by the individual and
confined to the faithful or disobedient phases of his life. Some attempt
has been made to account for this supposed shift in thought. Thus,
Chronicles has been seen as reflecting a growth in the biblical tradition
of the notion of individual moral responsibility (Noth, von Rad, Japhet,
Dillard), or reacting against speculation about post-mortem retribution
(North).

This summary represents the general consensus in scholarship about a
central feature of the writer's theology. Nevertheless, a fresh investigation of the problem is a desideratum, for the following reasons. First, the
historical explanations offered for the 'individual' and 'immediate'
character of the Chronicler's doctrine are unconvincing. Both
'individual' and 'corporate' aspects of responsibility can be found in
many different strata of the biblical tradition, including some of the
earliest,[31] with no simple pattern of historical development.[32] The notion
that the writer's emphasis on the 'individual' is a reflection of a late

31. E.g. Abraham's prayer for the righteous in Sodom in Gen. 18.23-32.
Similarly, the 'collectivist' interpretation of the punishment of Achan's family
(Josh. 7.24-25) is increasingly questioned; cf. the following note.
32. See Rogerson 1970; also 1981: 1156-57, and bibliography.

stage of religious psychology does not stand up to close scrutiny.

Secondly, the widespread assumption that Chronicles is essentially a piece of dogmatizing historiography has coloured evaluation of the work. Both as theology and history it has been depicted very much as inferior to the Deuteronomistic History. The theological character of the work, as well as its genre, needs to be considered afresh, as does the writer's understanding of the relationship of his work to the Deuteronomist's.[33]

33. See Chapter 9 for a discussion of some of the aspects of this latter issue.

Chapter 3

EXEGETICAL STUDIES (1): INTRODUCTION AND LEXICAL TERMS

1. *Introduction*

The Chronicler's retributive outlook is examined in detail in this and the following chapter, where it will be argued that the traditional under-standing of the writer's doctrine (as a theodicy focused rather narrowly upon the lifetime of an individual person or generation[1]) must be sub-stantially reformulated and re-evaluated. The writer's retributive thought is analysed in the following contexts:

1. the key lexical terms which express: (i) positive human responses of faith and repentance toward Yahweh; (ii) negative responses of apostasy and sin; (iii) Yahweh's reaction to these contrasting attitudes; and
2. the narrative notes in 1 Chronicles 1–9, and the self-contained pericopae within the narrative of 1 Chronicles 10–29 and 2 Chronicles 1–36.

The findings of these two chapters are taken up again in the conclusion to this study, which discusses the significance of the Chronicler's retributive doctrine in relation to other aspects of his thought, as these contribute toward the overall interpretation of the work.

Previous researches have of course stressed the close correspondence between piety and reward, or unfaithfulness and punishment, in the Chronicler's work. They have also usefully identified the writer's stock motifs of retribution (although some points of difference in interpretation about these remain[2]). However, the primary focus of this study lies, so

1. See especially Dillard 1987: 76-81.
2. See Braun 1979 and, more fully, the appendix at the end of this study, which presents the full distribution of these motifs in 2 Chron. 10–36. An important question concerns whether the Chronicler invariably perceives sickness as divine punishment; cf. the discussion below on Asa.

to speak, at the other end of the causal chain, with describing the nature of the relationship which subsists between Israel and Yahweh, and which finds expression in the characteristic motifs and language of the work. Although this bond is rarely spoken of in explicitly covenantal terms, it will be argued from several lines of evidence that the language and thought of covenantal theology underlie treatment of this theme, and that it is within this context that the writer's retributive outlook must be fundamentally understood.[3]

As well as the vocabulary and motifs, we must examine the nature and form of the discourse. Chronicles is a complex work whose *Gattung* is not easily decided, although it is generally agreed that it shares some of the characteristics and concerns of 'history' as that genre was understood in the ancient world.[4] Long (1984: 7-8) offers the following general definition:

> History is an extensive, continuous written composition made up of various materials [...] and devoted to a particular subject and historical period. The author describes events presumed to have actually occurred but assembles his sources [...] according to some cohering rubric of intelligibility. Thus he will impose structural and thematic connections which unify the work and implicitly or explicitly convey his evaluation of the importance of certain events.

'History' is distinguished from 'chronicle' or mere annalistic report by the element of interpretation, which for the Chronicler, no less than for the other narrators of the Old Testament, is explicitly theological. Here, the concept of retribution plays an evidently central role in the work's overall 'rubric of intelligibility', towards the task of ordering and understanding the events of the past. At the same time, the paraenetic style of the work has long been recognized, which is due in no small measure to the rhetorical character of its language and 'addresses' (royal and prophetic speeches and prayers).

A further definition of the literary genre of history stresses the description of the activity of personal agents within a specified period,

---

3. For the Chronicler the ברית *par excellence* is that which was made with David; nevertheless, this necessarily involves Israel as Yahweh's people; cf. 1 Chron. 17.9-10; 2 Chron. 7.14.

4. Welten (1973) dissents from this consensus; see Chapter 5.

and the causal connection between events.[5] Chronicles is distinguished
by the extent to which it attributes events to Yahweh's direct activity.[6]
At many points his activity in requiting piety or unfaithfulness is presented as explicit and direct,[7] whereas elsewhere this activity is implied,
usually through stock motifs of reward and punishment, and the
temporal conjunction of actions and results.[8]

However, it is less frequently observed that Yahweh does not only
respond to the conduct of his people, particularly as it is focused in cultic
fidelity,[9] but also *initiates* events. Chronicles presents Yahweh as
sovereign over human affairs generally, as well as being Israel's God.[10]
His own role in initiating and guiding the course of events is central to
the theology of the book. At times this activity is made explicit: most
notably, the impulse and opportunity to fetch the ark are attributed to
divine origin.[11] At other times, evidence of Yahweh's pro-active involvement may be deduced from the sequence of events, in the same way
that it is implied that certain outcomes are intended as divine reward
or punishment. The discussion therefore draws particular attention to
this pattern of divine activity, initiatory as well as reactive, and its
significance for understanding the author's retributive thought.

A concern with Yahweh's activity of rewarding and punishing pervades the work. This is most evident in the post-Solomonic narrative of
2 Chronicles 10–36, which is structured explicitly around this theme, but
the perspective is also reflected in the genealogies of 1 Chronicles 1–9
and is an important concern throughout the narratives of Saul (1 Chron.
10), David (1 Chron. 11–29) and Solomon (2 Chron. 1–9). It may be

5. Long 1984: 250.
6. Cf. Japhet 1989: 125-26.
7. Cf. 1 Chron. 10.14, Yahweh puts Saul to death and turns the kingdom over
to David; 2 Chron. 12.2b, Shishak's invasion; 13.15c, God routs Jeroboam and all
Israel; 14.6, Yahweh grants Asa rest.
8. Cf. 2 Chron. 13.21, Abijah's family flourishes; 15.19, Asa enjoys peace;
16.12, Asa's illness; cf. v. 10.
9. The Chronicler shows a greater interest in specifically cultic rather than more
general moral questions, as Japhet (1989: 262-65) notes, but that is a reflection of the
cultic orientation of his work, and the point should not be overpressed. The Law for
the Chronicler embraced the whole of Israel's existence (cf. 2 Chron. 19.10).
10. Cf. Japhet 1989: 41-53 on 'the monotheistic idea' in Chronicles.
11. 1 Chron. 13.2; cf. also the indications in 2 Chron. 10.15, 22.7 and 25.20 of
Yahweh's superintendence over human affairs.

added that the different forms reflected in the book, such as prophetic and royal speech, prayer and authorial comment, all have divine reward and punishment as a recurrent and often dominant theme.[12]

2. *Lexical Studies in the Chronicler's Theology of Retribution*

Investigations into the writer's special theological vocabulary have an established place in helping to define the theology of this work (as, indeed, they do in other branches of biblical studies), and several studies have focused closely on this aspect of the work.[13] However, two caveats are called for.

The first is the general principle that the interpretation of a work depends less on its vocabulary than on its larger sense-units. Thus the individual pericopae and the context of a given term are a surer guide to the Chronicler's meaning than atomistic concentration on terminology.[14] The writer's distinctive vocabulary is part of a larger set of theological ideas which can of course be expressed in different and more indirect ways. The pericopae may also help determine the content of this characteristic language, even where the terms are not expressly used.[15]

12. On this aspect in royal speech and prayer in Chronicles see Throntveit 1987: 84-85.

13. For recent studies of the Chronicler's vocabulary see especially Williamson 1979b: 149-51; 1982 *passim*; Braun 1979; McCarthy 1982; Johnstone 1986.

14. Moreover, the context(s) may define more closely the meaning of the vocabulary, whatever the traditional-historical (diachronic) background to the terms; cf. Barr 1961. On the contribution of linguistics and discourse analysis to hermeneutics, see Cotterell and Turner 1989.

15. For example, physical healing is implied in the account of Hezekiah's sickness and prayer in 2 Chron. 32.24: Yahweh 'answered him and gave him a sign'. Because the Chronicler has recast the relationship between Hezekiah and Isaiah over against the way it is presented in Kings, he omits the prophetic oracle:

'I have heard your prayer...; behold, I will heal you
'[שמעתי את תפלתך...הנני רפא לך] (2 Kgs 20.5).

However, the striking parallels in language between this passage and 2 Chron. 7.14 may suggest that the root רפא embraces physical healing for the Chronicler, as well as the sense in which it is usually taken, as a metaphor for 'forgiveness' or 'full restoration'. This suggestion is supported by the account of Asa who in his sickness 'did not seek Yahweh' (2 Chron. 16.12), and the description of Jehoram's disease (2 Chron. 21.18) as 'incurable' (לאין מרפא). The same expression is used in 2 Chron. 36.16 to describe the spiritual condition of the people. These allusions and

Secondly, the writer's special vocabulary is, to some extent, synonymous in usage: the individual terms often appear collectively in pericopae with some overlap in meaning, and it would be a mistake to
define the terms too discretely. In this stylistic fact we can detect something of the character of Chronicles as conscious rhetoric.[16]

With these caveats in mind, we may turn to a more detailed examination of the Chronicler's distinctive vocabulary. Many of these terms are
concentrated in the Chronistic additions in 2 Chron. 7.12b-16a,
especially כקש/דרש; התפלל; בנע niph.; and שוב.[17]

Examples of this vocabulary are also found earlier in the work than in
2 Chron. 7.12b-16a. Most of these earlier references are theologically
neutral, but some of them do contribute to an understanding of the
writer's thought. Yahweh's response is also typified in 2 Chron. 7.14 by
שמע, סלח, and רפא, terms which recur in varying degrees in the
subsequent narrative.

It is difficult to overstate the significance of 2 Chron. 7.12b-16a for
the interpretation of the work. This unit expresses *in nuce* the central
theological conviction of the work, a fuller statement of which is provided by the immediate context, the extended oracle of 2 Chron. 7.12-
22. As well as the positive vocabulary mentioned above, the Chronicler

examples of word-play suggest that the Chronicler also sees a relation between
spiritual health and physical healing, and that the theme of disease and healing is a
larger one in the work than is immediately apparent.

16. Alonso Schökel (1988: 67) comments on this aspect of Hebrew poetics:
'Synonymy has its privileged place in the genres which are dominated by emotion:
the emotion of the subject who expresses himself, or of a person whom the poet
wishes to influence. It is thus found in lyric poetry or in rhetoric.' Duke (1990)
argues that Chronicles employs rational modes of persuasion; indeed, he believes that
much of the work can be read as an extended demonstration of the consequences of
faithfulness, apostasy and repentance. At its linguistic level, however, the work must
also have appealed to the emotions of the Chronicler's community, with its synonymous and repetitious language echoing their earlier religious traditions. Mason
(1990) holds that the Chronicler's language and forms of address are a reflection of
contemporary preaching and paraenesis; certainly it can be readily imagined how
familiar turns of phrase might have been reminted to a new purpose.

17. Williamson (1982: 225-26) in particular has pointed to the programmatic
significance of 2 Chron. 7.14. He notes how each of the four verbs used there to
describe positive human responses to divine chastisement (כנע; התפלל; בקש/דרש
niph.; שוב) is taken up subsequently as an 'avenue of repentance' and a turning point
for miraculous deliverance. This insight, which is of the first importance for the
correct interpretation of the work, is developed and explored at length below.

also employs a parallel negative vocabulary, principally עזב and מעל. The results of a study of the distribution and significance of these terms are presented below.

However, before the terms are considered individually, it is useful to note the rhetorical force accorded them by their form and setting in the largely Chronistic unit of 2 Chron. 7.12b-16a:

v. 12b A   I have heard your prayer (שמעתי את תפלתך) and chosen (בחרתי) this place (במקום הזה) for myself as a house of sacrifice (לבית זבח).

v. 13   B   When I shut up the heavens (השמים) so that there is no rain, or command the locust to devour the land (לאכול הארץ) or send plague among my people (בעמי),

v. 14   C   if my people will humble themselves (ויכנעו עמי)— they who are called by my name—and pray (ויתפללו) and seek (ויבקשו) my face and turn (וישבו) from their evil ways,

        B′ I will hear from heaven (אשמע מן השמים) and forgive (ואסלח) their sin and heal their land (וארפא את ארצם).

v. 15   A′ Now my eyes will be open and my ears attentive to the prayer of this place (לתפלת המקום הזה). v. 16a For now I have chosen (בחרתי) and consecrated this house (הבית הזה)...

While the significance of v. 14 has been widely (if not always accurately) recognized, the emphatic chiastic form of this unit has not been commented on before. It is evident from this arrangement, with its degree of correspondence of components and repetition of key terms, that v. 14 is of central importance. It stands out as the point of reversal of circumstances, in which repentance is followed by divine restoration.

1. Positive Human Responses in Chronicles

(i) בִּקֵּשׁ/דָּרַשׁ; *associated motifs*. These are the most frequent and characteristic of the writer's terms, occurring in a theologically significant sense thirty-two times in the *Sondergut* and eight times in the synoptic sections.[18] Yahweh is typically the object of this verb, from which fact Begg (1982) and Duke (1990), following Schaefer (1972),[19] conclude

18. בקש/דרש is found in a theologically significant sense in the *Sondergut* in 1 Chron. 10.13, 14; 13.3; 15.13; 21.30; 22.19; 28.9; 2 Chron. 1.5; 7.14; 11.16; 12.14; 14.3, 7; 15.2, 12, 13, 15; 16.12; 17.3, 4; 19.3; 20.3, 4; 24.22; 25.15, 20; 26.5; 30.19; 34.3; and in synoptic passages in 1 Chron. 16.10-11 (= Ps. 105.3-4); 2 Chron. 18.4, 6, 7 (= 1 Kgs 22.5, 7, 8); 34.21, 26 (= 2 Kgs 22.13, 18).

19. G. Schaefer, 'The Significance of Seeking God in the Purpose of the

that 'seeking Yahweh' epitomizes the theme of the work. By this expression they understand a summons to trust Yahweh and worship him exclusively according to the Mosaic and Davidic cultic institutions. This is clearly a matter of importance for the writer, but this is too narrow a description of the writer's purposes. Moreover, it can be shown that the Chronicler uses בקש/דרש in more general, as well as quite specific (cult-centred), ways. Restricting our discussion to non-synoptic cases, we may identify the following principal usages:

1. 'Seeking Yahweh' is frequently used to typify commitment to Yahweh and his worship according to legitimate norms (כמשפט; cf. 1 Chron. 15.13). The contexts in which these verbs occur specify that 'seeking Yahweh' includes:

   a. sacrifice and prayer (1 Chron. 21.30; 2 Chron. 1.5; 11.16; 16.12);
   b. obedience to Yahweh's commandments (1 Chron. 22.19; 28.9; 2 Chron. 26.5);
   c. obedience to the Mosaic Law, probably with reference to cultic matters and reform (1 Chron. 10.13, 14; cf. 13.3; 15.13; 2 Chron. 14.3, 6 [E 4, 7]; 15.2, 12, 13, 15; 17.4; 19.3; 31.21; 34.3);
   d. intercession (2 Chron. 20.3-4).

The focus seems to be principally on faithfulness in cultic matters and does not have the old oracular sense of the expression דרש את יהוה.[20]

Accompanying descriptions confirm that the writer's interest in legitimacy and form in worship is not externalist nor overly formal but is balanced by a concern for motivation, integrity and religious experience. Thus, for example, Jehoshaphat is commended as one who 'sought Yahweh with all his heart' (2 Chron. 22.9; cf. 31.21 on Hezekiah).[21]

2. Yahweh is the subject in three passages, where the expression denotes his positive (1 Chron. 28.9; 2 Chron. 14.6 [E 7], following LXX) or negative (2 Chron. 24.22) orientation toward persons. The

Chronicler' (dissertation, Southern Baptist Theological Seminary, 1972); cited in Duke 1990: 49-50. Wagner suggests from his own survey that in the end the expression 'denotes nothing other than the Chronicler's ideal of piety' (*TDOT*: III, 301).

20. This is found probably only in 2 Chron. 18.4, 6, 7 (= 1 Kgs 22.5, 7, 8).

21. 'Seeking Yahweh' entails an act of will (2 Chron. 11.16; 12.14; 20.33; 30.19) and presupposes faith (cf. 2 Chron. 14.7, 10 [E 11]; 32.7-8). Japhet (1989) and Braun (1986) have also remarked on the writer's emphasis on joy as evidence of his concern with interior religious experience.

Chronicler's predilection for reciprocal word-play for rhetorical effect is evident in these examples.

3. The special focus of the expression in 1 Chron. 22.19 and 28.9-10 is on Solomon's commission to build the temple. It functions as an exhortation to future obedience to his given task.

4. As was remarked in the introductory discussion, the expression in 2 Chron. 7.14 denotes humble repentance associated with prayer in or towards the temple. A similar sense is reflected, for example, in the account of Hezekiah's Passover (2 Chron. 30.19) and in several passages noted below.

This last-mentioned meaning for בקש/דרש is not attested in the earlier chapters, and it imports a particular nuance into the usage from 2 Chronicles 6–7 onwards. While most uses signify positive, devoted commitment to Yahweh on the part of the king or community, especially as this is expressed in worship, the sense here is much closer to the summons to repentance and the assurance of divine restoration, a usage reflected in the exilic Deuteronomistic and prophetic writings. Deut. 4.29, Isa. 55.6-7, and Jer. 29.12-14 are important in this respect. In particular, the last-cited passage contains a number of expressions which recur in Chronicles.[22] In using such terms the author reflects the idiom of exilic proclamation, but retrojects that language and thought into the First Temple period. Subsequent references to 'seeking Yahweh' should be understood first in the light of the meaning of the temple for the Chronicler: at its most fundamental level, it is Yahweh's channel for forgiveness and restoration. This perspective will become clearer in our discussion of the narrative which depicts the extent of sinfulness in the people and the divine provision for this state of affairs. By the same token, we find in the Chronistic motif of cult reform that 'seeking Yahweh' denotes concrete acts of repentance to restore the nation to legitimate worship.[23] A correlation between 'seeking Yahweh' in this sense and obtaining success is certainly made in the work,[24] which is the complementary message to the Chronicler's emphasis on Yahweh's mercy and forgiveness.

22. The influence of Jeremiah on the writer is especially apparent in 2 Chron. 36.21-22, where the seventy-year exile and the return are both in accord with his prophetic word. Cf. Jer. 29.10-14.

23. Cf. 2 Chron. 14.3, 6 [E 4, 7]; 15.2, 12, 13; 19.3; 34.3.

24. Among many examples, Solomon (1 Chron. 22.13); Asa (2 Chron. 14.6; 15.2); Uzziah (26.5).

The above remarks have established the main lines of the discussion; the remaining terms may be considered more summarily.

(ii) הִתְפַּלֵּל. Prayer in Chronicles is an outward expression of 'seeking Yahweh'. Various terms are used to designate this activity,[25] which falls into two broad categories: a penitent appeal for restoration and forgiveness according to the meaning of 'seeking' in 2 Chron. 7.14 (cf. 2 Chron. 30.18; 33.13); and a plea for help in the face of external threats (cf. 2 Chron. 13.14; 14.11; 20.5-12; 32.20).[26]

Prayer in this work is set within the specific relationship between Yahweh and Israel mediated by the Davidic covenant. It will be seen that this covenant has a twofold expression, the Davidic dynasty and the temple. Accordingly, David's prayers (1 Chron. 17.16-27 [= 2 Sam. 7.18-29]; 29.10-19) concentrate on these related themes, while Solomon's dedicatory prayer (2 Chron. 6.4-42 [= 1 Kgs 8.23-53]) determines the meaning of prayer in or toward the temple. The centrality of temple prayer is also underscored by two special Chronistic emphases. In 1 Kgs 8.52 Solomon pleads that Yahweh may hear Israel's supplication, basing this appeal on the exodus (v. 53). 2 Chron. 6.40 paraphrases this, but ties it instead to the temple (לִתְפִלַּת הַמָּקוֹם הַזֶּה), and hence to the Davidic dynasty to which the temple testifies. The petition is reproduced verbatim in Yahweh's reply in 2 Chron. 7.15, reflecting the Chronicler's emphatic conviction that Yahweh hears and responds positively to the prayers of his people. This perception is demonstrated throughout 2 Chron. 10–36, where prayer is shown to be consistently efficacious.

In this respect Chronicles may give the impression of having a rather rationalistic or mechanical outlook over against other Old Testament writings. However, this simplified depiction is probably dictated by the writer's paraenetical intent. Prayer in Chronicles is evidence of piety: as Japhet (1989: 255 n. 185) notes, only the righteous (or more accurately,

---

25. The Chronistic vocabulary of prayer includes: הִתְפַּלֵּל (2 Chron. 7.1; 32.20, 24; 33.13); זָעַק (1 Chron. 5.20; 2 Chron. 13.14; 18.31; 20.9; 32.20; each case signifies an appeal for help in a situation of military distress); חלה (2 Chron. 33.12); שָׁאַל (1 Chron. 4.10; note also the paronomasia in 1 Chron. 10.13).

26. Wellhausen (1885: 204) argued that the invasion of the eastern coalition (2 Chron. 20) was in response to Jehoshaphat's disobedience (cf. 2 Chron. 19.2), but this claim is disputed below.

the penitent) are described in this work as praying.[27] No doubt as part of his purpose of encouraging prayer and engendering faith, the Chronicler depicts every recourse to the authentic Mosaic and Davidic cultic forms of piety in a positive light.[28]

(iii) שׁוּב. This verb occurs only infrequently in a theologically significant sense (2 Chron. 7.14; 15.4; 24.29; 30.6, 9; 36.13, out of 67 occurrences), but each instance corresponds to the idea of 'repentance'. The immediate source of the writer's usage is his *Vorlage* (1 Kgs 8.33-34 = 2 Chron. 6.24-25, from which 2 Chron. 7.14 is in part constructed), but the other examples have no parallel. The influence of the canonical prophets is probably to be discerned here: Holladay (1958: 116-17) shows that 113 of the 164 examples of שׁוּב used in a 'covenantal' sense belong to that corpus, notably Jeremiah (48×) and Ezekiel (16×). The influence of Jeremiah on Chronicles is, of course, well known (cf. 2 Chron. 36.13, 15-16, 20-21 for specific references; as well as general echoes of Jer. 29.12-14).

(iv) כָּנַע *niph.* Chronicles accounts for fourteen of the eighteen examples in the Hebrew Bible where this expression denotes a penitent attitude in prayer. In this respect it is synonymous with the other terms as an expression of the Chronicler's ideal of piety.

A more specific *Sitz im Leben* for this term has been suggested by McCarthy (1982), who maintains that כנע niph., דרשׁ, עזב and מעל (see below) are *termini technici* in acts of covenant-renewal. The purpose of these acts is said to be to revalidate the cult, purifying it 'so that God can *be* there with his people' (1982: 32, emphasis his). McCarthy bases his claim on three cases of cult reform instigated by prophetic calls to 'seek Yahweh', which speak of entering, making or renewing a covenant (2 Chron. 15.12-13; 29.10, 20-21; 34.31-32; McCarthy fails to mention the covenant under the 'priest-king' Jehoiada, 23.16). However, his attempt to reconstruct a hypothetical ceremony as the background for this language is unconvincing. As Japhet has shown (1989: 112-15),

---

27. This may have some bearing on the portrayal of Abijah (2 Chron. 13), which appears to diverge from Kings; note that Judah's army (v. 14), rather than Abijah himself, is described as crying out to Yahweh.

28. In contrast, for example, to the criticisms that the pre-exilic prophets often directed at the (ostensibly orthodox) religious practices of their day.

these 'covenants' are better understood as binding commitments between king and people to pursue a purified Yahwism, rather than any cultic reactivation of the bond between God and people. At no point is this bond actually severed.[29]

כנע niph. and the related terms are more properly the language of religious paraenesis rather than specific cultic terminology. The first occurrence of כנע niph. in the narrative (2 Chron. 12) corresponds to the first act of repentance in the face of divine judgment, while its fourfold repetition (vv. 6, 7 [*bis*], 12) makes it the leitmotif of that pericope. It may also serve the rhetorical intent of echoing 2 Chron. 7.14, where this verb is the first term of the protasis. In each of its occurrences it is stated or implied that those who humble themselves may avert Yahweh's wrath (2 Chron. 12.12; 30.8, 10; 32.25, 26; 34.25, 27; note the Chronistic repetition of the verb in this verse).

Underlying these examples is a sustained reflection on the meaning of the exile and return. The Chronicler's use is probably derived from Lev. 26.41-42, a passage whose influence is evident in 2 Chron. 36.21. Leviticus 26.41-42 envisages a situation of exile on account of מעל (v. 40; see below). It describes a transition in the exiles' condition 'when their uncircumcised heart is humbled (יכנע) and they accept [the punishment for] their guilt',[30] whereupon Yahweh remembers the land and his covenant with the patriarchs. Exile, impending or actual, forms the backcloth to the section in which this expression is concentrated, 2 Chronicles 30–36 (cf. 30.11; 32.26; 33.12; 34.27). The restored community was doubtless conscious of living still with the consequences of that event (not least of which must have been the continuing diaspora and the foreign occupation of their land). Against these harsh realities, the Chronicler strove to demonstrate that these consequences could be reversed by repentance.

---

29. As was remarked already, ברית in Chronicles denotes primarily the Davidic covenant, through which the king, people and cult are constituted into a special relationship with Yahweh. This covenant in turn is related by the Chronicler to the Mosaic and Abrahamic covenants; see further Chapter 7. Significantly, the Chronicler alters 2 Kgs 11.17a (= 2 Chron. 23.16, a passage ignored by McCarthy 1982) to make it simply into an act of solemn rededication.

30. Following Wenham's translation (1979: 332); cf. 2 Chron. 12.6 for a recognition of the people's guilt and Yahweh's justice.

2. *Negative Human Responses in Chronicles*

The Chronicler also employs a distinctive parallel vocabulary to characterize apostasy and other grievous types of sin.

(i) עָזַב. This term, the negative counterpart of דרשׁ, occurs in a theological sense fourteen times in Chronicles, usually denoting a forsaking of Yahweh which he reciprocates by withdrawing his presence and help (cf. 1 Chron. 28.9; 2 Chron. 7.19, 22; 12.1, 5; 13.10, 11: 15.2; 21.10; 24.18, 20, 24; 29.6; 34.25). In the conclusion to the oracle to Solomon (2 Chron. 7.19-22) the expression replaces the Deuteronomistic לא תשׁמרו.

While עזב is often used quite generally, a number of examples specify its cultic-religious content. Thus Rehoboam and all Israel 'forsook' Yahweh's law (2 Chron. 12.1; cf. v. 5); and Joash and the princes of Judah 'forsook' the temple for idolatry (2 Chron. 24.18; cf. 13.10-11; 29.6-7). The Chronicler's use does not depends on the *Vorlage* (except 2 Chron. 7.22 = 1 Kgs 9.9; 2 Chron. 34.25 = 2 Kgs 24.17) but is similar to those exilic/post-exilic texts which speak of Yahweh or his law or covenant being 'forsaken'.[31]

(ii) מעל. This is the most distinctive of the Chronicler's terms for sin (1 Chron. 2.3; 5.25; 9.1; 10.13; 2 Chron. 12.2; 26.16; 28.19; 29.19; 33.19; 36.14), and is unparalleled in Samuel–Kings. The term apparently originates from the realm of sacral law, where it denotes 'trespass against sancta' (cf. Milgrom 1976a). Mosis (1973: 29-30) follows Zimmerli and Elliger in taking it as a generalizing expression in Chronicles for 'serious sin against God'. Milgrom (p. 80) holds that where the context specifies the content of מעל, the term denotes a violation of the cult, including infringement of priestly prerogatives (cf. 2 Chron. 26.16, 18), but he does not discuss its wider contextual function in Chronicles.

Johnstone (1986), in contrast to Mosis, universalizes rather than generalizes the sacral law idea implicit in מעל. He holds that Chronicles is essentially a 'theological essay' on the theme of guilt and atonement in Israel's history. The writer is said to use מעל as a 'hermeneutical key' to interpret Israel's history in the land from beginning (cf. 1 Chron. 2.3) to end (cf. 2 Chron. 36.14) as one of sacrilege and robbing God, the

---

31. Cf. Deut. 28.20; Judg. 2.12-13; 1 Sam. 8.8; 1 Kgs 18.18; 2 Kgs 17.6; Jer. 9.12.

repeated failure of the elect nation to render God his due. Leviticus 5.14-26 (E 5.14–6.7) speaks discursively of מעל, and describes how the law of restitution and the *asham* offering constitute the appropriate offering for that offence. Chronicles is seen by Johnstone as an 'aggadic midrash' on this law of restitution. The cult which is established by David is the point at which the deadly course of מעל is overcome and, conversely, where the nation's life is consecrated through the presentation of the קדשׁים.

Johnstone's observations on these linguistic features orientate us to a significant sub-theme in the text, the question of holiness, but it is doubtful whether so uniform or thoroughgoing a schema is worked out in Chronicles. The book reflects numerous streams of tradition, including Pentateuchal, Deuteronomistic and prophetic, as well as the specifically priestly interest in sacrifice. It is certainly concerned with the matter of Israel's sinfulness (as we will see, Chronicles stresses more clearly than the *Vorlage* that the cult was instituted on account of this fact), but it subordinates this matter to a more comprehensive theme, that of Yahweh's kingdom, its realization and persistence.[32] I will argue in Chapter 7 that the Chronicler understands the earthly manifestation of that kingdom to be a much larger entity than simply the cult and the cultic community (although these are certainly central to his thought). Further, in using the expression מעל, the Chronicler does not refer to the law of restitution, as an aggadic interpretation might require.

Other usages of מעל would have been known to the writer from the traditions before him, especially Ezekiel, which makes repeated reference to מעל in contexts of national judgment and exile (cf. Ezek. 14.13; 15.8; 17.20; 18.24; 39.23, 26). However, the most likely source is Lev. 26.40-41, a passage whose significance for Chronicles has already been noted. Here the meaning is focused personally on God: for the writer, Israel's whole existence is lived *coram deo*. Chronicles is not concerned to distinguish between the comparative validity of the form and the content of the Mosaic religion. Those who 'seek Yahweh' do so sincerely according to legitimate cultic means; those who commit מעל forsake (√עזב) him, an apostasy which is demonstrated by their recourse to idolatry and their neglect or perversion of the legitimate cult (cf. 2 Chron. 29.6).

---

32. Cf. Chapters 7 and 8 for a discussion of Yahweh's kingdom in Chronicles. A helpful definition of 'theme' in Old Testament narrative is offered by Clines 1978.

3. *Lexical Terms Denoting Yahweh's Response to Repentance and Sin*
Up to this point, our discussion has concentrated for the most part on
2 Chron. 7.12-22, especially the Chronistic addition of vv. 12b-16a.
Important as this addition is, it belongs within a larger section which,
although derived from 1 Kgs 9.1-9, must also be taken as representing
the writer's viewpoint. The evidence for this is found in the numerous
adaptations, some minor and others more substantial, which the
Chronicler has made to his *Vorlage*.[33] 2 Chron. 7.12-22 corresponds
structurally and thematically to the other extended oracle of the work,
1 Chron. 17.4-14 (= 2 Sam. 7.5-16). Both oracles are concerned with
the mutually related themes of the temple and the dynastic promise, but
with differing emphases. The first passage concentrates on the promise
to David, while the second focuses predominantly on the meaning of the
temple.[34]

2 Chronicles 7 in its entirety may be rightly seen as the centrepiece of
Chronicles, as Solomon's great prayer of dedication is answered by a
theophany that evokes popular worship (vv. 1-3, no parallel), and is followed by festivities involving the whole nation (vv. 4-10). The
Chronicler understands the inauguration of the temple to mark a new
dispensation in Israel's history, and the significance of this event is
accordingly underlined by an oracle. Although in terms of historical time
thirteen years would have elapsed between the dedication of the temple
and the oracle (2 Chron. 7.11; 8.1; cf. 1 Kgs 6.38–7.1; 9.10), in
Chronicles (as in Kings) the two events are placed side by side to present
the divine message as the direct answer to the petitions of the prayer.
The connection and progression between the different units of the oracle
should be noted:

1. First, the chiastic insertion in 2 Chron. 7.12b-16a confirms the
    choice of the temple as the place where repentance is accepted
    and divine chastisement is reversed.
2. Next, vv. 17-18 concern the dynastic promise, according to the
    Chronicler's formulation.
3. Finally, vv. 19-22 describe the consequence of apostasy and
    persistent rebellion.

33. For a convenient comparison, see Bendavid 1972: 88-89.
34. The Chronicler's modifications to the *Vorlage* in 1 Chron. 17.4-14 are examined in Chapter 7, where it will be seen that this passage and 2 Chron. 7.12-22
together convey the central theological message of the work.

In their new context these last verses (which have also been slightly modified) act as a counterpoise to the first unit to indicate what will happen when no repentance is forthcoming. Selman (1994b: 342) remarks that the distinction between the salvation of v. 14 and the judgment of v. 20 is based not on the contrasting merits of the people concerned (for the same sinful people are in view), but rather on the presence or absence of repentance.

It is this decisive fact, more so than the question of just recompense, which dictates the Chronicler's subsequent presentation of history. Rehoboam and the leaders of Judah humble themselves before Shemaiah's word and are granted a partial deliverance (2 Chron. 12.6-7). Jehoshaphat submits to Jehu's rebuke (2 Chron. 19.3) after his disastrous alliance with Ahab, and he restores the nation to Yahweh's law (vv. 4-5). Even Manasseh is rehabilitated when he entreats Yahweh's favour (2 Chron. 33.12-13). Although the writer's overall assessment of Manasseh and Rehoboam remains negative,[35] he nevertheless wished to emphasize (no doubt for his own kerygmatic purpose) that even these unworthy descendants of David had been recipients of Yahweh's goodness.

Conversely, even those reigns which the writer looked on favourably could come to a bad end. Asa and Uzziah are probably judged positively by the Chronicler, at least to begin with (cf. 2 Chron. 16.14; 26.5), but both failed to heed the call to repentance (2 Chron. 16.9; 26.18). The same is unambiguously true for the majority of Judah's kings, who are viewed negatively by the writer.[36]

Yahweh's positive response to repentance is typified in 2 Chron. 7.14 by the verbs שׁמע, סלח, and רפא. This reply is constructed partly from the dedicatory prayer in 2 Chronicles 6 (which in turn depends on 1 Kings 8), where שׁמע and סלח are frequently found (2 Chron. 6.20, 21, 23, 25, 30, 33, 35, 39). This prayer and its reply have a much greater centrality and significance in Chronicles than in Kings. Its importance is underlined partly by allusions to the divine response at critical moments in the post-Solomonic history, such as Jehoshaphat facing invasion (2 Chron. 20.9), Hezekiah's Passover (2 Chron. 30.27), and Manasseh's captivity (2 Chron. 33.13).

---

35. This is clear from 2 Chron. 12.14 and the intensification of Manasseh's guilt in 2 Chron. 33.3, 6.

36. See the appendix at the end of this study, which includes the motif of heeding or rejecting the prophetic word.

Like שמע, the author's use of סלח is due to the *Vorlage* (2 Chron. 6.21 = 1 Kgs 8.30). The term is not used after 2 Chron. 7.14, although the idea is expressed in other ways.

רפא is the writer's own term, which he uses with reference to the land or the people. Brown[37] argues that the usage in Chronicles reflects a 'priestly' background in its emphasis on forgiveness or the declaration of cultic purity (cf. 2 Chron. 30.20). However, as I have suggested, the meaning of the root רפא should not be unduly limited to the 'spiritual' sense of forgiveness, and a cultic sense is also too restricted. The use in 2 Chron. 7.14 suggests relief for the land from the physical afflictions of drought, locusts or plague (cf. v. 13 and 2 Chron. 6.26-28), which is in keeping with the emphasis in 2 Chronicles 10–36 on the restoration of peace and security to the land.[38] By extension, the expression 'I will heal their land' also implies the return of the exiles. The Chronicler's usage closely echoes prophetic promises of restoration such as Jer. 30.17-18 and 33.6-37, which combine the spiritual and literal senses of a penitent people who have returned both to Yahweh and to the land.[39]

Yahweh's response to Israel's failure to repent (v. 20) consists of 'uprooting' the people from the land and rejecting the temple. The reference to 'uprooting' should probably be understood as an allusion to the Sinaitic covenant curses for disobedience as they are recorded in Deuteronomy 28–29. That association is, of course, already latent in the *Vorlage* (1 Kgs 9.9), but the Chronicler makes a closer link with Deut. 29.23-27 (E 24–28) by reading in v. 20 ונתשתים, in place of והכרתי את ישראל (1 Kgs 9.7). The Chronicler's sole use of this verb echoes Deut. 29.27 (E v. 28, ויתשם).[40]

---

37. *THAT*, II, col. 622.

38. Although in these cases the concern is exclusively with social and political well-being.

39. Cf. also the metaphorical use of the root רפא in Jer. 8.15; 14.19; 19.11.

40. Perhaps the Deuteronomist's expression had a note of finality about it that was foreign to the Chronicler's understanding of the people in Yahweh's purposes; see Chapter 9 for a discussion of the ways in which the Chronicler develops the Deuteronomistic History from his post-exilic perspective and makes it altogether more positive. It is of note that whereas *Israel* is made the proverb and byword in Kings, in Chronicles this refers instead to the temple (v. 20).

Additionally, the covenant blessing in Deut. 28.10, 'and all the nations of the earth will see that you are called by Yahweh's name' (ראו כל עמי הארץ כי שם יהוה נקרא עליך), may be the immediate source of the description of Israel in 2 Chron. 7.14 as עמי אשר נקרא שמי עליהם. In Solomon's prayer the expression 'to be called by (Yahweh's) name' referred to the temple (2 Chron. 6.33 = 1 Kgs 8.43), but in the divine response it is applied instead to the people of Israel. The expression denotes Yahweh's ownership and possession of Israel, and echoes a number of passages in prophetic literature, especially Jeremiah.[41]

3. *Conclusion*

The following preliminary conclusions have emerged from this discussion of the Chronicler's vocabulary. First, the extended oracle to Solomon in 2 Chron. 7.12-22 was seen to be of the first importance in defining the writer's principal theological terms. Although commonly called a 'vocabulary of retribution', the language of 2 Chron. 7.14 is primarily concerned with repentance and restoration, rather than strict retribution as such. The Chronistic insertion of vv. 12b-16a shows that repentance rather than merit is the deciding factor in many circumstances. Of course, in common with the whole witness of the Old Testament, Chronicles does affirm a close connection between actions and consequences, and it will be the task of the next section to describe this relationship more closely.

Secondly, it has been argued from much of the language that the Chronicler's thought is derived in part from reflection on the Sinaitic covenant, so that 'reward and punishment' are in fact closely related to the blessings and curses of that covenant.[42]

Thirdly, the writer is strongly influenced by the language and thought of the canonical prophets, especially Jeremiah.

41. Cf. Jer. 14.9; 15.16; and frequent references to the temple and Jerusalem as being 'called by Yahweh's name'; cf. also Isa. 63.19; Amos 9.12; Dan. 9.19; Num. 6.27.

42. In this respect, Japhet is too imprecise when she argues that Chronicles reflects 'a general religious awareness' which 'entails a desire to demonstrate that divine justice is at work in the world and can be discerned throughout Israelite history' (1989: 154). Rather, the Chronicler's moral world is to be understood against the backcloth of the Sinaitic covenant, as is the case for the Deuteronomistic Historian, on whose work the Chronicler depends in the first instance.

Such are the literary sources for the writer's language that can be positively identified. However, it is possible, indeed likely, that a work of paraenesis such as Chronicles would also draw on a living oral tradition of preaching and edification not otherwise known to us.[43]

43. Mason (1990) argues that the 'addresses' of Chronicles may reflect the homiletical practices of the Second Temple period; he rejects von Rad's theory of a recognizable literary genre of 'Levitical Sermon' as lacking sufficient objective criteria, but he identifies numerous rhetorical elements in the prophetic and royal speeches that point to an oral background in contemporary preaching and exegetical practice (pp. 137-44). Mason's work also involves a comparison of the 'addresses' in Chronicles with the 'speeches' in Ezra-Nehemiah, Zech. 1–8 and Malachi (pp. 145-256). An alternative view may be suggested by the work of Tangberg (1987). While Tangberg does not consider Chronicles or Ezra–Nehemiah, he does examine a wide range of pre- and post-exilic prophetic texts, including those analysed by Mason (Hag. 1.2-3; Zech. 1.2-3; Mal. 2.10-16; 3.6-12). He argues for the existence of an independent genre, the 'prophetic exhortation-speech', which consisted of two parts: (1) a call to repentance, often with the verbs דרשׁ, בקשׁ or שׁוב, and the appeal in the imperative or vetitive form; (2) motivation, usually in the form of a promise, threat or accusation. Tangberg argues that this genre underwent a transformation in the post-exilic period. 'In all the examples of the post-exilic prophets examined, the admonition to repent is connected with positive cultic demands in the service of the cultic restoration of the Jewish people. The polemic against the cult in classical prophecy is abolished and replaced by a new synthesis of cultic and prophetic piety' ('Bei sämtlichen untersuchten nachexilischen Propheten verbinden sich die Mahnungen zur Umkehr mit positivem kultischen Forderungen, die im Dienste der kultischen Restauration des jüdischen Volks stehen. Die Kultpolemik der klassischen Prophetie ist aufgehoben und durch eine neue Synthese von prophetischer und kultischer Frömmigkeit ersetzt worden') (1987: 148). If this interpretation of events is correct, Chronicles may echo (or indirectly witness to) a transformation in later prophetic activity. Certainly there are many affinities in language and thought between the post-exilic prophetic texts examined by Tangberg and the portrayal of prophecy in Chronicles. On cultic prophecy in Chronicles, see also Petersen 1977.

Chapter 4

EXEGETICAL STUDIES (2): NARRATIVE AND CONCLUSION

The structure of Chronicles is considered here according to the normally accepted divisions (1 Chron. 1–9; 10; 11–29; 2 Chron. 1–9; 10–36). The theme of reward and punishment here is generally associated with motifs or *topoi* in the non-synoptic sections, but the parallel passages have themselves been reworked to reflect the author's *Tendenzen*.[1] I will have occasion here to refer to lexical terms not discussed in Chapter 3, as well as other rhetorical and literary features which contribute to the overall composition. The sermonic-hortatory character of Chronicles as a whole is considered in the concluding chapter. In this chapter my concern is to determine how and to what extent a doctrine of retribution has motivated changes from, or additions to, the *Vorlage*.

1. *Retribution in the Genealogical Introduction (1 Chronicles 1–9)*

The narrative notes in the genealogies reflect the Chronicler's *Tendenzen* and anticipate the themes which will emerge in the narrative proper. Specific attention is given here to the way in which this section treats the subject of sin and punishment or piety and blessing.

1. *1 Chronicles 2.3*
The genealogies contain three notes about individuals which make rhetorical use of paronomasia to indicate the significance of these persons: Er, who did 'evil' (רע), Achar, who 'brings trouble' (עוכר) and Jabez, born 'in pain' (בעצב).

---

1. Older commentators often attributed minor differences to the Chronicler's supposed 'Priestly' outlook (cf. Curtis and Madsen 1910: 206 on 1 Chron. 13.14; a view qualified sharply by von Rad [1930]), but many of these differences, especially where Samuel is concerned, are now known to reflect the writer's text-type (Cross 1958; Lemke 1965; Ulrich 1978). Other differences are better taken more simply as stylistic variations (cf. Willi 1972).

The death notice of Er is the first example in Chronicles to state a relationship between sin and punishment. Characteristically it takes the form of direct divine intervention (וימיתהו, following Gen. 38.7; cf. 1 Chron. 10.14). Despite this unpropitious start, Judah's line is continued, albeit reprehensibly, through Tamar (v. 4). Williamson (1982: 50) rightly refers to the 'electing grace' which tolerated this situation.

2. *1 Chronicles 2.7*
The language of this note also depends on its source (Josh. 7.1), but the significance of מעל is often overlooked by commentators. The Chronicler draws attention to the fact that at the beginning of its occupation of the land, Israel is guilty of serious sin, through Achar's disobedience.[2] The allusion to the theft of the 'devoted things', which brought military disaster on the people, is specifically designated an act of מעל (Josh. 7.1; 22.20). The Chronicler will constantly underline the military consequences of מעל, the culmination of which is the exile of the entire guilty community. Johnstone lays great store by this incident, which he sees as anticipating *in nuce* the theme of Chronicles (see above). However, this must be balanced against the other, and more important, salvific message which is interwoven with this tale of sin, the election of both Judah, whose line proves to be expansive and numerous (1 Chron. 2.3–4.23), and the Davidic house (1 Chron. 3), whose line similarly continues into the post-exilic period.[3]

3. *1 Chronicles 4.9-10*
This brief account of Jabez and his prayer is an illustration of God acting for good in the life of an individual, and the Chronistic theme of the efficacy of prayer. The themes here of territorial expansion and divine protection are also prominent concerns of the work (cf. 1 Chron. 5.20-22; 2 Chron. 20.6-12).

4. *1 Chronicles 4.39-43*
This note describing Simeon's westward expansion and military success is said to display some of the criteria of what Welten designates the Chronistic *topos* 'war report with positive outcome' ('Kriegsbericht mit

---

2. Chronicles probably preserves the original form of the name; cf. LXX and Syr, and the word-play already reflected in Josh. 7.26.
3. 1973: 166-72; see Chapter 7 on the significance of this theme.

positivem Ausgang'),[4] such as the small number of warriors whose victory indicated it was achieved through God's help, and their peaceful occupation signifying 'rest'. This tribe acted in an exemplary way, observing the *herem* 'in the days of Hezekiah, king of Judah' and so enjoyed secure possession of the land. Mention of this ideal reforming king who trusted Yahweh for help against Judah's enemies (2 Chron. 29–32) may be an early indication to the Chronicler's readers of how the divine rewards of military success and territorial expansion may be secured.

5. *1 Chronicles 5.18-22, 23-26*

The author's understanding of war is also reflected in these passages which contain language and perspectives which will recur in the subsequent narrative.[5] In each case a theological rationale is given for the outcome: victory through trust in Yahweh, defeat on account of apostasy from him. The leitmotif of vv. 23-26, loss of land and exile for מעל, forms a counterpoint with the lesson of vv. 18-22, a stylized 'Yahweh war' account.[6] The writer typically makes a chronological division between periods of faithfulness and blessing, and apostasy and punishment. The theme of מעל is developed from the same source as 2.7. De Vries (1989: 62) holds that the Chronicler deduced the Transjordanians' guilt from their fate, but more probably the writer inferred this (albeit indirectly) from Joshua 22. There, they are charged with מעל over the erection of their illicit altar, and an explicit connection is made with Achan/Achar's sin (v. 20). While the situations described in Joshua 22 and 1 Chronicles 5 are not identical (the former is an alleged offence against the unity of the cult [cf. v. 29], rather than apostasy), a connection between the two can be inferred. The Chronicler is unexcelled in his insistence on the sole legitimacy of the Jerusalem cult (cf. 2 Chron. 13), so that anything which derogated from it indicated unfaithfulness. The key word מעל in Josh. 22.16, 20 (and the associated term קצף, vv. 18, 20)

---

4.   See Chapter 5. On the sources of this pericope see Williamson 1982: 61-62.

5.   Williamson (1982: 66-67) questions the originality of the second pericope, finding it awkward in its present place and out of keeping with the Chronicler's usual practice. On the other hand, its themes are Chronistic, and in its content and language (cf. וימעלו) it follows the structure and explanation of Judah's exile in 2 Chron. 36.14-20.

6.   Note especially the use of זעק and עזר, and the theme of trust leading to victory.

perhaps suggested just such a propensity among the Transjordanians which would issue in their exile.

6. *1 Chronicles 9.1a*

A clear parallel is made here with 5.25-26, as מעל leads to exile for Judah. However, the principal emphasis of this passage is on the return (vv. 2-3) and the personages through whom the restoration has begun. The message is basically a positive one, that the exile is past and a decisive new phase in the nation's history has commenced. At the centre of this description are the cultic personnel and their duties, restoring continuity with the past and testifying to the central place of the temple in the nation's life.

7. *Summary*

These pericopae anticipate many of the recurrent themes and *topoi* of the narrative proper. They indicate that serious sin was a fact of Israel's existence in the land from start (1 Chron. 2.7) to finish (1 Chron. 9.1), and that this led to its dispossession as an act of divine judgment. A countervailing theme of grace emphasizes the election of Judah and the Davidic house, the expansion of territory in the land for those who are faithful, divine help in time of war, and the efficacy of prayer. All of these motifs also cohere with the outlook of the narrative proper.

2. *Retribution in the Narrative* (*1 Chronicles 10–29, 2 Chronicles 1–36*)

As is discussed more fully in Chapter 7, Chronicles describes how Yahweh's kingdom (cf. 1 Chron. 17.14) is established in the earthly form of the Jerusalem cult and the Davidic dynasty, reaching its apogee in the portrayal of Solomon's realm (2 Chron. 9). 2 Chronicles 10–36 then relates the history of the post-Solomonic kingdom, ending in the fall of the state. Throughout, the narrative of Chronicles makes extensive use of the *Vorlage,* but it possesses a different shape and focus, since the writer has his own theological concerns and material which he fashions independently of Samuel–Kings.[7] The Chronicler's interests are readily

---

7. Willi (1972: 66-67) argues that Chronicles is related to its *Vorlage* as the 'exegesis' of sacred text. In support of this he assigns the differences in Chronicles to nine categories in three groups (text-critical differences, redaction and interpretation). At the other extreme, Fishbane (1985: 381-83) denies that the Chronicler

apparent in a synoptic comparison of the significant units, which is used here as the main methodological approach for determining how and to what extent he has transformed his *Vorlage* to express his retributive doctrine.

1. *Retribution in the Death of Saul (1 Chronicles 10)*

A synoptic comparison of this passage with its *Vorlage* is very straightforward:

> 10.1-12 = 1 Sam. 31.1-13, report of battle on Mount Gilboa and Saul's death.
> *10.13-14 (no par.), theological explanation of Saul's death and transfer of kingdom to David.*

There are numerous small but possibly significant differences in detail in the synoptic section (cf. Bendavid 1972: 30-31). Some of these may relate to a variant text-type of Samuel used by the Chronicler (cf. Lemke 1965) or minor grammatical variations for stylistic reasons (cf. Willi 1972: 88, 90), but other differences (e.g. v. 6, 'and all [Saul's] house died together') are evidently more significant. The Chronicler's editorial comment in vv. 13-14 is, of course, of the first importance in interpreting this unit.

The function of this passage in Chronicles is variously understood. Japhet (1989: 405) suggests that it is intended to give David's enthronement continuity with the past, while older views (for example, von Rad 1930: 79; Rudolph 1955: 96) stressed the contrast of characters. Mosis (1973: 17-43) and Ackroyd (1991: 313-14) argue that the pericope illustrates some of the Chronicler's principal thematic interests, and can be taken as a set-piece in how he handled and transformed his scriptural sources. According to Mosis, the writer intended a contrast between David and Saul primarily in terms of the periods they represent: Saul's reign as the paradigmatic period of defeat and exile, and David's (as 1 Chron. 13–16 shows) as the era of restoration. This approach is also supported by Williamson (1982: 92-96). By referring in v. 9 to Saul's head in the Philistine temple of Dagon (instead of his body on the walls of Beth-shan, 1 Sam. 31.10), the Chronicler depicts the reversal of the circumstances in 1 Samuel 4–6, in which Dagon is

___

intended a synoptic-comparative reading of his work in relation to Samuel–Kings. It is argued here instead that the Chronicler interprets his *Vorlage* in a basically conservative way, not substantially affecting its material contents,while still creating an account that is independent in its structure and concerns; cf. Williamson 1982: 22.

'decapitated' in his temple before the ark (Mosis 1973: 24-26). The theme of the correct disposition towards the ark, and therewith the reversal of Israel's 'exilic' state, emerges in the following Davidic narrative.

Mosis's interpretative approach to Chronicles is a strongly typological reading. On this pericope, Mosis argues from the fact that the story is presented *in medias res*, with the reduction of local detail from 1 Samuel 31, that it is concerned not with the historical fall of Saul's house, but with depicting a kind of 'primal model' of the possible relationships governing Yahweh, Israel and its king, and the world of nations (1973: 42).[8] Saul is not presented historically but 'idealtypisch', as a type of those kings whose disobedience brings disaster upon Judah.

The first difficulty with this claim is the writer's silence about Saul after 1 Chron. 26.28, in contrast to numerous statements of emulation made about various kings (positively in 2 Chron. 11.17; 22.9; 26.4; 27.2; 29.2; 34.2; negatively in 2 Chron. 21.12; 33.22; 34.2). It is true that the language of 1 Chron. 10.13-14, which reflects the Chronicler's evaluation of Saul, does recur frequently, but some of this has already been introduced (cf. 1 Chron. 2.7; 5.25; 9.1). Instead, the Saul pericope points in a different direction. First, the Chronicler adds מחו to v. 6, so creating an emphatic chiasm (Williamson 1982: 93). The fourfold repetition of this word in this pericope (cf. vv. 13-14) underlines how completely the Saulide dynasty has ended.

The editorial comment also signals the decisive new phase, Yahweh's transfer of the kingdom to David. Although other crises will occur, such as division, military defeat and exile, they will be of a different order, because the 'kingdom', which is Yahweh's, is to be given irrevocably to David and his descendants.[9]

By dehistoricizing 1 Chron. 10.12, Mosis obscures the significance of the Chronicler's criticisms in vv. 13-14a. Mosis takes these words as a general evaluation of Saul's reign, rather than a reference to the specific offences mentioned in 1 Samuel 13, 15: Saul's basic disposition was unfaithfulness ('Untreue'), which led to defeat and exile. Mosis links the expression דבר יהוה אשר לא שמר not with any particular prophetic

8. '...ein urgeschichtliches [...] Grundmuster; es zeigt in typisierter Reinheit eine mögliche Ausprägung des Verhältnisses der drei Größen: 1) Jahwe–2) Israel und sein König–3) Völkerwelt.'

9. Cf. 1 Chron. 17.13; 2 Chron. 13.5; this point is discussed in greater detail in Chapters 7 and 8.

messages but the usage of Deuteronomy and Psalm 119, where 'keeping Yahweh's word' is associated with life and possessing the land (1973: 33). However, this line of interpretation overlooks the Chronicler's common practice of assuming in his readers a knowledge of the *Vorlage*[10] (which is implied here in the reference to the medium in v. 13). Verses 13-14 are more probably dependent on 1 Sam. 13.13-14, 15.26-27, which speak of Saul's disobedience and rejection and the transfer of his kingdom to David. The phrases לא שמר and את דבר יהוה are derived from here, although דרש and מעל are, of course, the Chronicler's own expressions. Zalewski further notes the background to this incident in the *Vorlage*, to which. v. 13 alludes. The prelude to the battle on Gilboa is Saul's act of necromancy (1 Sam. 28), in which Samuel's shade repeats the prophetic word rejecting Saul from kingship and foretelling the destruction of his house and the transfer of his kingdom to David (vv. 17-19). These details concur precisely with 1 Chron. 10.13-14. The *Vorlage* provided ample evidence of Saul's gross impiety toward Yahweh (מעל). This fact provides an important pointer toward interpretation of the work, where the fundamental concern throughout is the attitude of king and people toward Yahweh, especially as this is expressed through legitimate worship.

We may now summarize the ways in which the Chronicler's understanding of retribution is reflected in this pericope. First, the editorial comment emphasizes that the outcome is Yahweh's personal action (וימיתהו; cf. 1 Chron. 2.3). This is already implied in the *Vorlage* (cf. 1 Sam. 28.19), but Chronicles is notable for its directness and the way in which it expresses Yahweh's close superintendence over events (cf. Japhet 1989: 132-36).

Secondly, the writer handles this narrative more as history than as typology or paradigm. Such examples are frequent in Chronicles, but the emphasis of this pericope lies principally in its concluding statement, that the kingdom was transferred to David. In the Chronicler's conception history is under the direction of the prophetic word.[11] This theme is

10. For example, in the background to the ark narrative (1 Chron. 13.5; cf. 1 Sam. 7.1) or the allusion to Solomon's later conduct (2 Chron. 9.29; cf. 1 Kgs 11.29-30) or Hezekiah and the Babylonian envoys (2 Chron. 32.25-26; cf. 2 Kgs 20.12-19).

11. It may be said that prophecy provides the Chronicles with both his understanding of history and his basis of hope. Through prophecy Saul's dynasty is ended and David's is founded (1 Chron. 11.3), along with the temple (1 Chron. 17.3-15).

demonstrated, first negatively in Saul's fate, and then positively in the choice of David. The Chronistic addition in 1 Chron. 11.3 (כדבר יהוה ביד שמואל) may be understood as linking these pericopae (cf. 1 Chron. 10.13 and 1 Sam. 13.13-14). Mosis's claim (1973: 19) that 1 Chronicles 10 is presented 'without presupposition and continuation' ('ohne Voraussetzung und ohne Fortsetzung') cannot really be sustained, all the more since Saul's background is given twice in the preceding genealogies (1 Chron. 8.29-40; 9.35-44),[12] and 1 Chronicles 11 onwards immediately recounts the history of the Davidic kingdom.

Thirdly, the widespread motif of prophecy strongly affects the presentation and interpretation of retribution. Japhet (1989: 176-91) has emphasized the role of the prophets as preachers of repentance and warning, which is really an expression of Yahweh's compassion (cf. 2 Chron. 36.15).[13] Williamson (1982: 415) refines Japhet's observations with the remark that judgment in Chronicles (ultimately, the exile) arises less from specific sins as such than from failure to heed the prophetic word. A survey of the post-Solomonic kings confirms this observation.[14] Although no prophetic speech is recorded in the Chronicler's Saul pericope, it is clear from v. 13 that Saul is condemned for his failure to keep Yahweh's word.

Finally, it is well known that Chronicles stresses the duty of the king to lead the people in the establishment and maintenance of proper

The prophetic word is active throughout the monarchy, and is fulfilled even in the destruction of the temple and state (2 Chron. 36.21). Cyrus's edict permitting the return is also the fulfilment of prophecy (v. 22).

12. Walters (1991) notes that Saul is the only person in the Chronicler's genealogies not to be linked with one of Jacob's twelve sons, but is linked instead with Gibeon (9.35). Walters finds a polemical note in this association: Gibeon is a city which typifies Canaanite religious and political traditions. Saul is therefore unsuitable to be king, and the future belongs to David (1991: 73-76).

13. Japhet (1989: 188) recognizes as much, but does not integrate this fact sufficiently into her overall interpretation of retribution.

14. The following examples show how punishment flows less from a specific sin than from rejection of the prophetic word: (1) Asa's decline follows his mistreatment of Hanani (2 Chron. 16.7-8); (2) punishment upon the apostate Joash and the princes comes after they ignored the prophet and the princes murdered Zechariah (2 Chron. 24.19-25); (3) Amaziah rejects prophetic counsel and so is condemned (2 Chron. 25.16-17); (4) leprosy breaks out on Uzziah only *after* he has angrily reacted to Azariah's command to leave the temple (2 Chron. 26.19); (5) Manasseh's captivity follows the failure to heed prophetic warnings (2 Chron. 33.10); (6) Zedekiah and the people repeatedly reject prophetic messages (2 Chron. 36.12, 16).

religious priorities, and judges the king according to his faithfulness in this matter. For the Chronicler, these priorities were spelled out in the Mosaic Law, which is used on several occasions as a standard for evaluating kings.[15] The allusions to Saul's conduct in vv. 13-14 (and later in 1 Chron. 13.3, where he is implicitly condemned for neglect of the ark) show how signally he failed in this respect. As I have indicated already, retribution in Chronicles is covenantal in basis, and largely cultic in its centre of interest: it reflects the identity of Israel as Yahweh's people (a relationship constituted through the Sinaitic and Davidic covenants) and the obligation to express that fact in legitimate worship. Saul's failure here leads to David as the faithful representative of this ideal.

2. *Retribution in the Davidic Narrative (1 Chronicles 11–29)*

Three sections are particularly interesting in this respect: the ark narrative (1 Chron. 13–16); David's census (1 Chron. 21); and David's disqualification and Solomon's election as temple builder (1 Chron. 22, 28).

(i) *1 Chronicles 13.1–16.4: the transfer of the ark.* A comparison of this unit with the *Vorlage* reveals the author's typical compositional methods of reordering his material and making some substantial additions, as well as smaller omissions and alterations. The structure of this section (considered synoptically) is as follows.

> *13.1-4 (no par.), David's consultation with the assembly of Israel to fetch the ark.*
> 13.5-14 = 2 Sam. 6.1-11, the first abortive mission.
> 14.1-16 = 2 Sam. 5.11-25, David's growth in power.
> *14.17 (no par.), statement of David's renown.*
> *15.1-24 (no par.), preparation of clergy for second mission.*
> > *2 Sam. 6.12a (no par.), report of blessing on Obed-Edom.*
> 15.25–16.3 = 2 Sam. 6.12b-19, the second mission and entry into City of David.

It is thus apparent that a new narrative structure has been created and older materials have been recontextualized. The most immediate question concerns the transposition of 2 Sam. 5.11-25 into the three-month period after the first mission. Older commentators understood the Chronicler to take this unit as a reference to secular matters which

---

15. Thus the Chronicler interpolates references to Torah into 2 Chron. 6.16 (cf. 1 Kgs 8.25); 14.3 (cf. 1 Kgs 15.11-13); 23.18 (cf. 2 Kgs 11.18); 35.26b (cf. 2 Kgs 23.28).

he subordinated to his true interest, the cult.[16] However, the material in 1 Chronicles 14 manifestly concerns events that were divinely assisted. Among more recent interpretations, Mosis (1973: 59-60) holds that the writer's dominant compositional device was word-play, using פרץ as a catchword in 1 Chron. 13.2, 11, 14.11, 15.13, to create a narrative link between these chapters. Yahweh's 'Riß' or 'breakout' against Uzzah is surpassed by a second 'Riß', David's campaigns against the Philistines. Such (proto-midrashic) word-play certainly appealed to the writer,[17] but it is already latent in the *Vorlage* (2 Sam. 5.20; 6.8) and of itself seems insufficient to explain the new order of the material. Mosis also argues that the Chronicler's portrayal here, as elsewhere, is typological rather than historical.[18]

Welten's (1979) interpretation is the inverse of Mosis's view: these chapters are said to describe the *Urzeit* of the Jerusalem cult rather than prefiguring the circumstances of the post-exilic community. The Chronicler deviated from the chronology and geography of the *Vorlage* so as to connect David's anointing as king directly with the mission to fetch the ark (1979: 176). David is now no longer a primarily political figure, but one whose first concern is to establish the cult. In their new setting, the campaigns of 1 Chron. 14.8-16 make sense as the necessary preliminaries for providing safe passage for the ark from Kiriath–Jearim, a theme absent from 2 Samuel 6. Welten argues that the Chronicler's interest in the ark and Davidic kingship, neither of which was extant in his day, was confined to their role in the foundation of the Jerusalem cult: the ark and David's efforts to secure a 'resting place' for it pro- vided the basis for the entry of Yahweh's כבוד into the temple (cf. 2 Chron. 7.1). Welten understands the Chronicler as teaching that the ark and Davidic kingship relate to a proper contemporary understanding

---

16. For a survey and bibliography of earlier views, including Wellhausen, Kittel, and more recently, Wilda, see Im 1985: 70-71.

17. Cf. the writer's use of הסית in 2 Chron. 18.2, 31; Williamson (1982: 279) also argues that קצף is used as a catchword in 2 Chron. 19.

18. Cf. Mosis (1973: 80) 'David's seeking the ark and the help granted to him and Israel [prefigure] the overcoming of the pagan opponents of post-exilic Israel' ('Davids Suchen der Lade und die ihm und Israel gewährte Hilfe [präfigurieren] die Überwindung der heidnischen Widersacher der nachexilischen Israel'). Mosis simi- larly explains the reduction of geographical detail in 1 Chron. 14 as in 1 Chron. 10 as part of the work's supposed dehistoricizing paradigmatic purpose, but this is an unlikely inference.

of the cult and not to any messianic or 'royalist' expectation (1979: 170).[19]

Although Welten's interpretation takes the historical and geographical data seriously, it is too one-sided in subsuming the monarchy into the cult. Chronistic additions in 1 Chron. 14.2, 17 show that David's kingship is a theme in its own right, and one which brackets that section as its leitmotif. In the first case, 2 Sam. 5.12b (וכי נשא ממלכתו) is altered to כי נשאת למעלה מלכותו, making Hiram's acknowledgment the ground for David's recognition of divine blessing on his kingship. The same point is made in v. 17, where it appears as a consequence of David's victories over the Philistines. The advancement of David's kingship (as well as its dynastic continuance) is nevertheless closely linked with a right disposition toward the cult. This is emphasized by Im (1985: 180-81), whose explanation for the reordering of the *Vorlage* is followed here with some modifications. Im argues that the new position of 2 Sam. 5.11-25 is explained principally as a consequence of the writer's 'dogma of retribution', which he applied 'more scrupulously' than the Deuteronomist to the individual (1985: 80-81):

> [The Chronicler] wishes to show the reader in 1 Chron. 14 that Yahweh has richly compensated David's accomplishments for the ark of God in 1 Chron 13. [...] Just as he showed a typical example of negative retribution in the case of Saul in 1 Chron. 10, he now shows here in 1 Chron. 14 a typical example of positive reward in the case of David.[20]

This suggestion has the merit of accounting for all the material in 1 Chronicles 14 (building, progeny, military success and recognition), which are all conventional signs of reward in Chronicles (although the events in 1 Chronicles 13–14 are not really 'typical': the ark is more than 'ein Symbol des Jahwekults' [p. 73], since it betokens the temple

---

19. Cf. Welten 1979: 182: 'The ark marks to some extent Yahweh's path to Jerusalem, into the temple. The fact that the Chronicler gives an extensive description of the long lost ark has really to do with God's presence in the Jerusalem temple cult, which was celebrated at his time.' ('Die Lade markiert [...] gewissermaßen den Weg Jahwes nach Jerusalem, in den Tempel. Wenn der Chronist so ausführlich die Geschichte der längst verlorenen Lade darstellt, dann geht es um die Präsenz Gottes im Gottesdienst, im Tempel in Jerusalem, der zu seiner Zeit gefeiert wird.')

20. '(Der Chronist) will in 1 Chr 14 den Leser zeigen, daß Jahwe reichlich vergütet hat, was David für die Lade Gottes in 1 Chr 13 geleistet hat. [...] Während er ein typisches Beispiel der negativen Vergeltung im Falle von Saul in 1 Chr 10 zeigte, zeigt er jetzt hier in 1 Chr 14 ein typisches Beispiel der positiven Vergeltung im Falle von David.'

to come, while the children born to David in Jerusalem [1 Chron. 14.3-7] are a proleptic indication of the Davidic dynasty, and not simply a conventional sign of blessing). Im's argument is an inference drawn from the narrative line and a general interpretative approach to the work. It can, however, be supported by (a) a consideration of the writer's exegetical methods, and (b) the points of contrast which the Chronicler draws between the portrayals of Saul and David.

a. It is increasingly recognized that the Chronicler employed interpretative methods which represent an early form of the techniques that characterized later rabbinic exegesis.[21] Of particular note is the method of *semukin* or 'conjunctions', which is defined thus by R. Aqiba (*Sifre Num* 131): 'every Scripture passage which is close to another must be interpreted with respect to it'. Other instances of exegesis by *semukin* have been identified elsewhere in Chronicles, making it likely that the Chronicler intended 1 Chronicles 13–14 to be read in this way.[22] Here the narrative is reordered to express the theme of Yahweh's blessing upon those who 'seek' him. This theme is introduced by the Chronistic unit 1 Chron. 13.1-4, in which David summons the קהל to fetch the ark. As a result, the *Vorlage* is accorded a new context, and 1 Chronicles 14 now appears as the evidence of divine approval of the leitmotif of David's rule, the preoccupation to fetch the ark which leads to divine blessing on his kingdom.

b. The Chronicler develops a number of contrasts between Saul and

21. It is perhaps not appropriate to term these 'midrash' given the imprecise associations of that term; cf. Porton 1981: 55-92; although the term is readily used with reference to Chronicles by Shinan and Zakovitch (1986: 257-77), and Seeligmann (1953: 150-51; 1979–80: 14-32). It should be noted in particular that Japhet (1989: 184-85) uses later rabbinical methods of interpretation to illuminate Chronicles' retributive doctrine, as she interprets it. Fishbane (1985) prefers to speak of 'innerbiblical exegesis' and 'aggadic midrash', and finds the origin of such exegesis at least as early as the exile. Shinan and Zakovitch find in Chronicles the following proto-midrashic procedures: the solving of contradictions posed by the traditum; the juxtapositioning of units (*semukin*); name derivations; and the avoiding of ambiguities. Fishbane (1985: 380-400) speaks of a number of 'aggadic transformations' in Chronicles, including the addition of new theological explanations, and especially the use of *semukin* (pp. 399-400; see below).

22. For other examples in Chronicles of exegesis by *semukin*, see Shinan and Zakovitch 1986: 268-69; and Fishbane 1985: 399-403 (though his interpretations here are contestable). Already Seeligmann (1953: 159) referred generally to the phenomenon with reference to Chronicles, as did Willi (1972: 219 n. 12). See the discussion of the relation between 1 Chron. 21 and 22 below.

David.[23] Confining our attention to those changes introduced into 1 Chronicles 10 by the Chronicler, we may note David's exemplary attitude toward the ark (1 Chron. 13.3; 10.14); the growth of his house and the end of Saul's (1 Chron. 14.3-7; 10.6); and the different fates of their kingdoms (1 Chron. 14.2, 17; 10.14).

The Chronicler thus shows a reversal by David of Israel's sorry condition under Saul. However, the understanding of Yahweh's activity in this unit is rather different from a strict doctrine of individual retribution (that is, that piety is rewarded while disobedience is punished). It will be shown in fact that the dominant motif is *blessing,* in an unexpected and undeserved form.

First, the Chronicler depicts the private military venture of 2 Samuel 6 as a religious act of Israel as a קהל and ascribes a divine initiative to the venture: ומן יהוה אלהינו נפרצה (1 Chron. 13.2). Thus far, David is evidently commended. However, in the light of the mission's now pronouncedly religious character and the Chronicler's well-known concern for cultic norms, the subsequent debacle (1 Chron. 13.9-13) can only be understood as a serious criticism of David, the human instigator and overseer of the mission. This is the first indication in the work that it does not present a one-sidedly idealized portrait of David, as many commentators maintain.[24] The manner in which David conducted the first mission, the transition in his emotions from joy to anger and fear (vv. 8, 11-12), and his failure to bring the ark all reflect badly on him.[25] The significance for the Chronicler of this initial failure is heightened over against the *Vorlage,* given the greater prominence that the ark has in his narrative and the manner in which he has introduced David as a zealous promoter of the cult. Yet in 1 Chronicles 14 Yahweh exalts David's kingdom, bestowing on him buildings (v. 1), progeny (vv. 3-7), military success (vv. 8-16) and fame (v. 17). The narrative line indicates that blessing has befallen David not only because of his right attitude, but also—somewhat surprisingly—*in spite of* his failure to understand and respect the nature of Yahweh's holiness.

This remark leads naturally to a consideration of the writer's outlook on reward and punishment. As we saw with reference to Saul, the

23. Cf. Im 1985: 82; Selman 1994a: 155-56.

24. This was classically expressed by Wellhausen 1885: 172-82.

25. There are numerous small differences between Chronicles and Samuel (e.g. vv. 9b, 10b, 13a), but Rudolph (1955: 113) argues that these are stylistic, not substantial (*contra* Fishbane 1985: 394).

Chronicler's conception of retribution is largely cultic in orientation: the right worship of Yahweh issues in blessing, whereas apostasy leads to punishment. While the presentation of this schema throughout the work is relatively straightforward, it has deeper theological reverberations. For the author the cultic norms (whether concerning ark or temple) express Israel's status as the covenant people, and they embody a profound awareness of Yahweh's holiness. Thus, Uzziah's presumption is labelled מעל (2 Chron. 26.16, 18), for he not only encroached on the Aaronic privilege but arrogantly sought a manifestation of Yahweh's glory.[26] The same concern for Yahweh's holiness informs the narrative of 1 Chronicles 13–15, but it does not reflect simple or rigidly legalistic notions of retribution. This can be illustrated by comparing the fates of Uzzah and Obed-Edom.

It is frequently noted that, whereas 2 Sam. 6.6-7 provides no explanation for Yahweh's outburst against Uzzah, the Chronicler adds his own interpretative comment in 1 Chron. 15.13: Uzzah's death arose from a breach of the Mosaic code concerning the transport of the ark by the Levites (cf. 1 Chron. 15.15; Exod. 25.12-15; Num. 4.15; 7.9). This comment has been variously estimated: negatively, as the Chronicler's falsification of history through anachronistically harmonizing his *Vorlage* with the Priestly Writing (thus de Wette, followed by Wellhausen); more positively (though equally unhistorical), as 'aggadic exegesis', in keeping with the writer's normative piety of how he imagined the past (Fishbane). Braun (1986: 176) offers an explicitly theological (cultic) interpretation according to his understanding of the Chronicler's outlook:

> While one explanation of this [*sc.*, why the mission failed] is given in vv 9-14, derived from Samuel, a second will be found in 15.2, 13—the failure to deal with the ark in the prescribed way. The writer thus adheres consistently to the dogma of retribution: disobedience to Yahweh and his word (15.13-15) cannot go unpunished and, in the same way, failure may always be explained by disobedience.

However, it must be remarked that however valid this interpretation may be for the fate of Uzzah, it stands in some tension with the subsequent description of blessing not only on David (1 Chron. 14.1-17), but also on Obed-Edom (1 Chron. 13.14).

The identity and status of this latter figure is a matter of some uncertainty. According to the most common line of interpretation,

26. Cf. Ackroyd 1973: 170.

reflected as far back as Josephus (*Ant.* 7.4), the Chronicler thought of
Obed-Edom as a Levite and was therefore observing cultic propriety in
placing the ark in his custody.[27] The assumption arises from references
to that name in Levitical connection in 1 Chron. 15.18, 21, 24; cf. also
1 Chron. 16.5, 38; 26.4-6; 2 Chron. 25.24.[28] It cannot, however, be
assumed that the Chronicler thought of Obed-Edom as *originally* a
Levite. This is evidently not the sense of 2 Sam. 6.10, where he is a
Philistine, a native of Gath on whom David apparently foisted the ark
'without regard to either his feelings or his credentials' (Gordon 1986:
233). The Chronicler probably shared this same understanding of Obed-
Edom's origin and David's motive (Rudolph 1955: 113). In this light,
the comment in 1 Chron. 13.14 (reinforced in 1 Chron. 26.5) recounting
the blessing enjoyed by Obed-Edom's household is all the more
noteworthy: what David may have intended for harm redounds for
blessing, in which David himself participates. This is suggested by the
new position of 2 Sam. 5.11-25 in 1 Chron. 14.1-16. This report of
David's successes now follows directly from the report of blessing on
Obed-Edom's household. In 2 Sam. 6.12a the account of the blessing on
Obed-Edom forms part of the message reported to David and so
provides the motive for the second mission, but in 1 Chron. 13.14 it is
worked into the narrative.[29]

27. Cf. Ackroyd 1973: 58; Braun 1986: 175. Curtis and Madsen (1910: 125) see
a deliberate tendentious change: 'This historical Philistine caretaker of the ark, a
native of Gath, 2 S. 6.10f., is transformed by the Chronicler [...] into a Levite of
the division of the gatekeepers, v. 24, 16.38, 26.4f., and as a Korahite gatekeeper
(26.1-4), he is a Kehathite.' Myers' position (1966: 103) is unclear. Williamson
(1982: 116) is guarded on the Chronicler's actual understanding of Obed-Edom's
original status, while also arguing for glosses over the role of his family in the cult
(pp. 125-26, 130, 169-70).

28. Various explanations are given for the inconcinnities in these traditions.
1 Chron. 15.21, 16.5 refer to Obed-Edom's liturgical service, while the other verses
refer to the work of gatekeepers and storekeepers. Keil [1988: 219] held that two
persons of the same name were distinguished in 1 Chron. 16.38. Most commentators
suggest tradition-critical reconstructions; cf. De Vries 1989: 150.

29. Im (1985: 81) comments: 'because the Chronicler places 1 Chr 14 immediately after the sentence "Yahweh blessed the house of Obed-Edom and everything
that he had" (1 Chr 13.14b), he also makes 1 Chr 14 appear in the context of the
thought of blessing for the ark' ('dadurch, daß der Chronist 1 Chr 14 gerade hinter
den Satz "Jahwe segnete das Haus Obed-Edoms und alles, was er hatte" (1 Chr 13,
14b) setzt, läßt er auch 1 Chr 14 im Kontext des Segensgedankens für die Lade
erscheinen').

We may summarize this unit as follows. Punishment is meted out for impiety (1 Chron. 13.9-10), but the dominant motif of this unit is not retribution in the sense of strict recompense for actions. Rather it emphasizes Yahweh's initiative on Israel's behalf, and his activity of blessing those who 'seek' him, even imperfectly. Such blessing is shown to be surprising in its scope: it extends to the Philistine Obed-Edom (a fact that runs counter to the older assumptions about the Chronicler's sense of cultic propriety and ethnic-religious exclusivism), and to David, despite his failure to observe properly the cultic law.

(ii) *1 Chronicles 21.1–22.1: David's census and the plague.* This pericope raises numerous textual and exegetical difficulties, which bear directly on the theme of how the Chronicler conceived of retribution. It will be seen, however, that the writer is concerned above all to emphasize divine mercy and forgiveness. David is shown to be guilty of grave sin and is certainly punished. Nevertheless, Yahweh turns David's disobedience which threatened Israel with destruction into an occasion for providing lasting atonement and restoration for his people.

Since Cross's work,[30] it has been clear that a different recension of Samuel (as represented by 4QSam[a]) underlay the Chronicler's account. However, the significance of this fact should not be overstated. As Dion notes, many substantial differences must still be attributed to the Chronicler (cf. 1 Chron. 21.1, 6, 12, 27, 30; 22.1). A brief synopsis of the two accounts suggests the special emphases and the climax of the Chronicler's version:

21.1	שׂטן incites David to number Israel.
2 Sam. 24.1	*Yahweh* incites David to number Israel.
21.2-6 = 2 Sam. 24.2-9	David commands Joab to conduct a census.
21.7	*God* smites *Israel.*
2 Sam. 24.10	*David's heart* smites *him.*
21.8-14 = 2 Sam. 24.10b-15	David's confession and choice of punishment.
21.16 (no par.)	David's vision of the angel (but cf. 2 Sam. 24.17a).
21.17-26a = 2 Sam. 24.17-25	David's second confession, erection of altar, sacrifice.
21.26b–22.1 (no par.)	*Yahweh answers with fire, withdraws the angel; David designates the temple site.*

---

30. Cross 1958: 141; cf. Lemke 1965; Ulrich 1978: 156-58.

The first exegetical (and theological) difficulty concerns the relation of 1 Chron. 21.1 to 2 Sam. 24.1. The reference to שָׂטָן instead of Yahweh has often been explained as an apologetic for the deity, in line with the Chronicler's supposed developed angelology. This assumes, however, that שָׂטָן is a proper name, a usage not otherwise attested before the second century BCE (Day 1988: 128-29). The Chronicler's use is non-articular, making 'a (human) adversary' a natural translation.

Sailhamer argues that the Chronicler's Deuteronomistic sources provide the best explanation. He points out first that 1 Kgs 11.14, 23, 25 refer to '(human) adversaries' whom Yahweh in his anger (v. 9) raised up against Solomon for his disobedience, and then suggests that the Chronicler intended 1 Chron. 21.1a as an elliptical statement expressing his (proto-midrashic) understanding of 2 Sam. 21.1, that Yahweh was punishing Israel by sending an invasion of enemies (1989: 44; cf. v. 12). This interpretation is somewhat different from Japhet, who also takes שָׂטָן in a human sense (1989: 145-49), but both agree that no dualistic or spiritual explanation for evil is being offered here.[31] It is not clear that Chronicles is concerned with this aspect of theodicy, which became such an important part of later Judaism.

We consider next the place of this chapter within the narrative and its presentation of David and Yahweh. Compared with the *Vorlage*, in which 2 Samuel 24 is part of an appendix of material (chs. 21–24) only loosely connected with the preceding chapters (Gordon 1986: 298-99), 1 Chronicles 21 has a central place, standing between David's wars of conquest (1 Chron. 18–20) and his temple preparations (1 Chron. 22–29), into which it immediately leads (22.1-2). It has also been seen to act as a narrative turning point in much the same way that the account of David's sin with Bathsheba does in 2 Samuel 11–12. Johnstone describes its function thus (1986: 123):

> It is the guilt of David himself, the king and cult-founder, which determines the selection [of the temple site]. As David's adultery with Bathsheba is the hinge of the presentation of the reign of David in 2 Samuel (2 Sam. 11f.), so David's census [...] is the pivot of the presentation of [him] in 1 Chronicles.

---

31. However, contrast Selman 1994a: 202-204. For a discussion of other views, cf. Rothstein and Hänel 1927: 379, 384; von Rad 1930: 8; Kittel 1902: 80; McKenzie 1985: 67. Willi (1972: 155-56; cf. Williamson 1982: 143) takes a mediating position, while Schenker (1982: 72) argues that the role of the adversary in Zechariah and Job is fundamentally different from 1 Chron. 21.1.

Selman (1994a: 201) independently supports this claim with a number of verbal and thematic correspondences which he identifies between the Bathsheba narrative and this pericope: (i) David's confession חָטָאתִי (2 Sam. 12.13; 24.10 = 1 Chron. 21.8), which is a turning point in both narratives; (ii) David's sin, which brings death to Israel (2 Sam. 11.17-26; 12.15-19; 24.15 = 1 Chron. 21.14); (iii) the prophetic rebuke (2 Sam. 12.1-4; 24.11-14 = 1 Chron. 21.9-13); (iv) divine punishment effected through the sword (2 Sam. 12.10; 1 Chron. 21.12, 16, 27); and (v) prophetic declarations of forgiveness (2 Sam. 12.13; 24.16 = 1 Chron. 21.15).

Since most of these parallels were already present in the *Vorlage*, it is hard to assess this claim. Only the references to the sword in vv. 12, 27 (and 30) are not paralleled in 2 Samuel 24.[32] It is, however, possible that the Chronicler was thinking of the Bathsheba narrative when he developed this motif. 2 Sam. 24.1 gives no clear explanation for Yahweh's anger, but the preceding chapter concludes with a list of David's warriors (2 Sam. 23.24-39 = 1 Chron. 11.26-41), ending with mention of Uriah the Hittite. The Chronicler may have deduced an associative link (*semuk*) here with 2 Sam. 24.1a, just as he spells out the implicit significance of that passage for designating the future temple site. I would add the further observation that 2 Sam. 11.27 expresses Yahweh's displeasure with the remark that 'the thing that David had done was evil in Yahweh's eyes' (וַיֵּרַע הַדָּבָר אֲשֶׁר עָשָׂה דָוִד בְּעֵינֵי יְהוָה). This is closely paralleled by the addition in 1 Chron. 21.7a 'this thing was evil in God's eyes' (וַיֵּרַע בְּעֵינֵי אֱלֹהִים עַל הַדָּבָר הַזֶּה).

The Chronicler does not specify why this census was so sinful (as opposed to the others he draws on elsewhere; cf. Johnson 1988: 62-68), but probably he saw David's act as a usurpation of Yahweh's prerogatives. In slight additions to the *Vorlage* in vv. 3 and 17 the Chronicler affirms that the people are Yahweh's, and so David's actions in numbering them must appear presumptuous and self-seeking. This census (in contrast, for example, to those in Exod. 30.12 and Num. 1.2, 26.2, which are sacral and commanded by Yahweh) lacked authorization and legitimacy. Moreover, it was apparently for a military purpose (cf. vv. 2, 5), and betrayed lack of trust in Yahweh who had so far acted as Israel's commander in war.[33]

---

32. Although the equivalent of v. 16 was probably present in the Chronicler's recension; cf. Ulrich 1978: 156.

33. Becker 1986: 85; cf. 1 Chron. 18.13.

The Chronicler heightens David's culpability over against the *Vorlage* (*contra* Rudolph) through a number of additional comments and changes. In v. 3 Joab charges David with bringing 'guilt upon Israel' (לאשמה לישראל). Other uses of the root אשם appear with קצף (or synonyms) to denote grave acts which incur God's wrath on his people (2 Chron. 19.10 [2×]; 28.10-11, 13 [3×]; cf. 24.18; 33.23). In v. 6 the Chronicler adds the remark that 'the king's command was repulsive to Joab', and, as noted above, in v. 7 that it was 'evil in God's eyes, so that he smote (ויך) Israel'. This is a reference to the plague of v. 14, and so the sense is quite different from 2 Sam. 24.10, where it is stated that 'David was conscience-stricken (ויך לב דוד אתו) after he had numbered the people'. It appears that David does not accept full responsibility for his act until v. 17, where his confession is more complete and accentuated than in 2 Sam. 24.17.

The choice of punishments with which David is confronted (v. 12; cf. 2 Sam. 24.13) has a covenantal basis in the curses of Lev. 26.25-26. These verses speak of Yahweh bringing a sword upon Israel for covenant-violation and mention plague, defeat by enemies and famine. It may be that the Chronicler has assimilated his text to reflect the language and imagery of this passage, particularly since Leviticus 26.40-41 is an influential passage elsewhere in Chronicles (cf. 2 Chron. 36.21; see above on מעל and כנע niph.). The description of the angel as 'destroying' (משחית, vv. 12, 15) also evokes Exod. 12.23, and indicates the extreme danger into which David's sin had plunged the nation.

Sin and its deserved judgment are thus an important interest of this chapter. The matter is expressed most poignantly in the case of David, the exemplary Yahweh-worshipper who had reversed the destructive consequences of Saul's disobedience (1 Chron. 13–16). Nevertheless, the Chronicler's fundamental concern here is not with punishment as such (vv. 9-14), but with stressing Yahweh's mercy and forgiveness (vv. 15-27). Already in v. 13, in a small addition to the *Vorlage* David declares that Yahweh's mercy is 'very (מאד) great'. This conviction is demonstrated in v. 15, where Yahweh withholds his punishment of Jerusalem; and in vv. 18-27, in the provision in the city of a new altar for the atonement of this offence, the way to Gibeon being barred (vv. 29-30). The climax of this unit is David's designation of Ornan's threshing floor as the future temple site (1 Chron. 22.1, no parallel). This association may already be implied in 2 Samuel 24 (von Rad 1962: 318; Gordon 1986: 317), but the Chronicler makes the link explicit and emphasizes that the temple is to be the place of atonement and forgiveness for Israel's sin (2 Chron. 7.12b, 14), just as this site was for David. This point is further underlined by the parallel fire-theophanies on the altars of burnt-offering (1 Chron. 21.26b; 2 Chron. 7.1).

Thus, in making this incident, the nadir of his Davidic narrative, the turning point of his presentation, the Chronicler affirms that the forgiveness of sins is integral to the meaning of the temple and the Davidic covenant, through which the temple is established (1 Chron. 17.12). Yahweh's covenant mercy (1 Chron. 17.13) is the fundamental conviction against which the Chronicler's doctrine of sin, punishment and forgiveness must be assessed.

(iii) *1 Chronicles 22, 28: David's disqualification from temple building and Solomon's commissioning*. These two chapters belong to a transitional unit (1 Chron. 22–29) which leads immediately from the designation of the temple site to David's preparations (1 Chron. 22.2-3) and Solomon's accession as king (1 Chron. 29.22b) and fulfilment of the task (2 Chron. 1–8). There is no real equivalent to this unit in the *Vorlage*, although it presupposes the account of David's charge to Solomon in 1 Kgs 2.1-12 (cf. 1 Chron. 22.13 and 1 Kgs 2.3). The basic model, however, is Moses' charge to Joshua, entrusting him with the task of possessing the land (cf. Deut. 31.7-8; Josh. 1.6-7).

1 Chronicles 22 and 28 have numerous thematic and verbal correspondences,[34] as David summons his son to his appointed task within the covenant, first privately and then before all the leaders of Israel. These chapters bracket David's cultic preparations (1 Chron. 23–27) and act as a bridge between the accounts of the census (1 Chron. 21.1–22.1) and Solomon's commissioning and accession (1 Chron. 28.10–29.30). The parallels between these chapters may be summarized as follows:

22.2-5/28.2	David's preparations.
22.3/28.8	David is forbidden to build.
22.9/28.6	Solomon is chosen to build.
22.10/28.7	Dynastic promise to David.
22.11-13/28.9-10	Exhortation to Solomon.

The question of reward and punishment appears to be reflected in David's exclusion from the task and the promise of success that will attend Solomon's obedience.

34. Cf. Braun 1976; Williamson 1976.

a. Chronicles diverges markedly in 1 Chron. 22.8 and 28.3 from the *Vorlage*, which relates David's failure to build as merely circumstantial: he was too preoccupied in wars to undertake this task (1 Kgs 5.17 [E 5.3]). In Chronicles David's failure to build is attributed additionally to Yahweh's express refusal:

> You have shed much blood (דם לרב שפכת) and waged great wars: you shall not build a house to my name, because you have shed so much blood before me on the earth; [...] you are a warrior and have shed blood.

Commentators are divided in taking these words in an ethical or non-ethical (e.g. ritual or literary) sense. Rudolph (1955: 151) and Fishbane (1985: 397) find in them a moral censure of warfare.[35] However, this reading is anachronistic and out of keeping with the Chronicler's own portrayal of God's activity in warfare on behalf of Israel, which is shown to be in close conjunction with religious ceremonial and in answer to prayer (Williamson 1982: 154).

Among non-ethical interpretations, Mosis (1973: 96-97) holds that David's disqualification reflects the Chronicler's periodization of history: David's reign is the time of war, whereas Solomon's era is the time of rest and peace. The ritual interpretation is derived from the statement that David shed blood לפני, thus bringing his action into the sacral realm. Goettsberger (1939: 163) suggests that the Chronicler reflects a religious psychology and concern for purity in which 'warfare and shedding blood make one unfit for work that brings one into close relation to God'.[36]

The expression ארצה is also difficult; perhaps an allusion is intended to Num. 35.33, where bloodguiltiness pollutes the land. In any case, the notion that war as such renders persons ritually unfit is not otherwise attested in the Old Testament. The above interpretations implicitly assume that שפך דם and עשה מלחמות are synonymous expressions. However, the first expression is not used anywhere in the Old Testament to denote warfare. This has been demonstrated by H. Christ's exhaustive study of דם in the Old Testament,[37] which distinguishes two

---

35. For rabbinical antecedents to this view, cf. Japhet 1989: 476-77.

36. '(D)as Kriegshandwerk und Blutvergießen als solches [machen] ungeeignet zu einem Werke, das in enge Beziehung zu Gott brachte. Das liegt in dem "vor mir", das die Doppelung V.8e nachträgt.'

37. Christ (1977) finds it 'odd' ('merkwürdig') that 'shedding blood' is never used as a description for killing in warfare, and suggests that 1 Chron. 22.8 forms

senses of שָׁפֵךְ דָּם. The first concerns priestly-sacrificial rites which describe participation in, rather than exclusion from the cult.[38] The second and larger group refers not to killing in war but to unlawful acts which cause death and incur bloodguiltiness. Especially in Jeremiah and Ezekiel שָׁפֵךְ דָּם is used as a *terminus technicus* for Israel's sin, including violence toward the weak, which incurred the wrath of exile.[39]

Since David's disqualification comes immediately after the unlawful census which brought death to great numbers in Israel (1 Chron. 21.14), that culpable act is probably intended by the expression 'shedding much blood' before Yahweh. The accounts of his sin and disbarment from building appear adjacently as 'conjunctions' or mutually interpretative *semukin* (cf. the contrasting theme of blessing upon David in the *semukin* to do with the ark narrative in 1 Chron. 13–14).

1 Chron. 22.8 and 28.3 thus recount not one but two reasons for David's exclusion from temple building: the guilt he incurred before God through the census, and the factual grounds given in the *Vorlage* that he was preoccupied in waging war. This interpretation construes these verses grammatically in the same way as the mediaeval commentator Qimhi (as a twofold reason, not synonymously), but without the reference to Uriah which he inferred from 'shedding blood'.[40] The charge of 'shedding much blood' occurs twice in 1 Chron. 22.8, which may suggest that the Chronicler considered this the principal reason for David's disqualification.

b. David's exclusion from the task leads directly to the designation of Solomon as heir and temple-builder. The Chronicler's retributive thought is expressed particularly in the key phrases in 1 Chron. 22.11-13 and 28.8-9, which belong respectively to the private and public commissionings.

In the first passage David prays for Solomon and admonishes him thus:

> Now, my son, may Yahweh be with you, and may you have success (וְהִצְלַחְתָּ) and build the house of Yahweh your God, as he said about you.

---

the sole exception (p. 148). However, his judgment appears to be based on the common understanding of that passage as referring exclusively to warfare.

38. Exod. 29.12; Lev. 4.7, 18, 25, 30, 34; Deut. 12.16, 24, 27; 15.23.

39. Jer. 7.6; 22.3, 7; Ezek. 16.38; 18.10; 22.3, 4, 6, 9, 12, 27; 23.45; 36.1; cf. also Gen. 9.6; 37.22; Lev. 17.4; Num. 35.33; Deut. 19.10; 1 Sam. 25.31; 1 Kgs 2.31; Pss. 79.3; 106.38; Prov. 6.17; Isa. 59.7, 8; Lam. 4.13.

40. Cf. Japhet 1989: 476-77.

> Only, may Yahweh give you discretion and understanding when he puts
> you in command of Israel, so that you may keep the law of Yahweh your
> God. Then you will have success (תצליח) if you are careful to observe the
> decrees and laws which Yahweh commanded Moses for Israel.

These words express the Chronicler's conviction that 'success' and even
obedience itself depend on Yahweh's presence and help.[41] 'Success'
(צלח√) is connected directly with obedience to the Mosaic Law, and so
has its basis in the blessings of the Sinaitic covenant, while Solomon's
election and commission depend on the Davidic covenant (cf. vv. 8-9),
to which he must be similarly obedient. The root צלה is repeatedly used
in Chronistic passages in the subsequent narrative to characterize the
results of 'seeking' Yahweh (or his commandments).[42]

The second passage contains charges to the leaders of Israel (v. 8), and
to Solomon, in the hearing of all the people (vv. 9-10). In the first case it
is stressed that possession of the land depends on keeping Yahweh's
commandments. Solomon is then exhorted to 'acknowledge' God and
serve him with heart and mind, since Yahweh 'seeks' (דורש) every heart
and understands every desire. This phrase combines the senses of
scrutiny of motive and Yahweh's positive orientation to Solomon, which
anticipates his own response of 'seeking'. The principle of retribution is
then succinctly stated in reciprocal language that will be echoed
throughout the narrative (cf. 2 Chron. 15.2):

> If you seek him (תדרשנו), he will be found by you; but if you forsake him
> (תעזבנו), he will cast you off for ever.

It must be noted, of course, that 'seeking (Yahweh)' here does not have
the overtone of repentance that 'seek my face' carries in 2 Chron. 7.14.
Further, while the second colon expresses the justice of Yahweh's acts
(cf. 2 Chron. 12.5-6), the whole phrase really functions as paraenesis,
assuring Solomon that Yahweh will respond positively to his obedience,
and warning him of the consequences of disobedience.

(iv) *Retributive doctrine in 1 Chronicles 11–29: a summary.* The
Chronicler's Davidic narrative is marked by contrasting episodes of
faithfulness and growing success, and disobedience and judgment.
Nevertheless, in spite of David's failures, it is shown that Yahweh has

---

41. Cf. 1 Chron. 29.14, 16, 18-19; 2 Chron. 13.10, 12.
42. Cf. 1 Chron. 29.23; 2 Chron. 7.11; 13.12; 14.6 [E 7]; 20.20; 24.20; 31.21;
32.30.

greatly blessed him and, indeed, has turned these failures to David's and Israel's benefit, first by greatly exalting David's kingdom (1 Chron. 14.2-3) and then by revealing the temple site, where henceforth atonement may be made for Israel's sin (1 Chron. 22.1).

These facts must significantly qualify the conventional understanding of the Chronicler's retributive doctrine. The writer is less concerned to demonstrate strict relationships between acts and consequences than to emphasize Yahweh's benevolence and mercy towards his people. It appears, however, that David's exclusion from temple building is due in part to his sinful act, a thought which is additional to the *Vorlage* and probably of greater weight in the Chronicler's eyes than David's military preoccupations. Solomon's response to his commission is also of critical importance for the benefit which he and the nation may derive from 'seeking' Yahweh and his commandments.

3. *Retribution in the Solomonic Narrative (2 Chronicles 1–9)*
This theme is reflected positively in this section in the form of the blessings that accrue to Solomon's kingdom following the organization of its religious life; in the special portrayal of Solomon; and in the presentation of the temple as the place of prayer, restoration and forgiveness.

(i) *The structure of 2 Chronicles 1–9.* By comparison with 1 Kings 1–11, the Chronicler's Solomonic narrative is a simplified account in which all its parts are related to some extent to the temple. A great deal of material in the *Vorlage* that reflects both negatively and positively on Solomon is omitted, as the Chronicler moves directly to his theme of illustrating the fulfilment of Solomon's commission, and the abiding significance of the temple for Israel's life.[43]

2 Chronicles 1–9 are properly a continuation of the Davidic narrative, without a thematic break: what David began, Solomon completes. Nevertheless, these chapters also possess their own unity from their large-scale chiastic structure and other internal literary patterns.[44] Among the different arrangements of the material that have been suggested,[45] Selman

---

43. The Chronicler's omissions include 1 Kgs 1–2, Solomon's accession and triumph over Adonijah; 3.16–4.34, his secular wisdom and administration; 7.1-12, the construction of his palace; 11.1-40, his polygamy, apostasy and opponents.

44. See Selman 1994b: 286-87 for a description of these patterns.

45. Dillard 1987: 5-7; De Vries 1989: 233; Duke 1990: 65. Dillard's intricate

(1994b: 285-86) provides the most satisfactory analysis. He finds the following correspondences of parts:

A	1.1-17	Solomon's wisdom, wealth and fame.
B	1.18–2.17	Solomon prepares for the temple.
C	3.1–5.1	Construction of the temple.
C′	5.2–7.22	Dedication of the temple.
B′	8.1-16	Solomon completes the temple and other building works.
A′	8.17–9.28	Solomon's wisdom, wealth and fame.

This analysis is confirmed by the editorial markers in 2 Chron. 1.18 (E 2.1), 3.1, 5.1, 7.11 and 8.16 which are mainly the Chronicler's own work and denote significant stages in the narrative. This arrangement reveals the focal interest of this unit as the construction and dedication of the temple.

The sections that bracket the narrative (A and A′) are also closely tied to the theme of the temple. The account of Solomon's wealth in 1 Kgs 10.26-29 has been transposed into 2 Chron. 1.14-17, to indicate that God has kept his promise of wealth (v. 12), which would have been used partly in temple-building. Similarly, God's gift of 'wisdom and knowledge' (v. 12) has temple-building primarily in mind, as Hiram's remark, considerably expanded over 1 Kgs 5.7, indicates: Yahweh has given David 'a wise son, endowed with discretion and understanding, who will build a house for Yahweh and a house for his kingdom' (2 Chron. 2.11b [E 12b], no parallel). Solomon's palace is associated with the temple throughout this narrative (cf. 2 Chron. 1.18 [E 2.1]; 7.11; 8.1, 11), probably as a symbol of the Davidic dynasty that is jointly established with the temple, in fulfilment of the Davidic covenant (cf. Selman 1994b: 298).

The definitive statement in 2 Chron. 8.16 marks the successful accomplishment of Solomon's task. Significantly, the 'completion of Yahweh's house' is related to other tasks detailed within 2 Chron. 8.1-16, including building works within the realm (vv. 1-6) and the organization of Gentiles in the kingdom (vv. 7-11). These 'secular' works, in fact, follow construction of the temple (v. 1), but are considered to be in the temple service 'because they made the land and people perfect for holiness' (De Vries 1989: 269). This work is crowned by the institution of the regular services (vv. 12-15), for the Chronicler considers the

analysis has been frequently cited, but Selman (1994b: 287) points out that his arrangement lacks a proper chiastic correspondence of parts.

temple 'completed' only with the inauguration of the cult. Indeed, the writer's interest in the temple has to do with its function within the life of the nation, especially as this is performed by the Levites, rather than the details of its design and construction.[46]

The completion of the temple-building is followed by the accounts of Solomon's trading ventures with Hiram (8.17-18) and the visit of the queen of Sheba (9.1-2). This section is introduced by the temporal marker אז (no parallel; cf. 8.12), implying that the superlative wealth and esteem of Solomon's kingdom are to be understood as the consequence of his faithfulness in establishing the correct religious priorities for the nation (Williamson 1982: 233). In this way, the narrative line suggests much the same message as that conveyed by the exaltation of David's kingdom after his (albeit abortive) mission to fetch the ark (1 Chron. 13–14). More so, the Chronicler intends this section to be read explicitly as the fulfilment to Solomon of the divine promise of wisdom, wealth and honour (2 Chron. 1.12; Selman 1994b: 294). This is confirmed by the repeated mention of these blessings (wisdom in 2 Chron. 9.2-8, 22-23; riches *passim* in the description; international renown in 2 Chron. 9.1, 5). The queen of Sheba affirms that Yahweh is the source of Solomon's exaltation, and has so acted out of his love for Israel:

> Because your God loved Israel (באהבת אלהיך את ישׂראל) and would establish them for ever, he has made you king over them (2 Chron. 9.8b).

This remark is closely paralleled by (and is probably the source of) the words attributed to Hiram at the start of the project:

> 'Because Yahweh loves his people (באהבת יהוה את עמו) he has made you king over them' (2 Chron. 2.10b [E 11b], no parallel in the *Vorlage*).

The temple-building is thus bracketed by the declarations of two Gentile monarchs, affirming that Solomon's reign is an expression of Yahweh's covenantal commitment to Israel.[47]

(ii) *The presentation of Solomon.* It is frequently held that the Chronicler has idealized Solomon and his reign as a paragon of faithfulness.[48] This

---

46. Thus 1 Kings devotes 46 verses to the account of the temple construction and 31 to its furnishings, whereas Chronicles' figures for the same are 17 and 23.

47. On אהב as a covenantal term see Thompson 1979.

48. Cf. Wellhausen 1885: 184-85; Curtis and Madsen 1910: 313; Rudolph 1955: 135, 225-26; Mosis 1973: 162; Braun 1973; 1986: xxxii-xxxv; Dillard 1980; Japhet 1993: 48.

claim (as with the similar one frequently made for David) is based largely on the omission of materials from the *Vorlage* that reflect negatively on him. Especially important here is 1 Kgs 11.1-40, the account of Solomon's foreign wives and later apostasy, his failings which, according to the Deuteronomist, led to the division of the kingdom.

In fact, the Chronicler has a more nuanced appreciation of Solomon's character and role than the conventional understanding allows. The omission (in detail) of critical materials is not intended as 'Solomonic apologetic' (*contra* Braun). Rather it is the Chronicler's means of concentrating on what he sees as the lasting significance of Solomon's reign, the fulfilment of the Davidic covenant through the building of the temple and the establishment of the Davidic dynasty.[49] Consequently, other materials, including those which reflect positively on Solomon,[50] are omitted as extraneous to the writer's purpose.

The Chronicler does depict Solomon at the start of his reign as acting in an exemplary, faithful manner. His first act to be described in detail, the journey to Gibeon to offer worship (2 Chron. 1.2-13), is modelled on David's mission to fetch the ark (1 Chron. 13.1-6) and is treated as an orthodox and zealous act of 'seeking Yahweh' (or the Mosaic altar, v. 5), in which 'all Israel' is involved. This is in marked contrast to the implied criticism of Solomon's religious practices in 1 Kgs 3.2-3. The act of 'seeking' leads directly to a divine appearance 'in that night' (v. 7), in which God grants him the wisdom needed for his responsibilities as king (v. 12). The rest of the narrative treats his reign positively, omitting mention of the corvée of Israelites under Adoniram (1 Kgs 5.13-14) and placing his dealings with Hiram over the Galilean towns in a favourable light (2 Chron. 8.2; cf. 1 Kgs 9.11-14). The apogee of Solomon's reign is described in 2 Chron. 9.22-28, a passage which largely parallels 1 Kgs 10.23-29. The Chronicler's Solomonic narrative breaks off here, while the Deuteronomist goes on to recount the king's later apostasy and military opposition (1 Kgs 11.1-40).

Thus far, the view would appear justified that the Chronicler has idealized Solomon, and various reasons have been proposed for such a presentation.[51] However, the Chronicler is not really concerned to conceal or deny Solomon's failings.[52] In his concluding note to this section

49. See further Chapter 7 on the fulfilment of the Davidic covenant.
50. 1 Kgs 3.16–4.34; 7.1-12; 9.15-17.
51. Cf. Mosis 1973: 162-68; Braun 1973; Williamson 1983.
52. Nor, properly speaking, his difficulties in establishing his reign. It is now

the writer refers to the rest of Solomon's acts 'from first to last', which are recorded in 'the words of Nathan the prophet and in the prophecy of Ahijah the Shilonite and the visions of Iddo the seer concerning Jeroboam the son of Nebat' (2 Chron. 9.29b, no parallel). Mention of Ahijah implies that the Chronicler's readers will be familiar with the account of Solomon's apostasy (cf. 1 Kgs 11.29-30).[53] Similarly, although the Chronicler does not directly mention Solomon's oppressive policy toward his fellow Israelites, criticism of the corvée is clearly reflected in 2 Chron. 10.4, 9-11, 14-15 (= 1 Kgs 12.4, 9-11, 14-15), without any attempt to suppress this detail. Readers of Chronicles are thus expected to know the narrative of 1 Kings 1–11, which concentrates much more on the details of Solomon's personal and political life. These facts are alluded to, but hardly emphasized, because the Chronicler treats Solomon as faithful in the all-important task of temple-building, which instituted a new phase in Israel's life. The Chronicler does not contradict his *Vorlage*, but rather concentrates on its essential meaning for his community. In other words, the writer's interest in Solomon is really centred on what Yahweh has accomplished through him and for his people, rather than on the more ambivalent figure of history.[54]

(iii) *The speeches in the centre of the chiasm (2 Chronicles 6–7).* Within the chiastic arrangement of 2 Chron. 1–9, Solomon's dedicatory address and prayer (2 Chron. 6.1-42) and Yahweh's word to him (2 Chron. 7.12-22) are the centre of thematic interest and theological significance.

generally recognized that 2 Chron. 1.1 (ויתחזק) contains an allusion to 1 Kgs 1–2, while 2 Chron. 8.2 (Solomon's receipt of cities from Hiram) does not contradict 1 Kgs 9.10-14 (cf. Williamson 1982: 193, 228).

53. Japhet (1993: 646) rejects the suggestion that 2 Chron. 9.29b is intended as an allusion to Kings because she thinks it doubtful that the Chronicler 'would direct his readers to the very material he had intentionally avoided'. But this presupposes a specific view of the writer's intention, and Japhet agrees that there is little or no evidence that sources other than 1 Kgs 1–11 were used in 2 Chron. 1–9.

54. Interestingly, the Chronicler omits the offer to Solomon of a long life, conditional on his obedience to Yahweh's statutes and commandments (1 Kgs 3.14). This verse was perhaps irrelevant for the Chronicler's interest in 2 Chron. 1 in emphasizing the promise of wisdom, wealth and honour (cf. vv. 11-12), and the writer duly records Solomon's forty-year reign (2 Chron. 9.30 = 1 Kgs 11.42). The omission may, however, reflect a recognition of Solomon's failings. The motif of a long life is not common in Chronicles, but it is used of David (1 Chron. 29.28) and Jehoiada (2 Chron. 24.15), possibly as an indication of reward.

These chapters are arranged according to a pattern of request and response, and are of the first importance in defining the meaning of the temple for the Chronicler and his community.

Solomon's speech is adopted for the most part without significant alteration from 1 Kgs 8.12-50a. In the first part it testifies to the fulfilment of Yahweh's promise to David, in the form of Solomon's accession and successful temple-building (2 Chron. 6.4, 10 = 1 Kgs 8.15, 20; cf. 1 Chron. 17.10-14; 22.10; 28.5-6). Yahweh's covenant faithfulness (vv. 14-15) is thus the basis of the following prayer, which asks first, for a continuing fulfilment of the dynastic promise (vv. 16-17), and secondly, that Yahweh would be attentive to temple prayer (vv. 22-40). A range of situations is described, most of which presuppose judgment for sin and request that repentance may secure forgiveness and restoration. The Chronicler is content here simply to reproduce his *Vorlage*, which was germane to his purpose, as he has shown that the temple has its origin both in Yahweh's will (1 Chron. 17.12) and in Israel's need for forgiveness, exemplified above all by David (cf. 1 Chron. 21.18; 22.1).

The form and tradition-historical background to the language of 2 Chron. 7.12-22 were discussed in greater detail above, where it was noted that the Chronistic addition of vv. 12b-16a describes the consequences of sacrifice and penitent prayer in the temple, whereas vv. 19-22 depict the results of persistent disobedience. A comparison with the *Vorlage* underlines the significance of this addition. 1 Kgs 8.56-61 (no parallel), the conclusion to Solomon's prayer, and 9.3-9, the divine reply, are essentially a summons to obedience to Yahweh's commandments, couched in typically Deuteronomistic language. This concern is readily appreciated, especially if these passages reflect traditional pre-exilic materials.[55] The Chronistic version, on the other hand, differs significantly in emphasis. In common with other post-exilic writings, Chronicles recognizes that Israel is a sinful people that has experienced judgment (1 Chron. 5.25-26; 9.1; 2 Chron. 36.16). Accordingly, the temple is presented as the point of reversal for Israel's circumstances, where sacrifice and prayer may secure forgiveness and restoration. The fact of punishment is not denied (vv. 19-22), but this takes second place to a stress on Yahweh's offer of mercy. Henceforth, it is affirmed (v. 12) that Yahweh will communicate his loving purpose for his people through the temple.

55. See further Chapter 9 on these verses.

This last point is plainly addressed to the Chronicler's own community. The presence of the second temple in the restored community (as well as the fact of the return itself) signals the continuity of the divine promises made in vv. 12-16, since both community and temple stand in continuity with the pre-exilic period (1 Chron. 9.2-34; 2 Chron. 36.22-23). The temple is not a talisman (cf. v. 20) but an incentive to expectant prayer and praise.

(iv) *Retribution in 2 Chronicles 1–9: a summary.* 2 Chronicles 1–9 is concerned with the public (and abiding) significance of Solomon's reign for Israel. As in the portrayal of David,[56] matters of a personal or secular nature are passed over, not from an apologetic motive but to allow the writer to concentrate on his central interest, Solomon's fulfilment of his commission. Everything is subordinated to this theme, and it appears that Solomon is rewarded not only for his faithful disposition but also, to some extent, despite his failings. This reflects a recognition of Yahweh's goodness to the inconsistent and undeserving. The message of Yahweh's mercy is highlighted in 2 Chronicles 6–7, where it is shown to be integral to the meaning of the temple and the Davidic covenant. It thus forms the basis for the following narrative (2 Chron. 10–36).

4. *Retribution in the Post-Solomonic Narrative (2 Chronicles 10–36)*
Most discussion of retribution in Chronicles has, understandably, focused on this section, where the stereotypical language and motifs of reward and punishment are particularly evident. Dillard (1987: 76) reflects the consensus view of these chapters when he asserts that they are governed by a 'theology of immediate retribution' which is said to provide the writer's 'dominant compositional technique' for his history of post-schism Judah. Dillard offers the following definition:

> 'Retribution theology' refers to the author's apparent conviction that reward and punishment are not deferred, but rather follow immediately on the heels of precipitating events. For the Chronicler sin always brings judgment and disaster, while obedience and righteousness yield the fruit of peace and prosperity.

It will be recalled as well that the Chronicler's retributive thought is also commonly seen as 'individual', that is, limited in its scope to the individual or generation concerned, so that notions of cumulative guilt and

56. Cf. the Chronicler's omission of 2 Sam. 9, 11–20.

deferment of punishment are excluded by definition.[57] Whether these judgments accurately reflect the outlook of 2 Chronicles 10–36 must be determined by a study of the way in which the theme of reward and punishment is articulated in these chapters. My discussion of this section has more of a summary character than that of the preceding chapters, partly because the theme of retribution here is a repetitive one which has been rehearsed in earlier studies (particularly in summarizing discussions of motifs and causality; cf. Wellhausen 1885; Braun 1979; Japhet 1989), but, more importantly, because the basic features of the Chronicler's theology have already been established by the conclusion of the Solomonic narrative. It therefore seemed more appropriate in this study to place the primary emphasis on the narratives of Saul, David and Solomon, as the context for understanding 2 Chronicles 10–36.

A synoptic comparison of this section with 1 Kings 12–2 Kings 25 indicates that the Chronicler's account of the post-Solomonic kingdom is largely self-contained, possessing its own structure and theological concerns over against the *Vorlage*. This result is due largely to the Chronicler's compositional methods, of which the most important are:

1.   the *omission* of materials dealing exclusively with the northern kingdom;
2.   the *insertion* into the *Vorlage* of periodizing chronological notices, theological rationales, stereotypical motifs of blessing and punishment, and prophetic speeches; and
3.   the *addition* of entire pericopae or the wholesale rewriting of passages.[58]

Further evidence of the work's theological design is found in the high degree of *patterning of reigns*, especially in comparative and contrastive groups. Much of this is achieved through the use of catchwords, especially the vocabulary of 2 Chron. 7.14, and common themes. The result

57. Cf. von Rad 1930: 13; 1962: 349; North 1963: 373; Braun 1986: xxxix; Dillard 1987: 80; Japhet 1989: 164-65.
58. Although the Chronicler omits all material from Kings which deals exclusively with the north, he recounts all the contacts between north and south. The additional periodizing chronological notices, retributive motifs and prophetic speeches are found in 2 Chron. 12.1, 2b, 3-9a, 12-14; 15.19–16.1a, 7-10, 12, 13b-14; 18.1-2, 31b; 20.33b, 37; 21.2-4; 22.1, 4b; 24.3-5; 25.5-16; 27.2b-6; 28.23-25; 32.22-23, 27-30; 33.11-17, 23; 34.3-7, 27b, 32-33; 35.21-25; while much larger additions to, or rewriting of the *Vorlage*, are found in 2 Chron. 11.5-23; 13.3-21; 14.3–15.15; 17.1-19; 19.1–20.30; 21.11-20; 24.15-22; 26.5-20; 28.8-15; 29–32; 35.16-17; 36).

of this patterning is a series of basically discrete sub-units which are used by the Chronicler to highlight the different types of behaviour displayed by Judah's kings toward a range of subjects, including: the cultic requirements of the covenant (reform and the upkeep of the temple), the theme of exclusive trust in Yahweh, repentance, obedience to the prophetic word, and the status of the northern tribes. The presentation is quite different from 1–2 Kings, not least because no material relating to the north in its own right is retained, while the accounts of some reigns have been expanded considerably.

Moreover, the Chronicler appears to present *a significantly different evaluation of certain reigns* over against Kings. It is this fact above all that has given rise to the most comment on—and criticism of—the author's presentation, and so will require a careful weighing of the evidence. The following overview of 2 Chronicles 10–36 considers the literary and narratological ways through which the writer's concerns are conveyed, paying particular attention to the basis of reward and punishment in each pericope.

(i) *2 Chronicles 10–12, Rehoboam.* Rehoboam's reign is judged negatively by Kings as a time of apostasy (1 Kgs 14.22-24). Several commentators[59] have asserted that the Chronicler took a contrary view of Rehoboam, chiefly because of the blessings that attended his reign, but this is refuted by the evaluation in 2 Chron. 12.14. The author depicts Rehoboam instead as an unworthy ruler who nevertheless received Yahweh's blessings and exhibited repentance at the critical moment. Rehoboam's foolishness leads to the division of the kingdom (2 Chron. 10.1-19), but he heeds Shemaiah's word to desist from the attempt to restore the north by force (2 Chron. 11.2-4). The Chronistic insertion in 2 Chron. 11.5-23 next describes blessings in the conventional form of buildings and fortifications (vv. 5-12) and a large family (vv. 18-23). These boons were evidently not confined to the three-year period when Rehoboam's realm obeyed the Law and the land enjoyed security (v. 17); in fact, no precise chronological connection is stated in this unit.[60] In the consolidation of his rule, Rehoboam receives help from the priests and Levites from the north (vv. 13-17), but, significantly, nothing

---

59. Cf. Wellhausen 1885: 209; Curtis and Madsen 1910: 362-63; Welten 1973: 127; more moderately, Dillard 1987: 94.

60. *Contra* Dillard 1987: 95.

is said about his own piety. Rather, 2 Chron. 12.14 condemns him as one who 'did not set his heart to seek Yahweh'.

The account of Rehoboam's and 'all Israel's' apostasy in 2 Chronicles 12 has been heavily shaped by the language of 2 Chron. 7.14 (cf. vv. 1, 2, 5, 6, 7, 12, 14). The Chronicler's theological rationale for Shishak's invasion is a deduction from the sequence of 1 Kgs 14.22-25. Judah's apostasy is an act of מעל which threatens to dispossess the people because of Yahweh's wrath (v. 7). However, the judgment is mitigated by repentance (כנע niph.) in response to Yahweh's prophet (vv. 5, 7).

The whole effect of this presentation is not to depict Rehoboam in a manner contrary to the *Vorlage* but to highlight Yahweh's mercy and faithfulness to the covenant promises of 2 Chron. 7.14. It depicts blessings on the undeserving and effectual repentance in the face of just chastisement.

(ii) *2 Chronicles 13–16, Abijah and Asa*. These accounts are united by the theme of reliance (√שׁען) on Yahweh (2 Chron. 13.18; 14.11; 16.7 [×2], 8; cf. Allen 1988: 29). Under Abijah, Judah's reliance on Yahweh leads to victory over Israel and Jeroboam, while Asa shows a conflicting attitude, relying first on Yahweh and then on the king of Aram.

The Chronicler's depiction of Abijah has also given rise to the charge that he has deviated from the critical assessment of 1 Kgs 15.3.[61] In reply, it must be said again that while Abijah is victorious in war and receives a large family, both conventional signs of blessing, the Chronicler is reticent about the king's own piety, as Deboys (1990: 51-52) observes. While Abijah is not criticized, neither is he personally commended in the manner of evidently faithful kings.[62] The writer also preserves indirect evidence of Abijah's failings in the details of the reforms carried out by his successor (2 Chron. 14.2-4 [E 3-5]; 15.8, 16-17). Dillard's statement (1987: 110), then, that the Chronicler 'has presented us with a prophet king, a preacher of righteousness' is somewhat exaggerated. Rather the point of 2 Chronicles 13 is to stress the greater reality of Yahweh's kingdom in Judah (vv. 5, 8), which has a twofold expression in the Davidic dynasty and the Jerusalem temple. Whatever his personal worthiness, Abijah is the legitimate Davidide under whom

---

61. Cf. Wellhausen 1885: 193; Curtis and Madsen 1910: 373-74; Welten 1973: 127; Dillard 1987: 104-105.

62. Contrast Asa (2 Chron. 14.1 [E 2]); Jehoshaphat (2 Chron. 17.4, 6; 19.3; 22.9); Jotham (2 Chron. 27.2); Hezekiah (2 Chron. 29.2).

the cult is conducted as the Law prescribes (vv. 10-11), in contrast to the rebel Jeroboam and his apostate practices (vv. 6, 9). Abijah's reign is described only briefly and ambivalently in 1 Kgs 15.1-8, where it is stressed that he is the recipient of Yahweh's promise of a 'lamp in Jerusalem' (v. 4). Perhaps this image prompted the reference to the lamps in 2 Chron. 13.11. Chronicles does not contradict Kings but emphasizes instead the presence of Yahweh's kingdom among sinners and the (corporate) loyalty of Judah to Yahweh's law, which leads to success (v. 18).

The Chronicler's Asa narrative (2 Chron. 14–16) is more complex and considerably expanded over against its *Vorlage* (1 Kgs 15.9-24). However, it can be divided essentially into contrasting periods of fidelity and unfaithfulness, with corresponding consequences. The turning point in this pericope is the note in 2 Chron. 15.19 that 'there was no war until the thirty-fifth year of Asa's reign'. Up to this point the king has acted in an exemplary way, promoting reform and compelling Judah to 'seek' Yahweh (cf. 2 Chron. 14.3, 6 [E 4, 7]; 15.1, 4, 12, 13). This programme is supported by the prophetic word (2 Chron. 15.1-7) and leads to rest and security for the land. Baasha's attack (2 Chron. 16.1) is certainly not an instance of divine punishment, no more than Zerah's (2 Chron. 14.8 [E 9]), but rather an opportunity to express faith in Yahweh's power to save. However, Asa completely reverses his former pattern of behaviour, making an alliance with Benhadad (2 Chron. 16.2-6), where previously he had relied on Yahweh. He rejects Hanani's word (contrast 2 Chron. 15.8) and mistreats him, together with some of the people (vv. 7-10), and in his last days 'has recourse to mediums'[63] rather than to Yahweh (contrast 2 Chron. 14.3 [E 4]). It is usually held that the Chronicler has inserted the Hanani episode to provide a theological rationale for Asa's illness. This is possible, although it is not expressly stated that the illness is punishment, in contrast to the writer's practice in 2 Chron. 21.18-19; 26.20. The Chronicler is more interested in placing Asa's persecution of Hanani (whatever the origin of this information) into a larger pattern of declension from previous faithfulness. Nevertheless, the description of the special honours at his funeral (2 Chron. 16.14) denotes a generally positive assessment of Asa.

63. See De Vries 1989: 304 for the suggestion that רפאים denotes 'mediums' rather than 'physicians'. The Chronicler's point, at any rate, is that Asa did not recognize Yahweh as his 'healer' (cf. 2 Chron. 7.14; Exod. 15.26).

(iii) *2 Chronicles 17–20, Jehoshaphat.* Jehoshaphat plays a much more extensive and important role in Chronicles than in Kings, where his reign is described only briefly (1 Kgs 22.41-50) and he is a secondary figure compared to Ahab (cf. 1 Kgs 22.1-38; 2 Kgs 3.4-27).

The structure and theological outlook of 2 Chronicles 17–20 have been variously analysed.[64] On the whole, the composition is rather loose and paratactic,[65] consisting of a series of tableaux showing contrasting attitudes of fidelity of Yahweh and his Law, and compromising involvement with Yahweh's enemies. The prophetic word (2 Chron. 18.16-22; 19.2-3; 20.37) and the consequences of these actions are the main ways in which the Chronicler's retributive thought is expressed here. At the same time, there is a strong emphasis on the availability of repentance. The structure follows the pattern of juxtaposing passages of *Sondergut* with material from Kings:

> *17.1-19 Jehoshaphat 'seeks' Yahweh and appoints Levites to teach the Law, leading to peace, tribute, buildings and an extensive army.*
> *18.1-2 Jehoshaphat has riches and honour (cf. 17.5), yet forms a marriage alliance with Ahab and is enticed into battle.*
> 18.3-34 = 1 Kgs 22.4-35 Disastrous campaign in Ramoth-gilead in defiance of Micaiah's word.
> *18.31b (no parallel): Yahweh rescues Jehoshaphat in battle.*
> *19.1–20.30 Jehu's condemnation; Jehoshaphat's legal reform; his prayer and deliverance from enemies.*
> 20.31–21.1 = 1 Kgs 22.42-50 Concluding note. Failed alliance with Ahaziah.
> *20.37 (no parallel): Eliezer's rebuke.*

The new introduction sets the Ramoth-gilead episode in a more reprehensible light. In 1 Kings 22 Jehoshaphat appears as the junior partner in the alliance, whereas in Chronicles it is emphasized that he possesses divinely accorded wealth and status (2 Chron. 17.5; 18.1) 'because he sought the God of his father and walked in his commandments and not according to the practice of Israel' (2 Chron. 17.4). Despite Jehoshaphat's disobedience in subsequently allying himself with Israel, he receives divine mercy at the critical moment, as his cry for help in battle is interpreted as a prayer and God reverses the effect of Ahab's

---

64. Cf. Williamson 1982: 277-80, who emphasizes thematic contrasts; Dillard 1987: 129-30, who argues unconvincingly that it is paralleled with Asa's reign; Knoppers 1991; Strübind 1991: 103-104.

65. Cf. Knoppers 1991.

enticement (ויסיתם, v. 31; cf. v. 2). Jehoshaphat then responds rightly to Jehu's prophetic admonishment (2 Chron. 19.2-11). In the following episode (2 Chron. 20.1-30) the king and people display exemplary trust in Yahweh in the face of the invading coalition, and so enjoy total victory. The Jehoshaphat narrative concludes, however, with a further example of how alliance with Yahweh's enemies leads to disaster (2 Chron. 20.35-37). This last episode detracts from the preceding climax, and is an ominous indicator of Jehoshaphat's legacy: it will be related next how his marriage alliance with Ahab will bring his own house to the brink of destruction (2 Chron. 21–23; see below).

In each section of this narrative, it is clear that Jehoshaphat's and Judah's fortunes are directly related to the way in which they express their covenantal status as Yahweh's people. Concern for the Law (2 Chron. 17, 19) and the right use of the temple (2 Chron. 20) are presented as the road to blessing, but involvement with the idolatrous northern kingdom (2 Chron. 18; 20.35-37) brings ruin. Even so, repentance always remains possible to mitigate or cancel the effects of disobedience, so that fidelity and sin are hardly equivalent forces (2 Chron. 18.31b; 19.4-5).

It is of interest in this context to mention Strübind's monograph (1991), which uses the Jehoshaphat narrative as a paradigm for investigating the writer's hermeneutics and theology (pp. 103-206). Strübind underestimates the degree to which the Chronicler condemns Jehoshaphat's behaviour in 2 Chronicles 18–19,[66] but drawing especially on the motif of repentance in this pericope, he concludes (as I have argued from the evidence marshalled in this chapter) that 'the assumption that Chronicles reflects a supposedly radical "dogma of retribution" represents a misunderstanding' of the work's intention (p. 170).[67] Further light on the Chronicler's view is shed by Jehoshaphat's temple prayer in 2 Chron. 20.3-12 in the face of invasion. There is no hint in this prayer of a confession of wrongdoing, nor any perception that the invasion is divine judgment. On the contrary, it is treated as unjustified act (v. 12). Strübind again comments pertinently (p. 182), 'The threatened catastrophe is not based upon a failure of the people or the king. This fact again illustrates how problematic is the assumption of a

---

66. 1991: 171: 'Jehoshaphat's declension from Yahweh... is treated as a "mere slip"' ('Josaphats Abfall von Jahwe wird... zum "Lapsus" bagatellisiert').

67. 'Die Annahme eines vermeintlich radikalen chronistischen "Vergeltungsdogmas" stellt ein Mißverständnis dar.'

Chronistic "dogma of retribution"'.[68] It is equally foreign to the Chronicler's intention to treat *every* misfortune as evidence of judgment, as it is to take divine blessing as evidence *simpliciter* of piety in individuals (*contra* Japhet 1989: 167).

(iv) *2 Chronicles 21–23, Jehoram, Ahaziah; Athaliah's interregnum.* These chapters constitute a unit in which the Davidic House is nearly annihilated as a result of Jehoshaphat's marriage alliance with Ahab. While this section provides graphic illustration of divine punishment of evil, paradoxically it is also used by the Chronicler to emphasize Yahweh's covenant mercy to the dynasty.[69]

The account of Jehoram's reign (2 Chron. 21.1b-20) is considerably expanded beyond 2 Kgs 8.16-24 and magnifies his evil character. This is readily appreciated from the following synoptic comparison:

> *21.1b-4 (no parallel) Jehoram's accession and murder of his brothers.*
> 21.5-10a = 2 Kgs 8.17-22 Jehoram's imitation of the ways of the House of Ahab. Yahweh's promise to David (contrast v. 7 and 2 Kgs 8.19); Libnah and Edom revolt.
> *21.10b-20a (no par.) Theological rationale for loss of land. Jehoram's deepening apostasy; Elijah's condemnation; Jehoram's fatal disease and loss of family.*
> 2 Kgs 8.23-24 Burial notice (contrast 2 Chron. 21.20b, Jehoram not buried in the tomb of the kings).

Thus Jehoram, a relatively colourless figure in the *Vorlage*, is forcefully depicted as an apostate fratricide whose exceptional punishment is merited.

On the other hand, the Chronicler's account of Ahaziah (2 Chron. 22.1-9) is told more summarily, although with expansionary comments on the influence of evil counsel (vv. 3b, 4b, 5b). The writer's interest in this figure is seen from the perspective of Jehu's divine commission to destroy the House of Ahab (v. 7b): although a Davidide, Ahaziah is also related to the northern house by blood and imitation of its ways, and (in vv. 5-7) by deliberate association. He therefore shares in its divine condemnation.

---

68. 'Die drohende Katastrophe ist nicht in einer Verfehlung des Volkes oder des Königs begründet. Diese Tatsache zeigt erneut, wie problematisch die Annahme eines chronistischen "Vergeltungsdogma" ist.'

69. See further Chapter 7 below on the 'schema of dynastic endangerment' in these chapters.

In the following account of Athaliah's coup and Jehoiada's counter-measures (2 Chron. 22.10–23.21), the writer emphasizes Yahweh's faithfulness to the Davidic covenant. This results in the restoration of both legitimate ruler and legitimate worship (cf. 2 Chron. 23.3b, 18-19, no parallel), which together represent the Chronicler's conception of the theocracy.[70]

(v) *2 Chronicles 24–26, Joash, Amaziah, Uzziah.* The Chronicler has added theological rationales (2 Chron. 24.25b; 25.20b, 27a; 26.5) and narrative insertions (2 Chron. 24.15-22; 25.5-16; 26.16-20) to make these reigns conform to the common theme of beginning in (comparative) faithfulness and blessing but ending in apostasy and punishment.[71] This pattern has already been seen in the case of Asa (2 Chron. 14–16), but here the motifs of unfaithfulness and hostility toward prophets are intensified.

Joash's positive period is confined to 'the days of Jehoiada the priest' (2 Chron. 24.2). This is followed by his abandoning the temple for idolatry, rejecting prophetic warnings, and complicity in the murder of the prophet Zechariah (vv. 18-22). Joash's own fate, a severe wounding at the hands of the Aramaeans and then his 'slaying' (ויהרגהו) as a result of a conspiracy (v. 25), is evidently intended as fitting recompense for his treatment of Zechariah, who was himself the object of a conspiracy and 'slain' (ויהרג) by stoning (vv. 22-23).

Amaziah is not really presented as an exemplary figure in the first part of his reign (cf. 2 Chron. 25.2b, 6, 9), but he does pay heed to the man of God who urges him to dismiss his mercenaries (vv. 7-8), and as a result Amaziah receives a great victory (vv. 11-12). However, out of hubris he forsakes Yahweh for the powerless gods of Edom and rejects prophetic counsel for evil advice (vv. 14-17). In typical word-play the Chronicler underlines the fitting punishment that will befall Amaziah: because he has rejected the counsel of Yahweh's prophet (לעצתי), God has determined (יעץ) to destroy him (cf. also v. 27).

Pride also brings about Uzziah's downfall, after an unquestionably positive start (2 Chron. 26.4-15). His encroachment upon the temple to offer incense evokes the memory of Korah's rebellion before the tabernacle, where Yahweh's glory appeared (Num. 16.18-19), and was intended to seek a similar manifestation of the glory (v. 19b). Uzziah's

70. See further Chapter 8 on the relation of king to cult and high priest.
71. Cf. Allen 1988: 33.

sin is compounded by his angry defiance of the priests' warning (vv. 18-19), whereupon he is stricken with leprosy.[72] With Uzziah, the course of מעל once again appears in Judah's history (vv. 16, 18) and will recur to the end of the work (cf. 2 Chron. 28.19, 22; 29.6, 19; 30.7; 33.19; 36.14).

Grave as these kings' offences are, it is clear that divine punishment befalls them only once they have repudiated a prophetic (or priestly) warning. Their fate again illustrates the fact that punishment in Chronicles is *not* automatic or consecutive upon offending, but rather arises from the failure to avail oneself of the opportunity to repent (cf. 2 Chron. 7.19-22).

(vi) *2 Chronicles 27–32, Jotham, Ahaz, Hezekiah*. Both Dillard (1987: 80-81) and Japhet (1989: 161) refer to Ezekiel 18 as teaching a doctrine of strict individual responsibility and retribution and suggest that it underwrites the Chronicler's thought. While such a view probably does not reflect the meaning of Ezekiel 18,[73] the pattern in which a righteous man (Jotham) has an unrighteous son (Ahaz), who is succeeded by a righteous son (Hezekiah) is the sequence used in Ezek. 18.5-20, as Dillard (1987: 216) recognizes, and this thought at least probably underlies the writer's treatment of these reigns.

Jotham's reign (2 Chron. 27.1-9) is depicted in wholly positive terms, and the nation prospers from his obedience (vv. 4-6). By contrast, Ahaz's reign (2 Chron. 28.1-7, 16-17) is unrelievedly negative: his idolatry (heightened over against the *Vorlage;* cf. vv. 2-3) leads to defeat and exile for large numbers of the population (vv. 5-7). This portrayal (which is quite different from the impression of 2 Kgs 16.5, where Rezin and Pekah attack, but without success) culminates in Ahaz's suspension of the cult and promotion of idolatry through Judah (vv. 24-25, no parallel).

Ahaz's reign, then, represents the nadir of the monarchy prior to the exile. The point of this drastic portrayal is to create a foil for his successor, his righteous son Hezekiah. The writer's lengthy account of this reign (2 Chron. 29–32) is overwhelmingly positive. It has a quite

72. The style of this passage may be influenced by Num. 16.46-50.
73. Cf. Joyce 1979; Hals 1989: 118-27. Hals's interpretation of the disputation in Ezek. 18, that it does not propound one theory of responsibility in place of another but is rather a summons to repentance, is also a fair reflection of the Chronicler's outlook.

different focus from Kings, concentrating on Hezekiah's religious reforms rather than the political matters of the Assyrian invasion and the Babylonian envoys that interested the Deuteronomistic writer (cf. 2 Kgs 18.8–19.37; 20.1-19). Both incidents are severely abridged and confined to the latter part of Hezekiah's career (2 Chron. 32), whereas prior and extensive attention is given in 2 Chronicles 29–31 to showing how Hezekiah reversed the results of Ahaz's apostasy (and, to some extent, the original schism[74]). Thus the temple is rededicated (2 Chron. 29.3-36), Israelites from both north and south are summoned to a passover (2 Chron. 30.1-27), and the ideal round of worship and obedience is restored (2 Chron. 31.1-21).

Parallels with the thought and language of 2 Chron. 7.14 are particularly evident in the account of the passover (cf. 2 Chron. 30.6, 9, 19-20, 27), where the writer points to the temple worship as the way ahead to reunification of the people and restoration from the effects of exile. The description is thus a demonstration of the efficacy of repentance focused on the temple, as Yahweh had promised Solomon. Furthermore, the Chronicler has modelled his portrayal of Hezekiah's reign on that of the united reign of David and Solomon.[75] It follows, therefore, that just as these kings experienced blessing on their realm when they had established proper religious priorities for the nation (1 Chron. 14.2-3; 2 Chron. 8.17-18), so too does Hezekiah. Accordingly, his 'acts of faithfulness' (2 Chron. 32.1) are rewarded by victory over Sennacherib and renown in the sight of the nations (vv. 21-23).

The one shadow in this portrayal is the compressed account in 2 Chron. 32.24-31, a terse description of Hezekiah's illness and recovery, his wealth, and the visit of the Babylonian envoys. This passage implies that the reader is familiar with 2 Kgs 20.1-19. There, Hezekiah's proud bearing and display of wealth before the envoys (2 Kgs 20.13-15; cf. 2 Chron. 32.27-29) was understood as contributing to the fall of the kingdom (2 Kgs 20.16-19). The Chronicler does not contradict this view, but stresses instead that Hezekiah's and the people's self-humbling forestalled Yahweh's wrath from Jerusalem (2 Chron. 32.26). As De Vries (1989: 395) observes, a new element now emerges in the narrative (and indeed has been intimated already in

---

74. Williamson 1977a: 119-31. Williamson's view that the Chronicler's Hezekiah depicts a pre-exilic reunification in principle is challenged by Knoppers (1990).

75. See Throntveit 1988 for details.

2 Chronicles 28, where the shadow of exile has been cast and will become progressively longer). Judgment for Judah's sin may be delayed but now appears inevitable.

(vii) *2 Chronicles 33–35, Manasseh, Amon, Josiah.* The unifying theme of this section is the consequences of humble repentance.[76] Substantial additions have been made to these chapters (2 Chron. 32.11-17, 19; 33.23; 34.3, 27b; 35.1-17, 21-25), which recast them significantly over against Kings. Thematically, the most interesting of these is the emphatic use of כנע niph. as a catchword. Manasseh 'humbled himself' in exile (2 Chron. 33.12, 19) and was restored to the land, which also received blessings (vv. 14-16). The point of this presentation[77] is to highlight Yahweh's faithfulness to the covenant promise of restoration (2 Chron. 7.14), and his goodness even to the most notorious of sinners; as Lowery remarks (1991: 188), '(Manasseh's) restoration and prosperity is proof of God's surprising willingness to bless even those who must repent of serious sins. His cult reform shows the righteous action which follows true repentance.'

By contrast, Amon 'did not humble himself before Yahweh as Manasseh his father had humbled himself' (v. 23) but instead increased the guilt (אשמה) that incurred Yahweh's wrath. The addition of this verse sets up a rhetorical contrast between these reigns (and generations), whereas in 2 Kings 21 Manasseh and Amon are essentially paralleled.

The events of Josiah's reign (2 Chron. 34–35) are reordered and expanded from the *Vorlage* to convey the writer's own emphases. The discovery of the book of the law (2 Chron. 34.8-14), which is a turning point in Kings, is instead presented as the last stage of a process which began with Josiah's early piety and reform (vv. 3-7), and thus is a consequence of 'seeking' God (v. 3). Josiah's exemplary response to the commandments of the law book is underscored by the repetition of the root כנע in Huldah's prophecy in 2 Chron. 34.27. Because of his obedience in promoting reform, he will be spared seeing the destruction of the temple and Jerusalem.[78] This news is a stimulus to further reform

76. Cf. Selman 1994b: 517-18.

77. See further Chapter 9 on the Chronicler's portrayal of Manasseh.

78. Nevertheless, Josiah dies in battle, having refused to 'listen to the words of Neco from the mouth of God' (2 Chron. 35.22). The Chronicler's account of Josiah's death has given rise to a debate whether this report was already in his version of Kings or is his own composition; contrast Begg 1987a and Williamson 1982b; 1987a.

(2 Chron. 34.29–35.19), and although Judah's fate is sealed, the Chronicler once more points to repentance and the right use of the temple as the means of restoration from the consequences of exile (cf. 2 Chron. 30.6-9).

(viii) *2 Chronicles 36, Judah's last four kings.* The final chapter is severely abridged from the *Vorlage* as the history of Judah seemingly accelerates to its inevitable judgment. The last kings are treated very summarily, with the elimination of much personal information about them, and are typologically linked by the experience of exile, actual or implied. The history of מעל now reaches its climax in the description of Zedekiah's generation, where the Chronicler breaks off from his *Vorlage* to offer his own theological explanation for the destruction and exile. The effect is very different from the factual account in 2 Kgs 25.1-22. The Chronicler emphasizes instead the grave sinfulness of Zedekiah and the populace (הרבו למעול מעל, v. 14), and their refusal to repent: vv. 12-16 reflect the language of 2 Chron. 7.14, but in the negative. Accordingly, the deserved judgment of 2 Chron. 7.19-22 finally befalls the temple and nation. Nevertheless, as part of a pattern of surprising reversals that marks the writer's presentation, the concluding note of the work, Cyrus's summons to return and rebuild (vv. 22-23), is a clear indication of hope and restoration.

Before the results of this study are summarized, two features of 2 Chronicles 10–36 call for brief comment. The first is the use of stereotypical motifs of reward and punishment. These are remarked on by Braun (1979: 53-55), who notes that 'apart from those additions to his work directly related to the cult, it is difficult to find an addition which the Chronicler has made to his *Vorlage* which does not function in these terms'.

The second question concerns the Chronistic burial notices. Special honours are reported of Asa (2 Chron. 16.14) and Hezekiah (2 Chron. 32.33), while it is expressly stated of Jehoram (2 Chron. 21.20), Joash (2 Chron. 24.25) and Ahaz (2 Chron. 28.27) that they were not buried 'in the tombs of the kings'. It was noted in Chapter 2 that this feature has been interpreted as a reflex of the writer's supposed 'earth-bound retributionism'.[79] This is quite doubtful, since the Chronicler nowhere plainly addresses the question of post-mortem retribution.[80] It is clear,

79. North 1963; cf. von Rad 1962: 350.
80. Although, interestingly, Ackroyd (1987: 176-80) suggests that the portrayal

however, that the burial notices do express the writer's theological verdict on particular reigns.

3. *Summary and Conclusion*

It has long been agreed that a concern with divine reward and punishment is central to the Chronicler's work, but this fact has rarely redounded to the writer's credit, whether as theologian or historian. Our study of the Chronicler's special vocabulary and the narrative units that give expression to his retributive doctrine lead us instead to a substantially different appraisal of the writer's thought and intention. It appears that insufficient attention has been paid in the course of research to the Chronicler's basic theological convictions, and that the literary form of his presentation has been insufficiently appreciated. For these reasons I have sought in these chapters to define more exactly the significance of the central divine address in 2 Chron. 7.12-22, and to view each narrative unit in its own terms. The following results have emerged from this study.

The theme of reward and punishment in Chronicles has its meaning not within a general theory of divine action in history but specifically as part of the covenantal relationship between Yahweh, 'the God of Israel',[81] and his people. The thought and language of such passages as Deut. 28.10-11 and Lev. 26.40-41 appear to underlie the writer's usage (cf. 2 Chron. 7.14, 20; 34.24) and suggest as a traditio-historical setting the *blessings and curses of the Sinaitic covenant* as they are represented in the Pentateuch. The Chronicler develops this idea by showing that the Sinaitic (and for that matter, the Abrahamic) covenant underlie the Davidic covenant, which carries with it its own (temple-orientated) promises of forgiveness and restoration. The Sinaitic and Davidic covenants are in fact more closely related to each other in the Chronicler's view than the usual approach to this question, which tends to see the former covenant displaced by the latter in the Chronicler's outlook, has hitherto allowed.[82] It seems better to speak of the Davidic covenant as consolidating and culminating what was earlier achieved

---

of the death of Hezekiah in 2 Chron. 32.33 hints in this direction.

81. An epithet found thirty-three times in Chronicles; cf. Japhet 1989: 19.

82. Japhet presents the most extreme interpretation of this view, according to which the Chronicler effectively denies the significance of the exodus and Sinai, in favour of a belief in continuous settlement in the land since the patriarchs.

through Abraham and Moses. The Chronicler's retributive thought is properly a development of a central part of his community's religious tradition.

Other streams of biblical tradition (such as the canonical prophetic corpus, the Deuteronomistic History and the Psalms) have contributed to the Chronicler's expression and outlook here; the work should not be considered simply or primarily as 'aggadic midrash' on the 'Levitical doctrine of guilt and atonement' (thus Johnstone 1986), but as a summation of the various scriptural currents that contributed to Israel's religious, and especially its liturgical, life.

The Chronicler handles the theme of reward and punishment vis-à-vis his *Vorlage* with exegetical techniques which appear to be early forms of methods attested in rabbinic exegesis, especially *semukin*.[83] Much of the Chronicler's interpolated material in 2 Chron. 10–36 (whatever its origins) is also readily understandable as amplifying or rendering explicit relationships which he saw already implied in Samuel–Kings. In his relation to his *Vorlage* the writer intensifies the presentation in his traditum (or, as in the case of Hezekiah, he may underplay his failings) but does not contradict it, nor does he really impose a foreign construction on his sources.[84] Where he appears to be at variance with the judgments of Kings (e.g., over Solomon, Rehoboam, Abijah and Manasseh), a more careful reading of the text shows that the Chronicler's purpose is not to attribute an unsullied piety to these kings, in defiance of the earlier tradition, but to stress Yahweh's covenantal goodness to them or their place in Yahweh's purposes (which is summed up in his covenant with David).

The Chronicler is not concerned to show 'the systematization of history' according to absolute divine justice,[85] nor with 'rationalizing' the action of the deity.[86] The traditional concerns of theodicy, such as the origin of evil and its final requiting, are not really addressed in the book. Nor is there any attempt to answer (or repudiate) the question of innocent suffering (cf. 1 Chron. 21.17; 2 Chron. 25.13), which we might expect as part of a rigorous theory of retribution. Nowhere is it stated or implied that every misfortune (typically in Chronicles, a foreign invasion,

---

83. Cf. 1 Chron. 13–14; 1 Chron. 21–22; cf. the specific studies in proto-midrash by Seeligmann 1953; Fishbane 1979–80; Shinan 1985; and Zakovitch 1986.

84. As Childs (1979: 651-53) rightly recognizes.

85. Thus Japhet 1989: 156-76.

86. Cf. von Rad 1930; 1962.

but illness as well) is the consequence of sin (*contra* Wellhausen 1885: 203). On the other hand, where punishment is meted out, it is shown to be deserved and appropriate for the sin .[87]

The writer uses the theme of blessing and punishment to demonstrate a much more fundamental concern than retribution, namely, *Yahweh's mercy and restorative will toward his sinful people.* This has sometimes been observed with reference to the role of the prophets in Chronicles, but such a perception of the divine will pervades the whole presentation. As Johnstone emphasizes, Chronicles depicts sin as touching every part of Israel's life, most outstandingly in the case of David (cf. 1 Chron. 13, 21), who otherwise represents the writer's ideal. It is precisely because every reign is marked by some failing that the temple stands in the nation's midst. There, the destructive course of sin may be halted, Israel's life sanctified and the land made secure and fruitful (cf. 2 Chron. 31.10).

There is, however, nothing *ex opere operato* about the temple's function, because behind it, Yahweh controls the course of history for Israel's sake. Thus, David's serious cultic failure toward the ark (which prefigures the temple) is nevertheless followed by blessing on his kingdom (1 Chron. 13–14); the suspension of the cult under Ahaz (2 Chron. 28.24) is succeeded by the reform under Hezekiah (2 Chron. 29.3); while the destruction of the temple only gives rise to a new divine initiative through Cyrus (2 Chron. 36.22-23). Certainly there is nothing mechanical about this narrative pattern. Rather we should note the *surprising* and *gracious* character of these transitions in Israel's fortunes. There is no balance between blessing, which comes *consistently* whenever Israel 'seeks Yahweh', and judgment, which can be mitigated or remitted entirely.

The 'individual' and 'immediate' character of the doctrine (Dillard 1987) as it has usually been represented must be qualified and reassessed. The Chronicler can speak of collective judgment in Jehu's purge (2 Chron. 22.7-8), while the destruction and exile are not exclusively the fault of Zedekiah and his generation: exile is intimated already in 2 Chronicles 28 and becomes a steadily more insistent motif until the end of the work. Hezekiah's pride (2 Chron. 32.25) also contributes to that fate, though he, like Josiah (2 Chron. 34.26-28), is spared from seeing it. Their reforms can delay but not decisively avert the fall of

---

87. Cf. Japhet 1989: 170, 'measure for measure'.

judgment. *Contra* Japhet (1989: 163), 2 Chron. 36.15-16 probably refers to the continuous history of the monarchy which incurred the mounting wrath. It appears therefore that the Chronicler does recognize corporate and cumulative guilt, and the notion that punishment may be deferred. His differences in outlook over these questions with the Deuteronomistic History are more a matter of emphasis than substance.

It is nevertheless true that the Chronicler stresses the 'individual' character of actions and their consequences. This fact is not related to the supposed late development of Old Testament thought on the status of the individual,[88] nor is it simply a reflection of the Chronicler's 'deductive' manner of explaining the past, supplying acceptable theological reasons where the *Vorlage* was content merely to report events (cf. De Vries 1989). Instead, this emphasis belongs to the paraenetic nature and purpose of the work. While it affirms Yahweh's justice, it is above all the writer's means of underlining the opportunity that his own age has to pursue the path of full restoration, assisted by the institution of the temple (which signifies the Davidic covenant, along with the dynasty), and untrammelled by the consequences of past disobedience and judgment. The point is expressed most clearly in Hezekiah's summons to the Levites to purify the cult after the extreme unfaithfulness of Ahaz's reign (2 Chron. 29.5-6). In this speech Hezekiah remarks (v. 8) that because of the previous generation's sinful behaviour,

> Yahweh's wrath came upon Judah and Jerusalem, and he has made them an object of dread and horror and scorn, as you can see with your own eyes, and see, our fathers have fallen by the sword and our sons, daughters and wives are in captivity for this.

While the immediate reference is to the reign of Ahaz (cf. 2 Chron. 28.5), the precise verbal allusions in this verse to Jer. 29.18 especially ('an object of dread..., horror and scorn') plainly evoke thought of the Babylonian exile.[89] Hezekiah's cult reform is intended 'so that Yahweh will turn his fierce anger away from us' (v. 10). The Chronicler's community stands in an analogous situation, and is instructed through this

88. Thus von Rad 1962: 349-50; Japhet 1989.

89. Williamson 1982: 353. Cf. Ackroyd 1973: 181: 'Prophetic judgement themes underline this sermonic address. The point is made still clearer in the emphasis on the people *actually seeing with their own eyes* (v. 8) the present conditions of the land and city [...] (T)he Chronicler is here commenting on the exilic situation.'

and numerous other examples that the guilt and failings of previous generations need not be visited upon it. In this respect, the writer's emphasis upon the 'individual' character of retribution emerges as fundamentally positive.[90]

---

90. Strübind (1991: 50) more accurately describes this aspect as 'generationen-immanent'.

Chapter 5

THE USE OF SOURCES IN MOTIFS OF REWARD AND PUNISHMENT IN 2 CHRONICLES 10–36

1. *Sources in Chronicles: Welten's Critique*

A cursory examination of the Chronicler's *Sondergut* in 2 Chronicles 10–36 indicates that the greater part of this material serves to illustrate his doctrine of divine reward and punishment. Recognition of this evident theological purpose has contributed to the suspicion that has prevailed for much of the modern period that the author was unreliable as a witness to the pre-exilic history of Israel, and indeed possessed little historical sense. Already in the sixteenth century doubts had been expressed about the historical worth of the book,[1] but these became general with the advent of modern biblical criticism. Graham (1990) has charted the course of nineteenth-century Chronicles studies as a series of challenges to, and defences of, the work's historical reliability, beginning with de Wette's (1806) judgment that it was a tendentious falsification ('Verfälschung') of the events of the distant past.[2] Wellhausen (1885) extended de Wette's critique on several levels, particularly on the historical basis of the pericopae describing reward and punishment in 2 Chronicles 10–36. The theological character of these sections and the author's plan of writing revealed these sections to be 'inventions of the

---

1.   For the history of research up to Wellhausen see Willi 1972: 12-47.

2.   De Wette (1806: I, 42-132) compares Chronicles unfavourably with Samuel–Kings according to several criteria. De Wette's theological critique of Chronicles was directed mainly against its depiction of the cult, and the bias he perceived in the work against Israel and in favour of Judah. A forceful defence of the historicity of Chronicles was mounted by Keil ('Apologetischer Versuch', 1833; 1872), who argued that the Chronicler drew on a common source as did the authors of Samuel and Kings. It is, however, scarcely doubted today that the Chronicler was directly dependent on Samuel–Kings, whatever his use of extrabiblical sources (Japhet 1993: 14-23). Auld (1994) has recently revived the older theory.

most circumstantial kind' (p. 207), and as a late date for the Priestly Writing was increasingly accepted, the historical value of Chronicles was correspondingly depreciated.[3] The work was now studied primarily as an adjunct to Pentateuchal criticism or as a witness to the life and thought of the later post-exilic period.

The more negative judgments about the historicity of the work that characterized the latter part of the nineteenth century have in turn been significantly moderated.[4] Two related factors here have been the growth of archaeological knowledge of the monarchic period,[5] and the detection of extrabiblical pre-exilic sources incorporated by the writer. Since Noth (1943), there has been a gradual expansion of the amount of material in Chronicles that can be attributed to such sources. Noth held that two passages at least (2 Chron. 32.30, the description of Hezekiah's tunnel; and 2 Chron. 35.20-24, the account of Josiah's death) could be confidently assigned to monarchic sources. The modern period of Chronicles studies, inaugurated by Rudolph (1955), has added significantly to this list, largely through literary source criticism. The researches of Myers (1965), Johnson (1969) and Williamson (1982) in particular have taken a positive view toward the presence of pre-exilic traditional material in Chronicles, and have sought to identify it through literary analysis.

If the use of such sources can be confirmed, it may provide an important pointer to the character of the Chronicler's work, suggesting that he did not compose his narrative out of whole cloth, but rather that his evidently theological message has a historical basis. This point must be made with the following caveats.

First, it must be expected that for much of the writer's *Sondergut* there may be little evidence either way that extrabiblical sources have been used. While the style and outlook of the post-exilic author may be readily identified, it remains possible that he assimilated earlier materials to conform to these. It may in practice be difficult to distinguish redaction from tradition.

Secondly, the form of the work, in which the *Vorlage* is represented

3.   See the summary in Graham 1990: 128-34 of Graf's dating of P using Chronicles, arguments which were adopted and amplified by Wellhausen.
4.   Cf. Japhet 1985 for a survey of the major trends in scholarship.
5.   On the contribution of archaeology see especially Japhet 1985: 94-95. Besides Welten (see below), North (1974) takes a categorically negative view on this matter.

in a highly patterned and selective way, indicates that the writer's primary concern was to address and instruct his readers in a homiletical manner, and to draw out the significance of these past events for them, rather than to compose either a parallel or a 'strongly "revisionist" history' using the Pentateuch and Deuteronomistic History.[6] This need not imply, however, that the Chronicler was indifferent to historical matters. As Deboys (1990) and Schniedewind (1991) indicate in their respective studies of Abijah and Manasseh, homiletic and historical concerns are not necessarily opposed to each other in the Chronicler's work.

However, while English-language scholarship increasingly affirms the use of pre-exilic sources in Chronicles,[7] a divergent approach to this question has been taken in recent German work.[8] The most extensive challenge has come from Welten (1973), endorsed by Strübind (1991).[9]

Welten's work is a study of some parts of the *Sondergut* in 2 Chronicles 10–36 which have usually been seen as stereotypical motifs of reward. From his analysis of the literary and linguistic characteristics of these sections, as well as an appraisal of archaeological and other historical evidence, Welten concludes that the Chronicler made very little use of earlier extrabiblical sources. Only a few brief notices from the time of Rehoboam, Uzziah and Hezekiah are accepted as authentic, while three other portions are judged possible but less likely.[10] Welten's study is confined mainly to the categories or *topoi* of building notices (especially fortifications), descriptions of Judah's army, and military victories. He examines the texts belonging to each category in the light of

6.   Thus Van Seters (1983: 361) on the Chronicler's purpose. This presupposition also underlies Japhet's work (1989; 1993). Cf. Chapter 2 n. 10 above on the view that Chronicles is to be understood as a work of history intended to supplant (or supplement) the Deuteronomistic History. Von Rad (1930: 133) denied that the author intended to write history, but apparently treated Chronicles as such a work in his *Theology* (1962: 347-48).

7.   Cf. Myers, Johnson, Williamson, Dillard, Selman. Braun (1986: xxiii) takes a rather negative view on this, but his discussion is very brief.

8.   Cf. Chapter 2 n. 10, on recent German approaches to the genre of Chronicles.

9.   Strübind 1991: 177.

10.   Welten accepts as evidence of earlier sources the list of Rehoboam's fortresses (11.5b, 6-10a), the notice of Uzziah's war against the Philistines and his agricultural works (26.6a, 10), and the description of Hezekiah's tunnel (32.30). He also allows that the family details in 11.22-23 and 21.1-4 and the report of Josiah's death (35.20-25) could reflect pre-exilic sources (1973: 191-94).

their literary and historical evidence, as well as the category as a whole in relation to the author's literary methods and purposes. Like Torrey (to whom, however, he makes no reference), Welten concludes that the vast majority of the *Sondergut* is the author's own creation. Chronicles has no real historical interests, but instead represents a new literary phenomenon (1973: 205):

> With the Books of Chronicles history writing in Israel enters a new phase, in which traditions are no longer collected and edited, or an existing work appears in a new version. The Chronicler writes the history from beginning to end in a new and independent way.[11]

The best analogy for this new genre is said to be the book of Judith, which E. Haag described as a 'free, parabolic representation of history ("Geschichtsdarstellung")' (Welten 1973: 206) that purports to narrate history but is actually edifying fiction. In the same way, the contents of Chronicles really reflect the social, religious and political circumstances of the author's Hellenistic period rather than pre-exilic times. According to Welten, this era was one of permanent external threat to the small, beleaguered community of Judah. The *topoi* of fortifications and army notices do not convey authentic information, since the description makes it clear that neither fortresses nor armies played any real military role. Rather they are to be understood as reflexes of the motif of 'rest', the security which Judah enjoys when it 'seeks Yahweh'. Similarly, the four 'Yahweh war' reports do not reflect pre-exilic traditions but are a schematic demonstration of the divine protection Judah can expect on every side ('nach allen vier Himmelsrichtungen') from its hostile neighbours, provided it faithfully observes the cult (1973: 201-204).[12]

In the following discussion it is argued that the sharp distinction that Welten draws between theology and history in Chronicles is overdrawn.

---

11. 'Mit den Chronikbüchern tritt die Geschichtsschreibung in Israel in eine ganz neue Phase, wo nicht mehr Traditionen gesammelt und redigiert werden, wo nicht mehr ein vorgebenes Werk in eine neue Bearbeitung aufgeht. Der Chronist schreibt die Geschichte von Anfang bis Ende neu und selbständig durch.'

12. Welten (p. 169) observes that prior to the Chronicler's time, Neh. 2.11–7.3 showed the province of Yehud facing threats from each direction (Sanballat and his sons in the north, Geshem the Arab in the south, Tobiah and the Ammonites in the east, and the Ashdodites in the west). He argues that the Chronicler's 'Yahweh war' accounts are literary projections of the post-exilic community's disputes with its surrounding neighbours, and are intended to show the schematic defence of Judah in the north (13.2-19), south (14.8-14 [E 9-15]), east (20.1-30), and west (26.6-8).

It will be maintained instead that the retributive motifs of 2 Chronicles 10–36 reflect earlier traditions to a much greater extent than Welten allows, and that this is an important feature in understanding the nature of the work.

2. *The Chronicler's Sondergut in 2 Chronicles 10–36*

This material falls into two broad groups, both of which are related to the author's doctrine of retribution. The first group includes signs of divine reward in the form of buildings, army organization, military victory, progeny, wealth and tribute; and its negative counterpart, divine punishment in the form of military defeat, disease and death. The second group recounts information about the religious life of Judah, including accounts of the reforms and apostasies of individual kings. Examples from each group are discussed below for evidence of the use of extrabiblical sources.

1. *Motifs of Divine Reward*
(i) *Building notices* ('Baunotizen'). References to building works are confined to those reigns (or portions thereof) that are judged positively by the Chronicler. Thus, such works are (apparently) ascribed to Rehoboam's positive period (11.5-12; cf. vv. 13-17; although, in fact, no chronological notice is given), and to Asa (14.5-6 [E 6–7]; cf. v. 2), Jehoshaphat (17.12-13; cf. 3-10), Uzziah (26.2, 6c, 9-10a; cf. v. 4), Hezekiah (32.5, 29-30) and Manasseh, following repentance (33.14; cf. v. 12). Of these reigns, the first and last are on the whole judged negatively by the Chronicler, while the others are judged on the whole positively, despite lapses.[13] Some of these notices are only brief and stereotypical, but in at least four cases there is fuller information which suggests underlying sources.

First, there is widespread agreement that the account of Rehoboam's fortifications (11.5-12) is based on a pre-exilic document (reflected in vv. 6a-10a) to which the Chronicler has attached introductory and concluding notes.[14] The details are not paralleled in any other biblical lists, and they make good sense as a defensive perimeter for Judah on

---

13. Welten's theory that the author wished to present the first four kings of Judah in a positive light (1973: 127, supported by Klein 1983: 214-15) is criticized below.

14. Welten (1973: 15) also accepts its authenticity.

the east, south and west.[15] Largely on archaeological grounds, the list
has been attributed to the time of Josiah or Hezekiah.[16] However, it does
accord with the political circumstances of Rehoboam's time, either
before or after Shishak's invasion.[17] Aharoni (1979: 293) also points to
the internal evidence of Chronicles that this line did play a defensive role
in the first half of the ninth century: the defeat of Zerah at Mareshah
(14.8-14 [E 9–15]), and the eastern coalition near Tekoa (20.1-24).[18] By
contrast, Na'aman (1986) objects that the archaeological evidence for

15. See Miller 1987: 277 for a map showing the distribution of these fortresses.
Aharoni suggests that there was no northern line because Rehoboam wished to
expand in that direction (1979: 292), but Williamson argues that no town in the north
may have been suitable, and Rehoboam may not have felt a threat from that quarter
(1982: 241). The absence of mention of fortresses on the north side may, however,
be explained by the fact that Rehoboam retained control of Gezer, Lower Beth-Horon
and Baalah, towns which Solomon had built (1 Kgs 9.15-18), presumably to guard
the north approach to Jerusalem via the Ascent of Beth-horon.

16. See Na'aman 1986: 9-10 for a brief discussion of Junge, Alt and Fritz who
assign the list to Josiah's time, and Na'aman's own view that it reflects measures
taken by Hezekiah to prepare against Sennacherib's attack. His arguments are based
on the distribution of *lmlk* stamps (from jars which he thinks contained siege rations)
and the assumption that the Chronicler omitted northern cities from the list for ideological reasons. Na'aman's arguments are criticized by Garfinkel (1988), who points
out that the present known distribution of *lmlk* stamps does not match the list very
closely, while there is no biblical evidence that Hezekiah fortified any city other than
Jerusalem. However, it is very likely that Hezekiah did undertake other defensive
measures (see further below). Na'aman reaffirms his views in a reply to Garfinkel
(1986: 74-75). For a critique of Fritz's views, see Miller 1987: 278-79. Japhet
(1993: 665-67) accepts that the list comes from Rehoboam's time, taking it as a
summary of his activity throughout his reign.

17. If the fortifications were begun before Shishak's invasion, this may suggest
the threat Judah feared from Egypt, to whom Jeroboam probably owed fealty (Dillard
1987: 95); if afterwards, it was as a result of his attack (Aharoni 1979: 292). It seems
unlikely, though, that Rehoboam would have been allowed to fortify his southeast
border after a campaign which left him a vassal, according to 2 Chron. 12.8.

18. This assumes, of course, that there is a historical kernel to these accounts, for
all that they are presented in the extreme, stylized form of 'Yahweh war' narratives.
Welten objects 'that the reports of military constructions have no relation to the
numerous campaigns within the Chronistic work. In no war report in Chronicles do
the fortresses play a role' ('daß die Berichte über militärische Bauten keine
Beziehung zu den zahlreichen Feldzügen innerhalb des chronistischen Werkes haben.
In keinem Kriegsbericht der Chronik spielen die Festungen eine Rolle') (p. 10).
However, these geographical notices may suggest otherwise. See below on 'military
victory'.

Beth-zur and Lachish for Rehoboam's time is quite ambiguous, and that Philistine Gath (v. 8) was not part of his kingdom. However, 'Gath' in the list probably denotes Moresheth-Gath, which may have lost the first part of its name from haplography (Dillard 1987: 97; Japhet 1993: 667).

The account of Uzziah's military and agricultural activities (26.9-13) is also generally accepted, largely on the basis of extensive archaeological finds assigned to this period.[19]

A description of Hezekiah's defensive measures against Sennacherib is given in 32.5, 30. The latter note is widely accepted as evidence of an earlier source.[20] Welten argues from the grammar of v. 5 (*waw*-consecutive imperfect without a substantive subject immediately following v. 4) and the typically Chronistic language that the author composed this note himself without any source (1973: 29-31), but as an expansion of Isa. 22.9b-11 (1973: 72). However, more recent archaeological indications appear to support the implications of this verse, that Hezekiah did in fact undertake a considerable expansion of the defended area of the city. Broshi has deduced from excavations in the Jewish Quarter and the Armenian Garden that around 700 BCE Jerusalem increased to three or four times its former size, after changing very little from Solomon's time. Broshi attributes this to immigration from the north after 721 and from western Judah after 701. Shiloh's excavations at the north end of the City of David also found little evidence of activity in the ninth century, but considerable evidence of activity in the eighth century which he thinks probably points to the work of Hezekiah.[21]

Finally, the detailed description of Manasseh's building works (33.14a) may reflect a pre-exilic source, as Noth maintained (1967: 141). The topographical and textual difficulties are discussed by Welten, who argues instead that it reflects the Chronicler's own time (1973: 72-78).

19. Cf. Williamson 1982: 336-37; Japhet 1993: 876-77. Dillard (1987: 209) also refers to the discovery of a seal bearing Uzziah's name in a cistern in Tell Beit Mirsim. The evidence of pre-exilic sources for v. 9 is less secure than for v. 10: the reference to the Corner Gate could have been deduced from 25.23 (= 2 Kgs 14.13), while Welten (1973: 63-66) holds that the topography and special use of מגדל reflect post-exilic times. On the other hand, it is very likely that Uzziah would have undertaken such repairs; moreover, Amos 1.1 and Zech. 14.5 may suggest that Jerusalem sustained significant damage from the earthquake during his reign (Selman 1994b: 469).

20. The case was strongly put by Noth (1967: 139). North (1974: 379) rejects this conclusion, but cf. Japhet 1993: 977-78.

21. Broshi 1974; Shiloh 1984: 28a.

In particular, Welten holds that 'Ophel' does not denote the spur connecting the temple mount to the City of David,[22] but is post-exilic usage for the northern part of the city, including the temple area and the quarters for the cult personnel (pp. 67, 77). Thus, according to Welten, v. 14 makes the improbable ascription to Manasseh of building works around the entire perimeter of the city, from the southeast to the Fish Gate in the northwest and thence to the temple area. However, such an identification of Ophel is far from certain.[23] Following Broshi, the passage may also be understood as a westward expansion of the city, as a continuation of Hezekiah's policies (cf. 32.5).[24]

On the other hand, other references to building works are much less certain. Where they are expressed in generalized terms that bear the strong imprint of the Chronicler's style (e.g. 14.5-6 [E 6–7]; 17.12-13a) or as a parallel with a preceding reign (27.3-4 with 26.9, 15), there is less reason to postulate another source.

(ii) *Army Notices* ('Heeresverfassung'). A number of notices purporting to give information about the composition and equipment of Judah's army at various times during the monarchy forms the next *topos* examined by Welten (1973: 79-114). In his view these notices are marked by a unitary Chronistic style and by anachronisms, and function as a measure of theological evaluation of particular reigns. From such features he concludes that the notices have no authenticity, but are the author's own compositions, reflecting the Hellenistic armies of the Chronicler's own

22. The identification is made in Josephus, *War* 5.145.

23. Welten's view is based in part on the versional evidence, which is at best ambivalent. The Targum renders Ophel as *pltyryn* (= 'praetorium'), whereas Syr and Arab read 'all Jerusalem'. By contrast, LXX and Vulg transcribe as *opla* or Ophel. A more serious difficulty for Welten's theory is presented by Shiloh's observation (1984: 27) that 'Ophel' is not a name particular to Jerusalem but is an urban architectural term denoting the outstanding site of a citadel or acropolis. The term is used in 2 Kgs 5.24 for the citadel of Samaria, and also for that built by Mesha at Dibon. Shiloh argues that from the tenth century BCE the hill of the City of David was divided into three main units, of which the central one was the 'Ophel' where the citadel may have been located. Welten also fails to reckon with the use of the term in Isa. 32.14.

24. Kenyon (1974: 150-51) assigned the wall she discovered on the eastern slope of the southeastern ridge of the City of David to Hezekiah. However, Bahat (1981) argues that it is to be attributed to Manasseh because it meets the description of 33.14.

late post-exilic period (1973: 98-114). Again, it is likely that these notes are intended for the most part to reflect blessing upon a reign (or part of one) which is judged positively. However, in taking such a historically sceptical position Welten parts company with many scholars preceding him who discerned in these notices evidence of earlier sources.[25]

The subject is helpfully reviewed by Williamson, who argues that at a number of points Welten has misinterpreted the evidence and that in one case certainly (25.5) the description is both an integral part of its context and features in a passage (vv. 6-13) in which the king, Amaziah, is acting in a way of which the Chronicler disapproves. The general authenticity of this passage is also affirmed by Rainey.[26] Williamson comments that this exception should warn against placing these notices automatically on the same level as those about building. Moreover, they are fewer in number compared with the building notices, suggesting that the Chronicler was constrained by regard for the sources from which he drew this material (1982: 261-62).

The texts in question are 14.7 [E 8]; 17.13b-19; 26.11-15; and 25.5. Welten recognizes that the last-named verse forms an exception (1973: 95-96 n. 97) but does not otherwise discuss it. He attributes the first three to the Chronicler's own composition largely on formal and linguistic grounds. Each is concerned with enumerating the forces, while two begin with similar formulae: ויהי לאסא or ויהי לעזיהו (14.7; 26.11). The passages also describe the organization of the army according to equipment and tribal divisions (Judah and Benjamin) and employ a number of expressions particularly common in P and Chronicles (יצא צבא ;פקדה ;בית אבות). Welten considers that these texts present a unitary picture. The absence of reference to horses and chariots is considered remarkable (p. 99), given the putative period of these notices (c. 900–750 BCE) and our knowledge of this time from earlier traditions (cf. 2 Kgs 3.7; 8.21; Isa. 2.7). The neat division of weapons along tribal lines (large shields and spears for Judah, small shields and bows for Benjamin) is also unlikely, and was probably composed by the Chronicler on the basis of Judg. 20.16 (p. 102). The real source of this

25. Junge (1937: 37-45) attributed the Chronicler's notices to dislocated material from Josiah's time, since they concerned only conscript armies and made no reference to chariots. This dating was rejected by others who nevertheless accepted that the author made use of sources here (Goettsberger, Rudolph, Michaeli, Myers, Cazelles).

26. Rainey 1988.

division into heavily and lightly armed forces was the Chronicler's knowledge of the Hellenistic armies that had long been present in Palestine, first as mercenaries, and then immediately prior to the Chronicler's time under Alexander (pp. 106-111). Finally, 26.15a appears to ascribe defensive catapults to Uzziah's time, against the evidence that such devices were unknown before the fifth century BCE (p. 113).

These arguments are criticized at a number of points by Williamson. Following Junge, he observes that the notices are themselves free of any moralizing or religious elements. Moreover, they give details not of standing armies but of conscripts (1982: 261). This explains the absence of reference to horses and chariots. Williamson also notes that the argument from style is partly offset by the nature of the comparable technical material that is being treated. Although the reports do contain expressions from Late Biblical Hebrew, stylistic considerations may also point to the use of sources. In 17.13b-19 details of the standing army (vv. 13b, 19 and the names of individual commanders) appear to be confused with details of the conscript army. Moreover, Amasiah is described in v. 16 as המתנדב ליהוה, which Williamson notes is not explained in any way and is unparalleled in comparable cases (1982: 284). Both details suggest that inherited materials underlie this account, which the Chronicler passes on as a tradent. Welten maintains that the description of Amasiah is 'expressly Chronistic' (1973: 84) and points to the evidence of Curtis's list that התנדב is found almost exclusively in Chronicles and Ezra–Nehemiah. However, the examples which are clearly by the authors of these works have to do exclusively with freewill offerings or the decision of returnees to live in Jerusalem.[27] By contrast, the military sense of the expression is attested in Judg. 5.2, 9, which is undeniably ancient.[28]

Finally, Welten's interpretation of 26.15a as an anachronistic reference to catapults, an identification important for his late dating of the work, is probably mistaken. Yadin had long ago suggested that חשבנות מחשבת חושב referred not to torsion-operated weapons but rather (as the Hebrew suggests) 'skilfully made' defensive structures built onto the towers and battlements for archers and throwers. The reliefs of Sennacherib's assault on Lachish, from a time shortly after Uzziah, show just such protective structures.[29]

27. Cf. 1 Chron. 29.5, 6, 9, 14, 17; Ezra 2.68; 3.5; 7.13, 15, 16; Neh. 11.2.
28. Cf. Soggin 1981: 80-81.
29. Yadin 1963: 325-27. Williamson (1982: 338) also points to more recent

So far our discussion has been limited to indications of extrabiblical sources underlying the army notices of 2 Chronicles 10–36. This positive evidence is also of a piece with the other military Chronistic material in 1 Chronicles 11–12. Williamson (1982: 104) observes that the additional list of David's heroes in 1 Chron. 11.41b-47 is unlikely to be a post-exilic fabrication (thus Noth), since all the identifiable places of origin are in Transjordan, an area regarded with suspicion by the post-exilic community. The material in 1 Chronicles 12 could well stem from the Davidic period, although the structure and style of that unit belong to the Chronicler. Johnson (1988: 63-68) has demonstrated that military census materials underlie much of 1 Chronicles 2–8 (particularly for the genealogies of Issachar, Benjamin, Asher and the Transjordanian tribes), so it is a reasonable surmise that other similar material is reflected in the scattered notices in the post-Solomonic narrative.

(iii) *Military victories* ('Kriegsberichte mit positivem Ausgang'). Military victories constitute the third *topos* examined in detail by Welten (1973: 115-75). 2 Chronicles 10–36 contains fifteen accounts of war without parallel in the *Vorlage*, of which six describe victories which occur during reigns (or parts thereof) that are apparently judged positively by the Chronicler.[30] Although these reports are presented in a highly schematized way, with moralizing comment and the imprint of the Chronicler's style (catalogued by Welten on pp. 117-22, 133-35, 142-43), they also contain onomastic and geographical details which may reflect earlier forms of the traditions.

Before considering such details, we must first review Welten's basic approach to these texts. As with the other *topoi*, he holds these accounts to be the author's own compositions, written without recourse to other sources. Welten argues that the writer was motivated by two main considerations. First, he wished to present the first four kings of Judah in a positive light so as to bolster the legitimacy of the post-exilic community over against its northern neighbour (p. 127). This is said to explain the significant divergences from Kings which Welten sees in the

archaeological evidence of rather earlier use of catapults in the near east.

30. The Chronicler's *Sondergut* of victories is related in: 13.3-20 (Abijah); 14.8-14 [E 9-15] (Asa); 20.1-30 (Jehoshaphat); 25.10-13 (Amaziah; but cf. 2 Kgs 14.7); 26.6-8 (Uzziah); 27.5-6 (Jotham). Defeats are recounted in: 21.16-17 (Jehoram); 28.5-8, 16-20 (Ahaz); 33.10-13 (Manasseh); 35.20-25 (Josiah); 36.6-7 (Jehoiachim); 36.10 (Jehoiachin); 36.17-20 (Zedekiah).

Chronicler's depiction of Rehoboam and Abijah (pp. 126-27). Secondly, it is likely that tense relations existed not only between Yehud and Samaria, but also with the other surrounding provinces of Ammon, Moab, Idumaea and Ashdod. Thus the real theme of the Chronistic war reports is the disputes of Yehud with its encircling neighbours who, it seems, posed a constant and considerable threat to the Chronicler's community, both territorially and religiously (pp. 169-70). The Chronicler transposed these disputes into a kind of paraenetic historical fiction set in the monarchy ('Geschichtsdarstellung' rather than 'Geschichte'), from which the Chronicler's community could rightly infer that the path to security vis-à-vis its neighbours lay in cultic fidelity. This moral is drawn especially in the 'Yahweh war' narratives, where 'in all four reports [viz. 13.3-19; 14.8-14 (E 9-15); 20.1-30; 26.6-8] Judah's military weakness is to be perceived just as clearly as Yahweh's miraculous intervention' (pp. 170-71).[31] These narratives present 'the striking picture of the cult community, humbly and obediently maintaining its worship through legitimate cult personnel, calling on God and seeking him, and obtaining rest in north, south, east and west' (pp. 171-72).[32]

In reply, it must be stated that while a paraenetic purpose has certainly shaped the *form* of these reports, Welten's wider interpretation is more questionable. First, the apologetic interpretation which he discerns in the presentation of the first four kings of Judah is certainly refuted by the overall evaluation of Rehoboam in 12.14. The presentation of Jehoshaphat is also complex, for while the Chronicler does evaluate him positively (cf. 21.12; 22.9), he also shows him in a negative light (cf. 18.1-2; 20.35-37). The Chronicler's portrayal of Abijah is more problematic. Although it is often seen to contradict the negative assessment in 1 Kgs 15.3 (cf. Curtis and Madsen 1910: 373; Michaeli 1967: 177; Dillard 1987: 110), there are indications in the text that the Chronicler's attitude toward Abijah is more ambivalent than has usually been allowed.[33] Whatever the significance 2 Chronicles 13 would have had in

31. '[I]n allen vier Berichten [ist] die militärische Ohnmacht Judas ebenso deutlich zu fassen wie das wunderhafte Eingreifen Jahwes.'

32. 'So begegnet in der Zusammenschau der vier Kriegsberichte das überraschende Bild der Kultgemeinde, die im Demut und Gehorsam ihre Gottesdienste hält durch legitimes Kultpersonal, die Gott anruft und ihn sucht, die Ruhe gewinnt, Ruhe geschenkt erhält, im Norden und im Süden, im Osten und im Westen.'

33. Cf. Deboys 1990.

the post-exilic community, it should certainly not be read as a piece of anti-Samaritan (or anti-Samarian) polemic.[34]

Welten's second argument also has only limited validity. First, the assumption that the 'Yahweh war' narratives are intended to give hope and consolation to a defenceless people is a fair inference from 2 Chronicles 20, where Judah's weakness is emphasized (v. 12) and the army does not participate at all in the fighting (v. 17). However, it is clear from 13.17-19 and 14.12-14 [E 13-15] that Judah's armies do participate in these battles, although the victories are conventionally ascribed to Yahweh (13.12; 14.11 [E 12]) and there are other features of 'Yahweh war' in the presentation.[35] Secondly, Welten includes 26.6-8 (Uzziah's campaigns against the Philistines, Arabs and Meunites) under the rubric of 'Yahweh war' to complete the circle of divine protection for Judah (pp. 168-69). However, this pericope is unlike the others in that it describes an offensive rather than defensive campaign and has none of the characteristic motifs of 'Yahweh war'. The suggestion that the Chronicler has composed a geographically based schema here is really quite doubtful.

Discussion of sources in 2 Chronicles 13 has usually focused on the geographical notices in vv. 4, 19. The location of Mount Zemaraim is uncertain, but Josh. 18.21-24 lists a Benjaminite town of that name, along with Bethel and Ophrah (Ephron). Klein holds that this list was the Chronicler's sole source for composing this account, but he is required to restore Jeshanah to the list for it to serve as the Chronicler's supposed *Vorlage* (1983: 215-16). This procedure is rejected by Deboys as circular and untenable on text-critical grounds (1990: 61). While there can be no doubt that the language and ideas expressed in Abijah's speech are the Chronicler's own work, the most likely reason for the inclusion of this narrative remains that suggested by Noth, that the Chronicler knew of a tradition which ascribed the capture of these towns to Abijah, from which he developed an account which modifies the portrayal (not the evaluation) in Kings.[36]

---

34. *Contra* Noth, Rudolph, Oeming. Cf. Williamson 1977a: 111-14.

35. See Chapter 8 for a discussion of these motifs and the theological significance of these accounts.

36. Noth 1967: 142. Deboys (1990: 54) also makes an interesting form-critical comparison with a passage from Thucydides (Book II Section 71) in which envoys from Plataea try unsuccessfully to dissuade a Lacedaemonian expedition by means of speeches invoking right and deity. One further point calls for comment. Welten lays

Three main positions are represented by those who hold that there is a historical basis to the account of Asa's defeat of Zerah the Cushite.[37] (1) Kitchen (1986: 309) proposes that it concerns an expedition led by a general of Nubian extraction serving under Osorkon I, who perhaps wished to emulate the exploits of his father Shoshenq. (2) Albright (1924) suggested that Shoshenq had established a garrison or buffer state around Gerar, which was peopled by Nubian mercenaries who eventually invaded Judah. (3) This is rejected on archaeological and textual grounds by S. Hidal,[38] who argues instead that the Chronicler magnified a local conflict involving Bedouin tribes south of Judah. In this respect the parallel sometimes drawn between 'Cushan' and 'Midian' is suggestive.[39]

There is no epigraphic or other extrabiblical evidence for this account, nor does the text preserve signs of an earlier source. The question of whether the Chronicler was dependent on an earlier tradition can be determined only by considering his procedure in analogous situations, and the coherence of the internal details of the account with our knowledge of the period. On the first matter, 13.3-19 presents just such an analogy. Although external evidence is similarly lacking in that case, no reason was found for preferring Welten's position that the account is simply a fabrication. The internal details also give grounds for accepting that 14.8-14 has a historical core, and of the main reconstructions proposed, Kitchen's seems the most plausible. Kitchen first points out that

much store by the fact that Chronicler describes battles between 'überdimensioniert' armies, indeed of 'Weltkriegdimensione', but places the combats within small, geographically defined areas. The numbers in Chronicles are problematic (though not outstandingly so in comparison with other historical books of the Old Testament), yet this incongruence hardly demonstrates that the reports lack a historical basis or are simply parabolic (as opposed to hyperbolic). An important observation is contributed indirectly by Younger's recent comparative analysis of ancient warfare accounts (1990). Younger draws attention to what he calls the 'common transmission codes' and stereotypical syntagms of ancient Near Eastern accounts of conquest and military victory, and in particular the universal use of hyperbole and the ascription of victory to the respective nation's deity. Neither feature militates against a historical basis to these reports.

37. Cf. Williamson 1982: 263-65 for a summary of the main views.

38. S. Hidal, *SEÅ* 41-42 (1976–77), 100-101, cited by Williamson 1982: 264.

39. Cf. Hab. 3.7. Dillard (1987: 119) also draws attention to the traditions that Moses, whose father-in-law was a priest of Midian (Exod. 2.16-21) had married a 'Cushite' woman (Num. 12.1), which might refer to Zipporah.

Zerah is not to be equated with Osorkon I, as earlier commentators sug-gested.[40] The absence of Egyptian epigraphic evidence is understandable in view of a defeat. A further reason supporting the African origin of this person is the association made between the Cushites and Libyans in 16.8; cf. 12.3. Bedouins are also unlikely to have had chariots (v. 8), while the course of the pursuit from Mareshah to Gerar would corre-spond to an attack from Egypt, but accords less easily with the location of Cushan to the south of Judah.[41] Finally, the reference to Mareshah (v. 8) corresponds to the internal evidence of 11.8. Such details do not amount to positive evidence, and there are clear examples of stylization and hyperbole (cf. v. 8). Nevertheless, a coherent case can be made out that the Chronicler here reflects an earlier tradition of a victory by Asa over a foreign force.

The account of the defeat of the eastern coalition in Jehoshaphat's time (20.1-30) raises similar evidential and source-critical questions as in the previous examples. Among those who ascribe a historical kernel to this report, it is generally seen as a magnification of a local conflict in the post-exilic period or as dependent in some distant way on a good local tradition.[42] Noth argued from the toponymic details and the appar-ent reference to 'Meunites' in v. 1 (derived from the LXX reading Μιναίων for MT מהעמונים) that the Chronicler had used a local oral tradi-tion of an attack by Nabataeans from Meun (or Ma'an) southeast of Petra in the late fourth or early third century. Rudolph (1955: 259)

40. Cf. Welten 1973: 132 n. 94. Kitchen (1986: 309-10) points out that Zerah is designated a Cushite rather than a Libyan or Egyptian; that he is not a king (which the Chronicler might have mentioned, if only to show the significance of the Israelite victory); and that the linguistic equation of Osorkon with Zerah is not tenable.

41. Cf. Aharoni 1979: 132 for the location of Cushan in the Canaanite period. The reference to the attack on the אהלי מקנה (v. 14) is taken to support the 'Bedouin' interpretation of this incident, but Dillard (1987: 119) explains this as part of the camp following for the invading army.

42. The historicity is again rejected by Welten (1973: 140-53) followed by Strübind (1991: 176-88). The older view that it is a historical midrash on 2 Kgs 3 (Wellhausen, Benzinger, Curtis) is increasingly rejected (most recently by Strübind 1991: 179), but upheld by Welten. P.R. Davies (1990) offers a sociological interpre-tation of the narrative as a projection of the struggle of the post-exilic community to define itself ethnically following the loss of its national identity. Davies assigns the emergence of the concept of 'Israel' to this period (cf. Davies 1992). Most recently, Beentjes (1993) agrees with Welten and thinks the narrative has been imaginatively constructed out of Exod. 14 and Isa. 7.9b.

modified Noth's arguments, rejecting the association of the Nabataeans with the Meunites, and arguing that the account did indeed come from Jehoshaphat's time; the Chronicler had followed a written source for his explanatory comment on Hazazon-tamar הִיא עֵין גֶּדִי (v. 2). Williamson attributes this comment to the Chronicler, but points to the aetiology in v. 26 as indicating the presence of a further layer in the literary or tradition history of the account.[43]

No attempt to identify more precisely the third group in v. 1 is likely to succeed, owing to the corrupt state of the text.[44] Nor does Noth's association of this group with the 'Meunites' accord well with what is suggested of that people in 26.7. Whatever the true reading of 20.1 should be, this group is later designated 'those from the hill country of Seir' (vv. 10, 22, 23) and they are clearly set apart from the Ammonites and Moabites. This is a synonymous expression in many biblical passages for Edom.[45] 'Edom' is not used as an ethnic designation in this chapter,[46] perhaps because at this point the Edomites were still subject to Jehoshaphat (cf. 1 Chron. 18.12-13). However, the term recurs in 21.8-10, where the Edomites regain their independence.[47]

Together these details point to small yet traditional elements underlying the Chronicler's account. Military victories are also related in two other Chronistic passages, 26.6-8 and 27.5. The first is universally agreed to reflect a pre-exilic source. The latter passage is expressed in more generalized terms, and its point is evidently to reflect positively on Jotham. However, it may also implicitly concede that tribute from Ammon ceased after three years as Aram's power increased.

43. See especially Noth 1967; Rudolph 1955: 259; Williamson 1982: 291-94.

44. The most recent proposal is by Bartlett (1989: 143-45), who suggests a local tradition about the people of Maon.

45. Cf. Gen. 32.3; 36.6-8; Num. 24.18; Deut. 2.4-5; Judg. 5.4; Isa. 21.11; Ezek. 25.8; 35.15.

46. Although it should probably be restored as a geographic description in v. 2 (instead of אֲרָם). Cf. 1 Chron. 18.11 (contrast 2 Sam. 8.12 MT).

47. Cf. Davies 1990: 7. The identification with Edom, Israel's close yet antagonistic relation, may be supported by the way in which 'those from the hill country of Seir' are distinguished from the Ammonites and Moabites. There is no extra-biblical reference to this or the other battles, but Wolff (1977: 76) allows the possibility that the memory of this event may have helped shape the apocalyptic description of divine judgment in the 'Valley of Jehoshaphat' in Joel 4.2-3. However, no firm dating or literary dependence can be determined. For a possible reconstruction of the invasion course see Dorsey 1991: 148.

(iv) *Other motifs of blessing*. Other Chronistic *topoi* of blessing include large families, tribute and wealth. These are (apparently) assigned by the writer to those portions of reigns that are judged positively (although, as I argued in Chapter 4, the Chronicler actually treats the theme of blessing much more flexibly than older theories of retribution allow). Notwithstanding the theological purpose of these notices, there are some indications that the author depended on earlier sources for this information.

The account of Rehoboam's family (11.18-23) contains names unknown from elsewhere and stands in some tension with other biblical passages, suggesting that an inherited source has been used here.[48] The content and style of the report of Jehoshaphat's sons (21.2-4) also probably reflect earlier materials,[49] although here it is not used to indicate blessing but to highlight Jehoram's wickedness (cf. v. 13). The details on Abijah's and Joash's families (13.21; 24.3) are too brief to indicate additional sources, although the reference to the otherwise unknown Zechariah in 24.20, along with the variant account of the Aramaean invasion in vv. 23-24, may suggest that the Chronicler had alternative information on Joash.[50]

The references to tribute and wealth also make good historical sense. Welten does consider briefly 'homage and tribute' as a further *topos* but holds that the Chronistic style of these passages (17.10-11; 27.5-6) and their association with positively judged kings makes a historical basis to the reports 'highly improbable' (1973: 186). This view is extended by Strübind (1991: 148), who argues that the report in 17.11 that 'some Philistines' and 'the Arabs' brought tribute to Jehoshaphat was composed to establish a parallel between that king's rule and David's through the use of typological motifs (cf. 1 Chron. 14.16-17). However, the parallels are not close, nor is there any reference in the earlier passage to tribute. By contrast, Williamson (1982: 283) holds that the

48. Cf. Williamson 1982: 244. Rudolph's (and Noth's) view that the passage is secondary does not take into consideration the fact that it is meant to signify the consolidation of Rehoboam's rule (cf. v. 17) (though naturally such a large family belongs to the whole of Rehoboam's reign, not just the first three years).

49. E.g. Rudolph, Michaeli, Williamson, Dillard. By contrast, in his discussion of the portrait of Jehoram in 2.21, Begg (1989: 37) attributes virtually every deviation from Kings to the literary creativity of the Chronicler who 'embellished' the Deuteronomic portrait with 'Ahabite' material from Kings and his own theological schema of 'exile and beyond'.

50. Williamson 1982: 323-26; Selman 1994b: 456.

guarded opening ('some Philistines'), the localized source of the tribute (an area where Asa had campaigned; cf. 14.13 [E 14]) and its modest nature create a favourable historical impression. The description of Hezekiah's wealth (32.27-29) also accords with the indications of more recent archaeological finds. While the syntagm עשׁר וכבוד is Chronistic (cf. 1 Chron. 29.28; 2 Chron. 1.11, 12; 9.22; 17.5; 18.1) and clearly denotes divine blessing, the references to storehouses and military measures (32.5-6) make sense as preparations for war with Sennacherib. Aharoni (1979: 340-46) argues from the dating and distribution of jar handles bearing the *lmlk* stamp that in the years prior to the invasion Hezekiah was involved in the reorganization of tax-collecting procedures and in the concentration of tribute in kind at four main store cities.[51]

2. *Motifs of Divine Punishment*
A balanced discussion of sources in Chronicles must also consider the corresponding motifs of divine punishment, which generally takes the form of sickness or death for the individual, and military defeat, diminution of power and exile for the nation. For the majority of these reports the author follows Kings, but he often inserts additional material or substantially rewrites his *Vorlage*. It must therefore be asked whether these expansions and revisions are purely his own compositions or instead reflect other sources at his disposal.

(i) *Sickness and death.* Three incidents in Chronicles may suggest that sickness is visited on kings for disobedience. One example (Jehoram, 21.18-19) has no parallel in the *Vorlage*. It is difficult to decide whether the writer's report here reflects an earlier tradition, although most recent discussions agree that the author did draw on other sources for at least parts of his *Sondergut* in 2 Chronicles 21 (especially vv. 2-4, 16-17).[52]

The other two accounts are expansions of Kings, where the question concerns not the illness but the nature of the preceding interpolated material. 16.7-10 recounts Asa's mistreatment of the prophet Hanani and some of the people, which precedes the king's foot disease. This incident is not otherwise attested and reflects the Chronicler's characteristic language and use of biblical allusions (cf. Jer. 20.2-3; Zech. 4.10). However, as was observed above, it is not certain that the Chronicler

---

51. See also Miller and Hayes 1986: 353-56.
52. *Contra* Begg 1989.

understood Asa's illness as retribution for his behaviour toward Hanani (*contra* Rudolph 1955: 248; Dillard 1987: 122-23), so it need not be inferred that the incident was invented to justify a doctrine (thus Wellhausen 1885: 204).

Similarly, Uzziah's leprosy is attributed to his cultic trespass (26.16-20), but the Chronicler is at one with 2 Kgs 15.5 in affirming that 'Yahweh struck him', an expression that can only denote punishment but is cryptic and unexplained in the *Vorlage*. Could such an incident have been known to the author of Kings and presupposed by him, as Hobbs (1985: 193) suggests? The historical nature of the Chronicler's account is questioned, in part because it is largely shaped by earlier traditions in which sickness or death is inflicted for certain cultic offences,[53] and partly because it is believed to reflect post-exilic cultic regulations (cf. Milgrom 1976: 81). The antiquity of the legitimate use of incense is certainly attested in Deut. 33.10 and 1 Sam. 2.28, but it must be admitted that there is no evidence for extrabiblical sources for this account. Perhaps the *Vorlage* itself provided the immediate impetus for the narrative, which the Chronicler composed in 'biblical' style. 2 Kgs 15.4 (omitted by Chronicles) reports that under Azariah (Uzziah) 'the people still sacrificed and burned incense on the high places', and then immediately notes that 'Yahweh struck the king so that he was a leper to the day of his death'. The writer's account would then be in the nature of an inference from the *Vorlage* in which cultic irregularity, divine punishment and leprosy feature together.

(ii) *Military defeat*. The Chronicler's account of Shishak's invasion (12.2-9) purports to give additional historical information, including details of his army (v. 3) and conquests (v. 4). Kitchen (1986: 293-300, 432-47) cites evidence from Shishak's (that is, Shoshenq I's) own record of that campaign which shows that this account is plausible and probably reflects an independent record of these events. However, as Williamson remarks (1982: 246-47), Kitchen also bases some aspects of his reconstruction of the campaign on the Chronicler's account alone, without independent evidence of its veracity. Kitchen considers the size of the chariot-force reasonable, although the number of horsemen may be a scribal error (cf. 2 Chron. 9.25; 1 Kgs 5.6). The description of the army as consisting of 'Libyans, Sukkiim and Nubians (כושים)' also accords

---

53. Lev. 10.1-3; Num. 12.10; 16.46-50; 1 Kgs 12.33-34; cf. 2 Kgs 5.36-37 (Gehazi).

with the data of the thirteenth-twelfth centuries BCE, with the second group probably representing the Egyptian Tjuk(ten) (Kitchen 1986: 295 n. 291). The Chronicler's note that Shishak captured the fortified cities of Judah and came to Jerusalem' (v. 4) is partially confirmed by Shishak's own topographical list at Karnak, which mentions the capture of Aijalon (cf. 11.10) and brings the course of his campaign at least to Gibeon, from where he could have secured the submission of Rehoboam in nearby Jerusalem (Kitchen 1986: 297, 446).

The attack of 'the Philistines and the Arabs who are near the Cushites (כושים)'[54] (21.16-17) against Jehoram's household is without parallel in the *Vorlage*, but this is consistent with the note in 21.8, 10 (= 2 Kgs 8.20, 22) that Libnah and Edom revolted against Judah. The failure to suppress these revolts in the southwest and southeast may have encouraged those groups subjugated by Jehoshaphat (17.11) who were close to these locales to similar rebellion.[55]

Chronicles contains three other passages recounting military defeat that differ significantly from the *Vorlage*: the Aramaean attack on Joash (24.23-25); its account of the Syro-Ephraimite war (28.5-21); and Josiah's defeat by Neco (35.20-25). The first passage is closely integrated in themes and language with the preceding unit (vv. 17-21) and illustrates fulfilment of Zechariah's imprecation on Joash and the leaders of Judah for apostasy and murder. The Chronicler may have had an alternative source for his account, which has few points of contact with 2 Kgs 12.17-18, but if so, it has been reworked according to his characteristic vocabulary, literary patterning and outlook. The same is true of his interpretation of the Syro-Ephraimite war, which has little overlap with 2 Kgs 15.37, 16.5 or the other Old Testament references (Isa. 7.1–9:6; Hos. 5.8–7.16). However, despite the differences in detail and emphasis, the accounts do not contradict each other in substance. Whereas 2 Kgs 16.5 and Isa. 7.1-2 note the failure of the coalition to capture Jerusalem, these armies evidently overran most of northern Judah, and it is this catastrophe which the Chronicler wishes to stress

54. כושים here may denote the nomadic people of Cushan, south of Judah (as the locative expression על יד suggests), who should be distinguished from the military force of Nubians in 14.8-14 [E 9-15]. It is not necessary to maintain that in the earlier passage a local bedouin incident has been magnified, or indeed that bedouin were involved.

55. Williamson (1982: 308) finds further evidence of a source in the use of 'Jehoahaz' instead of the normal 'Ahaziah' in 21.17 (cf. 22.1).

(cf. vv. 5, 8). The precise details in v. 7, otherwise unattested, may also reflect the Chronicler's source.[56] Ahaz's appeal to 'the kings of Assyria' (vv. 16-21) relates to circumstances somewhat later than those recounted in 2 Kgs 16.6-7, but the Chronicler's report of Edomite and Philistine activity, 'natural allies against Judah' (Bartlett 1989), and the Philistines' recovery of areas probably taken by Uzziah (26.6), is consistent with the general historical picture.[57]

3. *Religious Activities of Kings*

The *Sondergut* in 2 Chronicles 10–36 purports to relate a great deal of additional information about the religious activities of the kings of Judah, their reforms and apostasies. Only a limited engagement with the question of sources is undertaken here. Reform of the cult and instruction of the people are briefly considered by Welten as further *topoi* in the Chronistic *Sondergut* (1973: 180-85). Although he concedes the possibility of pre-exilic materials underlying these passages, he considers them to be most probably the author's own composition, since they are confined to positively judged reigns (or periods thereof) and are described in association with other (unhistorical) *topoi* of blessing. Nevertheless, it may be argued that these passages preserve some indications of earlier sources, and should not be attributed purely to the author's own composition.

Our first example is the extended report of Asa's religious reform (15.8-18).[58] This pericope is best taken as an independent doublet of

56. Rudolph 1955: 289. The description of Elkanah as משׁנה המלך does not serve a theological purpose, and is probably an indication of a source.

57. Cf. Williamson 1982: 347-48, and the bibliography cited there, and Bartlett 1989: 127-28, 140-41, for a discussion of Edomite and Philistine hostility to Judah, and archaeological evidence of Edomite extension of influence into the Negev of Judah.

58. The chronology of Asa's reign is a complex matter, on which a number of reconstructions have been proposed, each of which is problematic. Rudolph (1952) considered the chronological notes of these chapters confused or arbitrary, the product of the author's own theological creativity, whereas Thiele took them as historical, but related 15.19 and 16.1 (in tension with 1 Kgs 15.33; 16.8), not to Asa's reign but to the division of the monarchy. This harmonization is rejected by Dillard as anomalous to the whole practice of Old Testament chronology (1987: 124-25). A mediating position is suggested by Williamson (1982: 255-58), who allows that events have been reordered for theological reasons, but gives some credence to the chronological notices (though he thinks the Chronicler has deviated from his source in 15.19; 16.1).

14.2-4 [E 3-5].[59] Whereas the earlier passage is an elaboration of the *Vorlage* (probably influenced by 2 Kgs 18.4), an alternative source underlies this account. Specific mention is made of the extirpation of idolatry from the territory under Asa's control, the repair of the altar of burnt offering, and a national act of covenant renewal. While these could be simply conventional details, the passage also refers in v. 8 to reform in 'the towns which he [Asa] had captured in the hill country of Ephraim'. There is no antecedent reference for this note, which thus stands in some tension with the Chronicler's general depiction of Asa's reign as peaceful (cf. 15.19). Williamson (1982: 270) argues that 'the Chronicler was here drawing on an independent source which at this point he did not fully harmonise with his wider presentation'.

Secondly, the Chronicler's *Sondergut* attributes popular instruction in the Law (17.7-9) and judicial reform (19.4-11) to Jehoshaphat. The relationship of these passages to each other and their historical basis are also disputed, but there can be little doubt that pre-Chronistic material is reflected here.[60] Although v. 4 is clearly the writer's own composition, it does not sit easily with the Deuteronomistically couched material in vv. 5-11, which embraces wider legal and administrative concerns than the writer's cultic interests (as v. 4b suggests) and lacks the characteristic paraenetic vocabulary of royal speeches in Chronicles.[61]

Thirdly, the account of Hezekiah's passover (2 Chron. 30) has often been considered fictitious, written up on the basis of Josiah's passover. However, it also reports a number of irregularities: the date and duration of the festival, and the participation of cultically impure persons (vv. 1, 23, 17-20). It has long been observed that a writer such as the Chronicler, who is usually considered meticulous in cultic matters, would

59. So Rudolph, Williamson, De Vries.

60. The passages are sometimes considered doublets. Their historical basis was rejected by Wellhausen (1885: 191) as an aetiological legend based on the name יהושפט, with numerous anachronisms); of late, scepticism has been expressed by Ackroyd (1973: 143) and De Vries (1989: 322, 'the combination of sacral and secular courts [...] expresses ChrH's theocratic tendency'). However, De Vries fails to interact with Whitelam's arguments (1979: 185-206) for the historical basis of this system. The evidence that 17.7-9 reflects an earlier source is slight, but cf. Williamson 1982: 282.

61. Williamson (1982: 287-89); Dillard 1987: 147 on the language; though presumably v. 10d (קצף ;תאשמון) is the Chronicler's own composition. Throntveit (1987: 47-49) also notes the anomalous form of this speech compared to others in the work, but fails to attribute this to non-Chronistic sources.

hardly have invented such details, nor applied them to his idealized figure Hezekiah.[62] Selman (1994b: 494) also notes a number of differences in practice and detail between this report and 35.1-19 (perhaps the Chronicler's own stylized representation[63]) which argue against literary dependence.

3. *Summary and Conclusion*

This chapter has drawn together some of the more positive findings of source criticism of Chronicles from Rudolph and recent English-language scholarship, supplemented by more recent indications from archaeology. It has interacted with Welten's arguments as a detailed modern example of the older critical view that the Chronistic *Sondergut* contains little authentic pre-exilic material. The compass of Welten's study was extended to include further *topoi* of reward and the corresponding motifs of punishment. The historiographical and literary assumptions that underlie Welten's work were questioned, including his premiss that Chronistic style and outlook create a presumption that a particular section is simply the writer's own composition. Furthermore, a closer reading of certain sections shows that the author was not concerned to enhance the personal standing of certain kings, such as Rehoboam, Abijah and Manasseh, about whom he communicates additional information.

Not all the additional material could be assigned the same critical value, but it must be admitted that the full extent of the Chronicler's use of sources cannot be settled. Some of the material is of a generalized, stereotypical nature, while other parts are narrated according to 'scriptural' models rather than evident extrabiblical traditions. However, it is unlikely that the writer freely invented his accounts, and underlying kernels of tradition are still to be found, even where he has clearly composed according to literary conventions, such as his 'Yahweh war'

---

62. Moriarty 1965; also the commentaries of Williamson, Dillard and Selman follow this line, but disagree over the precise nature of the pre-Chronistic material and the festival. Segal (1963: 16-19, 226-30) assigned 2 Chron. 30 to a later hand than 2 Chron. 35, holding its differences to reflect 'a gradual process of development' toward a popular ceremony. However, the language and interests are clearly Chronistic. De Vries (1989: 264, 379) discerns a Chronistic 'Festival Schema' in this and other accounts of worship (2 Chron. 7.8-9; 15.9-15; 35.1-19).

63. So Segal 1963: 14-16; Williamson 1982: 403-404.

narratives. It may be added that for the Chronicler such a style would have been his most natural form of expression. It appears, too, that the Chronicler worked within the constraints of his sources, even where they did not accord well with his dominant outlook (cf. 25.5, 13). In all, the range of pericopae relating both rewards and punishments that can be fairly attributed to earlier sources may be considerably extended from the minimal core allowed by Welten.

These indications of the writer's working method lead me to conclude that Welten's description of Chronicles as a 'free, parabolic depiction of history' ('freie parabolische Geschichtsdarstellung') (1973: 206) misconstrues the character of this work and the Chronicler's understanding of his task. Although it was not the writer's *primary* concern to recount history (even a history of the foundation of the cult), he did retain evident historiographical concerns, recounting his understanding of the pre-exilic past and working within the constraints of his sources. The concluding chapter of this study will draw out some of the implications of the Chronicler's uses of history.

Chapter 6

ESCHATOLOGICAL THOUGHT IN CHRONICLES:
A SURVEY AND CRITIQUE OF RESEARCH

1. *Introduction*

This chapter surveys and evaluates the ways in which the controverted subject of eschatology in Chronicles has been handled in research, as a preliminary step to formulating an integrative approach to this question. This latter concern is taken up in Chapters 7 and 8.

While the importance of the Chronicler's doctrine of retribution is universally recognized, there is no consensus over the nature of the writer's eschatological outlook. Dillard (1987: 2) remarks that scholarly opinion on the subject

> is divided between two extremes and a host of mediating positions: on the one hand, many find the author's messianic/eschatological expectations central to the book, while others view the Chronicler as espousing the view that the purposes of God were so realized in the restoration community as to leave little if any place for eschatological expectation.

The disagreement turns in part on the definition of 'eschatology'. Mowinckel (1958: 125-26), for example, has defined this as a complex of ideas that looks for the end of the present world order through a cosmic catastrophe and the ushering in of a different and suprahistorical order by the power of God. Nothing, in that sense, is really applicable to Chronicles, nor indeed to most of the Old Testament. In a broader sense, however, eschatology is used by Old Testament scholars to denote not the suprahistorical termination of things but (more loosely) the expectation of better things to come, a future state brought about by God which is marked by 'the introduction of a situation discontinuous with the current evil one, the consummation of the divine purpose' (Bright 1977: 19). It is this second definition which forms the basis of my discussion, rather than the cosmological vision which surfaces in only a few Old Testament passages, particularly the apocalyptic chapters of Isaiah 24–27, Daniel and Zechariah. For Chronicles the question turns on the status and future of Judah, subsisting as a small temple state within the Persian empire. It must be asked what expectations, if any, the writer entertained for its subject people, the House of David, and the land of Israel.

Even within this restricted ambit, a wide diversity of views is held. At one extreme, Hanson (1975; 1986) sees the Chronicler's sights set firmly on the cult rather than the dynasty.[1] Mason (1990) also insists that the temple rather than the Davidic dynasty has a 'lasting soteriological function' for the writer.[2] By contrast, Im (1985) claims that the Chronicler's ideal *Davidbild* is a depiction of post-exilic expectation and that the writer looked forward to a dynastic restoration.[3]

Such conflicting interpretations point to the continuing necessity in research to investigate this dimension of the work. The most significant treatments of this aspect of the writer's thought are examined below. It will be seen that disagreement has arisen partly from differences of focus (for example, by concentrating on the presentation of David or

1.   'Hope resided not in realities to be revealed by a Messiah who would come in the future, but in the careful observation and presentation of the cultic institutions revealed by God to David, handed down by the priests and kings of Judah [...] and finding new life under the leadership of the Zadokite high priests once the true remnant had returned to Jerusalem' (1986: 301). In this later work Hanson presents much the same view of Chronicles' (anti-)eschatological outlook as in *The Dawn of Apocalyptic* (1975), but now accepts Cross's theory of multiple editions of Chronicles (cf. Chapter 1 above), that the 'Restorationist' 'Chr 1' was expanded by priestly circles into a final edition ('Chr 3') which was conciliatory toward proto-apocalyptic circles yet firmly 'theocratic' (i.e. anti-eschatological).

2.   Mason 1990: 32: '[The Chronicler appears] little concerned with the long-range issue of the dynasty itself. The temple survives the exile by its rebuilding, and the divinely appointed function of the dynasty finds itself fulfilled in the emergence of the temple community. Over this community God now reigns, exercising through priest and cult personnel the rule which was once exercised through kings, although seldom perfectly.'

3.   Im 1985: 184: 'The Jewish community could not be fully content with the modest situation of the post-exilic theocracy, because it lacked the kingdom of David. It expected the restoration of the kingdom and a Davidic king who could bring this expectation to fulfilment' ('Die jüdische Gemeinde konnte mit der bescheidenen Lage der nachexilischen Theokratie nicht ganz zufrieden sein, weil ihr das Königtum Davids fehlte. Sie erwartete die Wiederherstellung des Königtums und einen davidischen König, der diese Erwartung in Erfüllung bringen könnte').

Solomon), as well as from conflicting definitions (e.g. the scope of terms such as 'eschatology', 'theocracy' and 'messianism') and judgments on the unity, dating and extent of the Chronicler's work.

2. *Chronicles as a Non-eschatological Work*

Rudolph established the basic lines of a non-eschatological interpretation of the work, with an approach which has been supplemented by sociologically based studies in recent years. According to this view, the writer believed that the divine purpose was fully realized in the temple community of his time. Chronicles differed from the prophetic conception of theocracy by the virtual absence from its outlook of eschatological expectations (1955: xxiii). Undertones of the prophetic view could still be detected in the stress on the eternal duration of the Davidic covenant and the reference to the חסדי דויד (2 Chron. 6.42), but these notes were sparse and indistinct (in contrast, for example, to the clear expectation expressed in Jer. 33.14-26). This paucity of emphasis indicated that such a hope had little contemporary significance for the Chronicler. By contrast, the description of the post-exilic Jewish community in Nehemiah 12.44–13.3 represented in itself the realization of the theocratic ideal for the Chronicler. This passage describes how the liturgical services of the second temple were re-established, portions were assigned to the Levites and Aaronites, and those of mixed desent were 'separated out from Israel' (13.3). According to Rudolph, the Chronicler did not look beyond this state of affairs, but rather affirmed it as the 'ideal', in which there was no further need of an eschatological hope.[4]

Rudolph's interpretation at this point was challenged by Brunet (1959). In keeping with the virtual consensus of the time, Brunet accepted the common authorship of Chronicles with Ezra–Nehemiah.

---

4. Rudolph 1955: xxiii: 'The community could get over the lack of a Davidic dynasty, so long as the second pillar of the theocracy, the Jerusalem temple, stood firm (...), and the soteriological significance of the Davidic House was presently limited to the fact that David and Solomon had established the ordinances for the temple cult, on which the acceptable worship of the present community was based' ('Daß die davidische Dynastie fehlte, ließ sich verschmerzen, solange die zweite Säule der Theokratie, der Tempel in Jerusalem so feststand [...] und die heilsgeschichtliche Bedeutung des Hauses Davids beschränkte sich [...] derzeit darauf, daß David und Salomo für den Tempelkult die Ordnungen geschaffen hatten, auf denen der gottgefällige Gottesdienst der gegenwärtigen Gemeinde beruhte').

Along with Rudolph, he rejected Noordtzij's (1940) claim that the Chronicler intended to show the failure of the theocracy, but against Rudolph, he insisted on the abiding significance of the Davidic dynasty for the Chronicler.[5] Brunet also disputed Rudolph's interpretation of Nehemiah 12.44–13.3. This depicted a situation that was not yet the ideal anticipated by Deutero-Isaiah, for the people of God were still under foreign domination and occupying only a 'faible partie' of their inheritance (cf. Neh. 9.34-37).

Brunet thus discerned that Ezra–Nehemiah portrayed a situation that was as yet incomplete.[6] However, he argued (rather implausibly) that the silence over the dynastic question in that portion of 'the Chronicler's work' was an indication, not that the dynasty had no place in its outlook, but rather that the Restoration was slowly making its way to that end (1959: 396). No real evidence was adduced for this claim. This conflict in interpretation is an instance of the difficulties raised by the supposed 'Chronicler's History Work', which are satisfactorily resolved only by distinguishing the authorship of Chronicles from Ezra–Nehemiah.[7]

Rudolph highlighted two distinctive features of his non-eschatological understanding of theocracy in Chronicles. First, as we have noted, he interpreted the work as teaching that *the Jewish community of its own day* (rather than any messianic or royal figure) was now the embodiment of the theocracy.[8] Such an understanding sharply distinguished Chronicles from the 'essential Old Testament conception of theocracy' (1955: xxiv), and in this respect it stood theologically 'at the edge of the canon'.

---

5. Brunet 1959: 398: 'The Davidic dynasty is an essential and permanent element of the theocratic economy' ('La dynastie davidique est un élément essentiel et permanent de l'économie théocratique').

6. Cf. also more recently Williamson 1977a: 135: 'Certainly, the prayers of Ezra 9 and Neh. 1 and 9 give no indication of a situation beyond which no advance is contemplated, and the work as a whole seems to tail off in Neh. 13 without any suggestion that the problems and abuses have been finally settled.' See also Chapter 9 below.

7. As was noted in Chapter 1, whereas a Davidic interest is evident throughout Chronicles, it is virtually absent from Ezra–Nehemiah.

8. Riley (1993: 185-201) develops a similar idea that 'the cultic קהל constitutes Israel as the nation that is heir to the Davidic heritage' (p. 191) and Davidic covenant (see especially pp. 196-97), but without recourse to Rudolph's (questionable) interpretation of Neh. 12.44–13.3 (Riley distinguishes authorship of the works). These arguments are disputed in Chapters 7 and 8 below.

Secondly, Rudolph maintained that the Chronicler showed little interest in the religious fate of the Gentiles, because he was preoccupied in
debate with the Samaritans over the legitimacy of the Jerusalem cult.
Chronicles was seen to be focused wholly on the present concerns of the
cultic community, without a futurist, prophetic perspective.

The influence of Rudolph's views rests partly on the way they were
adopted and developed by Plöger (1957; ET 1968). For Plöger
Chronicles represented one of the two main currents of theological
thought which he believed characterized the post-exilic period. Far from
being united and peaceful, the Jewish community in the Persian and
Hellenistic eras was essentially divided into 'theocratic' and
'eschatological' circles, from which latter group, it is held, apocalyptic
eventually developed. These circles were marked by radically different
conceptions of Israel and the hopes of restoration. A particular self-
understanding of Israel was reflected in the Priestly Writing, which,
according to Plöger (1968: 40), contained 'the seeds of a non-
eschatological view of history in the Old Testament': Israel as the עדה at
Sinai represented the goal of God's ways with humanity (p. 32). As a
community constituted and ruled according to cultic and religious
principles rather than political ones, it experienced God's rule directly
and was no longer subject to changing political fortunes. Such a view
reflected a fundamental change in the structure of Israel from nation to
cultic community, one which rendered superfluous a historical
eschatology.

Chronicles was said to be oriented to that same understanding of
Israel, with an important distinction: whereas the *terminus a quo* in P for
this new conception of Israel is the Sinaitic covenant, in Chronicles Israel
is instead constituted by the Davidic covenant. Plöger attributed this difference in presentation to the author's assumed controversy with the
Samaritans: it was a means of affirming the legitimacy of the Jerusalem
cult against rival claims. The Chronicler's 'rejection of the Samaritan
heresy' and his 'refusal to entertain eschatological expectations of any
sort' (p. 41) were said to account for the polemical side of his work.
Plöger thus affirmed Rudolph's understanding of Nehemiah 12.44–13.3
as the climax of the Chronicler's work by setting the writer's work
within a larger framework, the supposed theological 'currents' of the
post-exilic period.[9]

---

9.   Rudolph 1955: viii: Neh. 12.44–13.3 depicts 'the realization of the theocracy
on the soil of Israel' ('die Verwirklichung der Theokratie auf dem Boden Israels').

Despite the influence of Plöger's theory,[10] it faces serious objections. His positive interpretation of Nehemiah 12.44–13.3, and the assumption of a unified 'Chronicler's History Work' are both very questionable. Further, the Samaritan schism as a background for the Chronicler's work is usually rejected today (although it still has its supporters[11]). Plöger's understanding of P and its relationship with Chronicles is also problematic. Rather less consensus exists now than did previously over the dating and provenance of P, and it may be significant that Chronicles does not actually designate the community by the common P expression עדה (except 2 Chron. 5.6 = 1 Kgs 8.5) but uniformly prefers קהל. Other differences in vocabulary may be cited which render more tenuous the older critical assumption that the Chronicler consciously worked with P (as a self-subsisting document) in 'revising' the pre-exilic history.[12]

The interpretation of P as anti-eschatological is also increasingly disputed, even where the traditional view of its provenance is accepted. Zimmerli (1968: 66-81) and Ackroyd (1968: 102) both observe that P is more than a collection of laws: it is also a history of progressive revelation which is in no sense closed to the future, but rather signifies for God's people the 'the possibility of a future, the opening up of hope' (Zimmerli 1968: 73). More specifically, Lohfink (1978: 216) argues that the basic aim of P as a whole was to engender hope in the exilic community. Its *communicative intention* differs from Deutero-Isaiah; that work grounds its message in prophetic eschatology, whereas P is focused in the past and communicates its message indirectly. However,

10. For details of those who have followed Plöger in general, see Williamson 1977a: 133. Plöger's views are developed by Steck (1968), though in a way that makes the thesis of a 'Chronicler's History Work' more difficult to maintain; cf. the criticisms by Strübind 1991: 41.

11. The Samaritan hypothesis was proposed by Torrey and Noth; it is rejected by Coggins, Williamson and Japhet, but accepted by Becker and Oeming.

12. This is an instance of the numerous lexical differences on the cult between P and Chronicles. These differences form part of the argument of those Israeli scholars who follow Kaufmann in seeing P as a pre-exilic work. Cf. especially Hurvitz (1974), who maintains that the linguistic differences between P on the one hand and Ezekiel, Chronicles and Ezra–Nehemiah on the other, are due to the chronological distinction between early BH and LBH. Alternatively, it has been doubted whether P ever existed as an independent document; cf. Wenham 1987: xxxi-ii, for survey and bibliography. However this issue should be decided, it is better to assume that the Chronicler was working with a text that already united J, E and P (Oeming 1990: 76).

in Lohfink's view, both works have the same *motive*.[13] He maintains that the real theme of P is to be found not in the cult but in the promised land of Canaan, which the exiles will regain once the sinful generation which caused the exile has died out.

Whatever the precise relationship between P and Chronicles, this last point is at least suggestive of the Chronicler's concerns: it will be argued in the following chapter that the writer also maintains an interest in the land and its secure possession and in fact holds out hopes for its fuller restoration. Such a concern is apparently absent from Plöger's interpretation of the post-exilic community, now no longer a nation with geo-political concerns and developing into a religious community founded exclusively on cult and law. Such a goal is said to make further hopes of restoration pointless (Plöger 1968: 43).

Hanson's work (1975; 1986) is also concerned with the theological currents that developed in post-exilic Judah. It is independent of Plöger's discussion, but parallels it in a number of respects, and an *anti-eschatological* interpretation of Chronicles is fundamental to his historical reconstruction. Hanson maintains that from the beginning of the post-exilic period there were two distinct groups, eschatologically minded 'visionaries' who were disciples of Deutero-Isaiah, and a theocratic (or hierocratic) party, associated with the restoration programme of Ezekiel. (Plöger traces the division in the community to a much later period.) The hierocratic party was dominated by the Zadokite priesthood and stood in unbroken continuity with the ruling classes of the temple prior to the exile. The visionaries opposed the hierocratic group because it rejected 'prophetic-eschatological perspectives' and had formed a compromising coalition with a foreign pagan power.

The hierocratic party triumphed in the ensuing struggle. With the passage of time it proved more accommodating to the 'visionaries', and 'the Chronicler's work', according to Hanson, reflected this spirit: it was a late attempt (c. 400 BCE) 'by the hierocratic tradition to heal the wounds of past controversy by presenting their program in a more conciliatory guise' (1975: 273). Such a motive is said to explain the differences between 'the Chronicler's work' and the 'Zadokite revision of Ezekiel'. These include the writer's interest in the Davidic dynasty and the adoption of elements of 'Yahweh war' tradition, perhaps 'to attract

---

13. See Brett 1991a for a discussion of 'communicative intention' and 'motive' in the Pentateuch.

the dissident prophetic element which held to the visionary concept of the Divine Warrior' (1975: 273).

Nevertheless, the Chronicler's outlook is non-eschatological: by Nehemiah 10 he has described the re-establishment of the people around the temple cult. This represents the fulfilment of the historical process the writer has been recounting. 'The work does not look for a future eschaton, for Israel's eschaton has been realized in the restoration of the institutions long ago established by David but lost' (1975: 277).

Like Rudolph and Plöger, Hanson presupposes the existence of a 'Chronicler's History Work' in his reconstruction. His interpretative frame for the work (the early emergence of apocalyptic in a community polarized over the eschatological question) is, of course, open to the criticism that it is speculative and draws one-sidedly on (rather contestable) sociological theory relating to the behaviour and ideology of religious groups. It may be argued that he has over-simplified the degree to which diverse views (e.g. on eschatology) can be maintained within one sociological group, such as the temple hierocracy. The actual function and treatment of such elements as the Davidic dynasty and the 'Yahweh war' motif must also be considered carefully in determining the Chronicler's outlook,[14] and in my view Hanson has not examined them closely enough. In his later work (1986) Hanson defends the same interpretation of the Chronicler's *Tendenz*, although he now accepts Cross's compositional theory of multiple editions. This shift introduces further difficulties into his reconstruction.[15]

---

14. Cf. Chapters 7 and 8 below.

15. For Cross's view see Chapter 1 and below. As noted above, Hanson now believes (1986) that the postulated 'Chr 1' was part of the 'Zadokite restoration program', which differed sharply from the visionaries over their understanding of the temple: whereas 1 Chron. 28.2 affirmed that the temple is the 'footstool of our God', the 'proto-apocalyptic' text Isa. 66.1-2 repudiated the temple. However, Westermann (1969: 412-13) refutes any idea of polemic against temple building here. Moreover, reference to the 'footstool' in 1 Chron. 28.2 is probably to the ark (cf. Ps. 132.7, but contrast Haran 1978: 256). A difficulty for Hanson in accepting Cross's recensional theory arises from the distinct purpose which Cross and others discern in 'Chr 1', its supposed association with a 'messianic movement' centred on Zerubbabel and the restoration of Judah according to dyarchic rule (Cross 1975: 15; see below). This 'restorationist' theory holds that the work was employed (necessarily with much revision and supplementation) in the very different circumstances of c. 400 BCE. Hanson also cites a number of texts that he believes reflect a later, conciliatory spirit

Caquot (1966) has propounded the non-eschatological interpretation of Chronicles in the greatest detail, and his historical and textual arguments have received renewed attention in Mason's study of post-exilic exegetical and teaching methods (1990: 31-32). These may be summarized as follows.

1. Chronicles is the work of hierocratic circles in the early Hellenistic period (332–323 BCE). This setting best explains its presentation and ideology. Achaemenid rule had granted the Jews two centuries of relative tranquility, during which time the high priest had been affirmed as representative of the nation, and the temple and the cult, 'the essential legacy' of the nation's past, had been restored.

2. The 'davidisme' of Chronicles (see below) is not intended to evoke the expectation of an exalted Davidic figure who will appear at the end of time. There is no messianism in Chronicles; moreover, it is not David, the man of wars, but Solomon, 'the wise and peaceful king', who is idealized in the interest of 'a hierocracy that is basically satisfied with the present' (1966: 120). Solomon is presented as 'the type of sovereign best suited to appeal to the Greeks' (p. 116).[16]

3. Solomon's essential work is finished with the construction of the temple. Caquot remarks on 1 Chron. 28.20 (ולא יעזבך עד לכלות כל מלאכת עבודת בית יהוה): 'It matters little what will happen afterwards: for the Chronicler the work of the dynasty is finished when the temple is built' (p. 118).

4. Other texts are said to support this conclusion. חסדי דויד (2 Chron. 6.42) is a subjective genitive, referring (in the spirit of Psalm 132) to the pains David took in establishing the cult, rather than an objective genitive referring to the Davidic covenant. 'If there is a future perspective in these verses, it concerns not the Davidic dynasty but the steriological function of the Temple' (p. 119). The Chronicler has suppressed most of

toward the Levites (1986: 302), but these surely belong to the primary layer of the composition.

16. Caquot (1966: 11) takes the note on Jaddua in Neh. 12.11 as the *terminus a quo* for the redaction of 'l'oeuvre du Chroniste'. Bickerman places the work earlier but finds a similar perspective: the tendency of the Chronicler 'is to recommend a kind of political quietism which should please the court of Susa as well as the High Priest's mansion in Jerusalem' (1966: 30). Hanson reflects similar views.

the texts from Kings concerning the preservation of a 'lamp' for David or divine action promised למען דוד (1 Kgs 11.13, 32, 36; 19.34; 20.6; only 2 Kgs 8.19 [= 2 Chron. 21.7] is retained). This indicates how little the Chronicler was interested in the Davidic line once its cultic work had been accomplished. The statement in 2 Chron. 13.5 ('Don't you know that Yahweh, the God of Israel, has given the kingship over Israel to David and his sons forever by a covenant of salt?') is an affirmation of Abijah's legitimacy over against the would-be usurper Jeroboam, rather than a profession of the Chronicler's faith.

Caquot's position depends in part on a historical view that can only be touched on here. However, it is doubtful to what extent the later Achaemenid period was marked by general peacefulness, especially in the western extremities of the empire. The most recent researches indicate how troubled some of this period was,[17] while Ezra 4.6-23 testifies to the opposition and interference the Jews experienced in the reigns of Xerxes (486–465) and Artaxerxes (465–424). Further, while it is true that the high priest came to assume the role of representative of the people vis-à-vis the imperial powers, the Chronicler has little to say on this figure, but concentrates instead much more on the activities of the kings and Levites. The writer's own view of the development in status and function of the high priest may instead be determined from the internal evidence of his work.[18]

Caquot's grammatical arguments may be disputed. עד in 1 Chron. 28.20 does not require the interpretation of 'until' in the temporally exclusive sense. Rather the sense is durative: it concerns the promise of divine help to Solomon throughout the period of building. The question of a subsequent, abiding divine presence remains open. Barr has pointed to uses of עד in adverbial phrases which are not temporally exclusive;[19] the durative sense (which is similar to the Aramaic עד) is attested also in Judg. 3.26; 1 Sam. 14.19; and 2 Kgs 9.22. As I argued in Chapter 4, the apogee of the Solomonic narrative (2 Chron. 9) is clearly intended to show the persistence of Yahweh's blessing upon the king throughout his reign, following the completion of the temple.

17. For recent discussions, cf. especially Cook 1983; Eph'al 1988: 139-64; Frye 1984; Gershevitch 1985.

18. This point is examined in Chaper 8 below.

19. Barr 1982. Barr also mentions Qoh. 12.1, 2, 6: Prov. 8.26 (p. 184). Cf. also 1 Sam. 7.12 ('Thus far has Yahweh helped us').

The meaning of הסדי דויד continues to attract scholarly attention.[20] In an earlier study Caquot maintained that the expression denoted '"David's faithful works" [i.e. his temple preparations], the demonstrations of his loyalty to God, and not the favours accorded by God to David' (1965: 59).[21] Caquot denied a direct dependence by the Chronicler on Isaiah 55.3b, but held that even this earlier passage had no messianic import: 'The originality of Isaiah 55 lies in seeing the guarantee of the new covenant in David's sacred deeds, i.e. establishing the divine residence in Jerusalem.'[22]

Williamson (1978) has presented a strong rebuttal of this interpretation. He disputes Caquot's use of the versional evidence and his understanding of חסדי דויד, and points to Acts 13.34 as evidence that in the first century CE at least the expression was understood as an objective genitive. Caquot also notes that חסדים elsewhere in Chronicles (2 Chron. 32.32; 35.26) denotes 'opera pia'. However, these examples do not concern the precise expression חסדי דויד, which is best taken as an allusion to Isaiah 55.3 and the Davidic covenant.[23]

The Chronicler's suppression of למען דוד from the *Vorlage* is not intended to deny the continuing validity of the Davidic covenant. Caquot does not take into account the actual ideological and compositional reasons the writer had for these omissions. Most of the references occur in 1 Kings 11 (cf. vv. 13, 32, 36) in a pericope which is omitted, probably because of its presentation of Solomon and the division of the kingdom. The omission of the oracle of 2 Kgs 19.34 (= Isa. 37.35) from Chronicles is due to the author's reworking of the *Vorlage* to present Hezekiah rather than Isaiah as the central figure, indeed, in 2 Chron. 32.7-8 as the mouthpiece of Isaiah's own oracles. Similar reasons account for the omission of 2 Kgs 20.6, which is part of a longer passage (2 Kgs 20.1-11) radically abbreviated by the Chronicler. On the other hand, Caquot passes over the Chronicler's *added* references to the Davidic covenant in 2 Chron. 21.7; 22.3.[24]

20. See most recently Kaiser 1989 and the bibliography cited there.
21. '"les oeuvres pies de David", les manifestations de sa loyauté envers Dieu, et non les faveurs accordées par Dieu à David.'
22. 'L'originalité d'Isaie 55 est de voir la garantie de la nouvelle alliance dans les oeuvres saintes de David, c'est-à-dire l'établissement à Jerusalem de la residence divine' (Caquot 1965: 55). However, Westermann (1969: 283-84) insists that Isa. 55.3 denotes 'the reliable tokens of grace vouchsafed to David'.
23. *Contra*, most recently, Riley 1993: ch. 3.
24. See the following chapter on the significance of these additions.

Other scholars holding to a traditional understanding of the 'Chronicler's History' (i.e. a complex comprising Chronicles–Ezra–Nehemiah) also argue for its essentially non-eschatological character, in which no role is envisaged for the Davidic house. Myers concludes from the absence of messianism in Ezra–Nehemiah that 'the messianic hope [in Chronicles] is more apparent than real' (1965: lxxxv). Similarly, Becker (1977; ET 1980) holds that Chronicles comes from a time of 'messianological vacuum'. Its hopes of salvation are not linked to a royal figure of Davidic lineage, and it is a mistake to read 'its glorification of David and Solomon, as though the Chronicler were writing history from prophetic perspectives to evoke the messianic kingdom' (1980: 80). The same views are represented in his more recent commentary (1986: 9).[25]

Japhet's work (1977; ET 1989) differs from the examples discussed above in separating Chronicles from Ezra–Nehemiah and reading it on its own terms. Several features of her interpretation call for comment. First, she finds a unified theological outlook in the work which reflects a 'distinct conceptualization which is non-messianic by its very nature' (1989: 499). This interpretation is structurally related to her rather rationalistic understanding of retribution in the work (*sc.*, the absolutization of divine justice in the world), and appears to owe much to Eichrodt's discussion of the Priestly attitude to 'the problem of human existence in time' (Eichrodt 1961: 424-30).

Eichrodt argued that P and Chronicles both looked upon history not eschatologically but 'as *the unfolding of a cosmic order planned for permanence and perfection*' (1961: 425, emphasis original). P depicted a world of 'carefully calculated architectonic perfection', of which the pivotal events were the manifestation of the law and the erection of the temple. The Chronicler expressed this view of history differently, retrojecting God's election perpetually from Adam onward (1961: 425):

> This view would seem to be related to the philosophical interpretation
> of the world which also sees truth as something constant and eternal,
> only revealed more and more in the course of history. Once God's full

25. 'David and Solomon do not have any meaning for the Chronicler for their own sake, not even as a messianic type, but only in so far as their time represents a present opportunity of salvation for Israel, which in any case is bound less to the kings than to the temple' ('David und Salomo haben für [den Chronisten] keine Bedeutung um ihrer selbst willen, auch nicht als messianischer Typos, sondern nur insofern ihre Zeit eine jeweilige Heilsbefindlichkeit Israels darstellt, die im übrigen weniger an die Könige als an den Tempel gebunden ist.').

revelation has been attained, however, all that is to be seen in history is the working out of permanent ordinances established once for all; gradually all obstacles will be overcome, but no room is left for the occurrence of anything really new.

This is the root of Japhet's conviction that the work is essentially non-eschatological, and her understanding of the work's retributive doctrine. Japhet buttresses this interpretation by finding in the work a 'positive anthropology', the innate human capacity to obey God's will. She allows that the work does entertain a 'hope of redemption', the restoration of the land and Israel's past glories, but sees this confidence grounded not in acts of divine intervention but in the given order of the world: 'The power to realize these hopes rests with the people; they need only follow God's ways and observe His commandments' (1989: 503). Finally, Japhet denies that the Davidic covenant is a central concern of the work (1989: 497): 'It rarely appears, and when it appears, it does so in passages of minor importance. Nathan's prophecy does indeed occupy a prominent position in Chronicles; however, it is stressed in texts dealing with the construction of the Temple.'

Each of these claims is open to question. First, as we have seen already, more recent writers reject the view that P reflects so fixed and static a view of the world, and emphasize instead its forward-looking dimensions. Although the cult celebrates Yahweh's present dominion over the world, it also anticipates it in some respects. Secondly, Japhet treats the work more from a 'systematic' than a narratological perspective, and so arguably does not give due weight to those frequent passages where Yahweh does intervene to reverse the effects of human sin, in keeping with his promises to his people (2 Chron. 7.14). As a result, Japhet understates the degree to which the work is really concerned with describing active divine grace in the history of Israel rather than a putative providential world order, in which human beings choose and act freely. The Chronicler notes that even the human will needs divine assistance to obey God's commandments (1 Chron. 22.12; 2 Chron. 30.12). Japhet's treatment of the Davidic covenant (1989: 453-57) is confined to two passages which make explicit mention of a ברית with David, 2 Chron. 13.5 and 21.7, but this ignores the considerable importance this theme has elsewhere (including its expansive treatment in non-synoptic passages) where the term ברית is not used but the concept is clearly implied.[26]

26. Cf. 1 Chron. 17.10-14; 22.6-13; 28.2-10; 2 Chron. 7.18; 13.8; 23.3. The

3. *Eschatological Interpretations of Chronicles*

The contrary trend in scholarship is represented by the following range of views, which are considered in their chronological order of appearance. They are loosely called eschatological because (with one exception) they focus on the abiding significance of the Davidic covenant and dynasty within the post-exilic community.

1. *'Davidism' in Chronicles*

The dominant approach among Christian interpreters has been to read the Chronicler's Davidic narrative not historically but typologically, as if the writer were really prefiguring an exalted messianic figure in his portrayal of David. The main arguments for this reading are the form of the dynastic oracle in Chronicles (1 Chron. 17.10-14, especially v. 11), and the author's supposed idealization of David.

The form and significance of the dynastic oracle is considered more closely in the following chapter. Here it may be noted that Keil (1988 [1870]: 223-24) took the wording of v. 11 (את זרעך אחריך אשר יהיה מבניך), which diverges from 2 Sam. 7.12 (יצא ממעיך), to refer not to Solomon but to a more distant descendant, the Messiah. Keil is followed in this interpretation by von Rad (1930: 119-32) and Im (1985: 120-24).

The omission of passages which reflect badly on David (for example, the Bathsheba narrative and the dispute over the succession in 2 Samuel 11–20), and the presentation of David as the zealous promoter of the cult, are the principal basis of the view that the Chronicler has idealized David as a type of his messianic expectation. This view was strongly expressed by Rothstein and Hänel (1927: x).[27] Von Rad concurred in this judgment, holding that the suppression of 2 Sam. 7.14b ('When he commits iniquity, I will chastise him with the rod of men, with the stripes of the sons of men') indicated that this king would stand outside 'the polar tension of judgment and grace' and signified 'something basically new', hinting obliquely at a form of end-time expectation (1930: 123).[28]

---

fundamental significance of the Davidic covenant for the Chronicler is examined more fully in the following chapter.

27. The Chronicler's 'Idealbild' of David is intended to evoke 'the type of the Davidic shoot of the end-time..., whom prophecy since Isaiah connected with every virtue' ('der Typus des Davidsproßes der Endzeit..., mit dem die Prophetie seit Jesaja die Fülle aller Untadeligkeit verband').

28. '...der polaren Spannung von Gericht und Gnade'; 'etwas Grundneues; wir

Independently Botterweck (1956), Stinespring (1961) and North (1963) argued for much the same interpretation of the Chronistic *Davidbild* and its omissions of negative passages from 2 Samuel 9–20.[29]

Im (1985) presents the most recent and thoroughgoing study of 'Davidism' in Chronicles. He argues that David is depicted as the ideal ruler of Israel (pp. 35-69) and the exemplary worshipper of Yahweh (pp. 70-112). The Chronicler's David is said to be a figure of hope and expectation for the post-exilic community, specifically 'a theocratic Messiah from the House of David' (p. 185). Im intends by this distinction a figure that is exalted yet fully continuous with the line of David and his earthly kingdom (p. 178): 'The Chronicler expected the restoration of the Davidic kingdom as in the time of David, and a Davidide who could accomplish this task. The kingdom belongs to this world and history and is not transcendental.'[30]

Im's work reflects the methodological difficulties that often beset studies of 'Davidism' in Chronicles. By restricting his investigation to 1 Chronicles 10–29, he was unable to explore how the issue of dynasty is developed in 2 Chronicles 1–36. In my view the essential question concerns not the *Davidbild* on its own but its meaning *in the context of the Davidic covenant*. It will be argued in the following chapter that in the Chronicler's presentation the Davidic covenant is an inclusive concept that embraces all of the writer's theological concerns, providing the basis of hope and expectation as well as the means of forgiveness and restoration.

To infer the Chronicler's future outlook from his *Davidbild* alone is an overly subjective approach that does not take account of other factors. Although David might appear as an idealized figure from the perspective of the post-exilic period, such a phenomenon (if, indeed, it is the case) need not reflect messianic longings, but is rather a standard motif in post-exilic literature (Japhet 1989: 498). I have argued, as well, in Chapter 4 that the Chronicler treats David more historically than typologically and highlights his serious failings as well as his positive achievements. There is no question of a one-sided portrayal of David as a cypher of hope.

---

haben es, wenn nur schüchtern angedeutet, mit einer Form von Endwartung zu tun.'

29. In comparable vein, see most recently Brueggemann 1985: 99-107.

30. 'Der Chronist erwartete die Wiederherstellung des "innerweltlichen" und "innergeschichtlichen", nicht transzendentalen Königtum Davids wie in der Davidzeit, und einen Davididen, der diese Aufgabe bewältigen kann.'

We are reminded, however, by Im's conclusion (that David is presented as a type of 'a theocratic Messiah') that the basic terms in this discussion ('eschatology', 'theocracy' and 'messiah') are often construed in conflicting ways by different scholars. For example, Japhet uses 'eschatology' in the suprahistorical sense when she denies that Chronicles has any such elements. 'Theocracy' has been used, especially since Plöger, to denote an anti-eschatological hierocracy, although it plainly has a wider range of meaning in the biblical tradition. 'Messianism' is also a polyvalent and developing concept in biblical theology. Saebø distinguishes between 'eschatological' and 'royal messianism' and finds in Chronicles a 'Davidic-theocratic messianism' (1980: 103). Certainly discussion would benefit from more precision over the use of such terms.

2. *'Restorative Eschatology'*

Freedman (1961), Cross (1975), Newsome (1975) and Throntveit (1987) all assign a fairly precise *Sitz im Leben* to Chronicles, the Judean restoration and temple-building under Zerubbabel and Joshua. These scholars maintain that Chronicles reflects a 'restorative eschatology' focused on the Davidic house. Thus Freedman argued that Chronicles was written 'to establish and defend the legitimate claims of the house of David to pre-eminence in Israel, and in particular its authoritative relationship to the temple and cult' (1961: 440-41). The Chronicler's work is said to be linked with the prophets Haggai and Zechariah, who designated Zerubbabel as the legitimate heir of the Davidic dynasty (1961: 441).[31]

This approach rightly recognizes the central place of the dynasty and the temple in Chronicles and its concern with prophecy. However, it is unlikely that Chronicles can be dated so early or tied so closely to the work of the Judean Restoration. The internal evidence of Chronicles suggests instead that it belongs to the fourth century, and there is no good reason for relegating 1 Chronicles 1–9 to a secondary level of composition, as this theory requires.

Secondly, the Chronicler does not appear to be a contemporary of Haggai and Zechariah, but rather one for whom Zechariah at least had authoritative status as a writing prophet. This is apparent from the citation of Zech. 4.10 in the 'Levitical sermon' in 2 Chronicles 16.7-10. Presumably the passage of some time was necessary before these prophetic words were received as 'scriptural'. The same holds for

---

31. Most proponents of this view endorse Cross's theory of multiple redactions. This argument is foundational to the work of McKenzie (1985) and Hanson (1986).

Hezekiah's words in 2 Chron. 30.6-9, which may be dependent on Zechariah 1.2-6.[32]

A third objection concerns the interpretation of the role of Zerubbabel. Even if Ezra 1.1–3.13 were part of the Chronicler's original composition, as Cross's theory holds, there is no evidence from these chapters that Zerubbabel's Davidic lineage was a focus of expectation. In fact, Ezra 2–3 (and 4) are completely silent about Zerubbabel's origins (other than his father's name) and his precise status. Japhet (1982: 72) remarks that silence on this matter concerning a descendant of David can only be intentional and reflects the view that the Davidic house is not presented here as a vehicle of aspirations.

3. *Mosis: Solomon as Eschatological Symbol*

Mosis (1973) offers the most original interpretation of the eschalogical question in Chronicles, although he has found few followers. He rejects solutions derived from the Chronicler's 'Davidism' and stresses instead the paradigmatic treatment of history which he discerns in the work. According to this view, Saul represents the time of apostasy and exile, David the 'turn toward salvation' ('Wende zum Heil'), and Solomon the era of final redemption, the eschatological rest. The character of this 'Heilszeit' is reflected in the depiction of the wealth and splendour of Jerusalem, the recognition accorded to Yahweh and his sanctuary by the heathen, and the end of the people's oppression (p. 163).

Thus the Chronicler presents his Solomonic narrative not as history but as a prefigurement of his expectation: it is 'an image of the salvation which is still outstanding at his time, the time of the second temple, and whose coming he expects for a yet future time' (p. 163).[33] The Solomonic temple is also intended as a perfect eschatological figure because it unites the tent and altar of the ideal Mosaic period with the ark, and thus transcends both the first temple and the second (p. 226).

Mosis argues that there is no place in this conception for the dynastic promise as it has been historically understood. He accordingly renders 1 Chron. 17.10b (וּבַיִת יִבְנֶה לְּךָ יְהוָה) not as a promise but as a preterite

---

32. The relationship between Haggai and Zechariah, their work and eponymous writings, is a complex matter as well. In particular, Haggai and Zech. 1–8 differ over the role of Zerubbabel (e.g. the dyarchic form of leadership involving Joshua envisaged in Zech. 1–8).

33. '... ein Bild des Heils, das zu seiner Zeit, der Zeit des zweiten Tempels, noch aussteht und dessen Kommen er für eine noch zukünftige Zeit erwartet.'

statement referring to the children already granted David in 1 Chron. 14.3-7 and 16.43. Mosis defends this reading on the basis of the tense uses in 1 Chron. 11.8b and Isa. 6.4 (pp. 85-87), but this overlooks the fact that the latter two passages are durative or circumstantial clauses (Williamson 1982: 135).

The objections to Mosis's approach may be briefly stated. First, as I argued in Chapter 4 in discussion of the Davidic narrative, the Chronicler's concern there is more historical than typological. Admittedly the writer uses a very distinctive patterned form of presentation for his homiletic purpose, but he does not sever an interest in history. Similarly, the Solomonic narrative cannot be dehistoricized. The portrayal is heightened but not 'endzeitlich' because the Chronicler bases his description of Hezekiah's reign (2 Chron. 29–32) on the united reign of David and Solomon,[34] implying the recurrence of those blessings in history. Secondly, it is recognized that the Chronicler presents the reigns of David and Solomon as complementary, 'a single "unified" event in the history of the people' (Williamson 1976: 356).[35] This 'event' belongs to the foundational past and refutes the sharp distinction Mosis draws between the Davidic and Solomonic eras (1973: 162). Thirdly, the 'Mosaic' elements in the Solomonic temple are a reflection not of end-time expectation but of the inclusive nature of the Davidic covenant. In the Chronicler's view this covenant is the new definitive basis of the nation, into which the earlier patriarchal and Mosaic expressions of Israel's relationship with Yahweh have been incorporated. The use of Abrahamic and Mosaic motifs in the portrayal of David is intended to show him fulfilling the work of his predecessors (cf. 1 Chron. 22.22, 24, 26; 28.12, 19), and Solomon is presented along similar lines (cf. 2 Chron. 1.9; 3.1; 7.1).[36]

34. Cf. Williamson 1977a: 119-25; Throntveit 1988.

35. Cf. also Braun 1973; Braun 1976; Throntveit 1987; Throntveit 1988. One of the large-scale structuring devices which the Chronicler uses for welding David's and Solomon's reigns together is the use of Moses–Joshua typology in describing Solomon's accession. The 'encouragement formula' (Braun) of Deut. 31.23/Josh. 1.6, 9 is found in 1 Chron. 22.11, 13; 28.10, 20. There is also a structural similarity in ideas: the completion of the divinely-appointed task (occupation of the land or temple-building) depends on the provision made by the predecessor and on obedience to the Law. The unity of their reigns is also reinforced by the unique way in which Solomon's accession is announced (1 Chron. 29.33-35) before the notice of David's death (vv. 26-30).

36. Williamson (1991: 27) suggests that the Chronicler had a conciliatory motive

It must be allowed, however, that just as the example of David's piety is held before the community, the Chronicler also intended his heightened portrayal of the Solomonic era as a spur to his own community, living in straitened conditions, to look for a restoration of past glories. Two details from 2 Chronicles 9 may hint at this. 1 Kgs 10.10b remarks on the queen of Sheba's gift of spices that 'never again were so many spices brought in' (לא בא כבשׂם ההוא עוד לרב), and v. 12b comments on the almug wood from which instruments were made '(such wood) has never been seen to this day' (ולא נראה עד היום הזה). The Chronicler alters both phrases to read 'there had never been such spices' (ולא היה כבשׂם ההוא, 2 Chron. 9.9b) and 'nothing like them [i.e. the instruments] had been seen previously in the land of Judah' (ולא נראו כהם כזה לפנים בארץ יהודה, v. 11b).[37] Mosis thinks that these phrases were altered to express the eschatological view that the 'Solomonic period' to come would be the time of incomparable splendour (cf. 1973: 160 on the omission of עוד: 'Solomon's time appears thereby as the full completion of the time "previously"').[38] It is more likely, however, that the difference should be explained by the more positive perspective of Chronicles in comparison with Kings. Whereas the exilic Deuteronomist could only look back ruefully over the devastation of judgment and the loss of Israel's greatness, the post-exilic Chronicler was more concerned to stress that restoration had begun and that nothing in principle stood in the way of the resumption of such blessings as had once characterized the Davidic-Solomonic past.[39]

in linking these ancient Mosaic cultic objects with the Jerusalem temple, viz. to unite around it groups that had lingering loyalties to the cultic centres of Gibeon (traditionally associated with the bronze altar and tabernacle) and Shiloh (the erstwhile home of the ark).

37. The LXX of 1 Kgs 10.10b reads: οὐκ ἐληλύθει κατὰ τὰ ἡδύσματα ἐκεῖνα ἔτι εἰς πλῆθος ἃ ἔδωκε βασίλισσα Σαβὰ τῷ βασιλεῖ Σαλωμών; while 1 Kgs 10.12b reads: οὐκ ἐληλύθει τοιαῦτα ξύλα ἀπελέκητα ἐπὶ τῆς γῆ οὐδὲ ὤφθησάν που ἕως τῇ ἡμέρας ταύτης. This could indicate assimilation of LXX (also Lucianic and Vaticanus) to Chronicles (cf. 2 Chron. 9.11b, בארץ יהודה). McKenzie (1985: 155) has demonstrated Chronicles' dependence on a Vorlage of Kings similar to the MT, so the differences in Chronicles probably reflect the writer's outlook.

38. '(D)ie Zeit Salomos erscheint somit als die letzte Vollendung der Zeiten "vorher".'

39. This point is examined further in Chapter 9.

4. *Williamson: 'Royalism' in Chronicles*

Williamson's influential treatment of this subject (1977b; 1983; *passim* in his commentary, 1982) is a point of departure for my own discussion in the following chapter. Adopting an immanentist sense of eschatology, he characterizes Chronicles as 'royalist', holding out the hope that the Davidic dynasty may yet be restored, in a way that is continuous with the history of the pre-exilic state.

The main basis of Williamson's argument is the form of the dynastic oracle and the presentation of Solomon. 1 Chron. 17.11 is found to refer not to a distant descendant (*contra* Keil and von Rad) but to Solomon, who shares with David a responsibility in the confirmation of this promise. This is seen as entailing a twofold obligation, to complete the temple and to be unswervingly obedient to the Law throughout his reign. According to Williamson, the form of the Solomonic narrative demonstrates that Solomon was obedient in both respects and it implies that, upon the death of this obedient king, the dynastic promise was irrevocably established. A number of texts in the post-Solomonic narrative relating to the dynastic promise (2 Chron. 13.5; 21.7b; 23.3) confirm that this remains the author's position throughout the work.

Williamson also discerns a structural connection between the writer's hope and his theology of retribution (1977b: 154):

> His doctrine of immediate and individual retribution, including as it does a
> firm belief in God's direct involvement in history, suggests both that the
> people themselves should be encouraged to look to the future for
> improvement in their present sorry condition, and that it is by no means
> incongruous that the Chronicler could have inherited and passed on a
> continuing tradition of hope centred on the Davidic family.

These arguments are examined and amplified in the following chapter, where I consider more closely the nature of Solomon's obedience and other literary indications of the continuing importance and validity of the dynastic promise. As I have remarked already, the dynastic promise is part of a more comprehensive theme within the Davidic covenant. The dimensions of this covenant must first be determined in any discussion of the futurist outlook of the work.

4. *Summary and Conclusion*

This chapter has surveyed the most important modern discussions of eschatology in Chronicles from 1927 (Rothstein and Hänel; but taking Keil 1870 into consideration as well) to the present. It has shown that the lack of consensus on this question is due principally to three disputed issues: opinions over the extent and dating of the Chronicler's work; the relationship of Chronicles to its wider sociological and theological milieu; and the significance accorded its presentation of David and the dynastic promise.

Our assessment of previous views has in turn been determined by the following critical judgments: Chronicles is a self-contained work (exclusive of Ezra–Nehemiah) from the fourth century BCE; it does not reflect the outlook of a supposedly non-eschatological Priestly writing; it does not depict David (or Solomon) in a one-sidedly idealized way, nor does it portray David as a cypher of messianic expectation. The next two chapters will attempt to characterize the futurist outlook of the work by describing the tendency of a wide range of themes.

Chapter 7

ESCHATOLOGY IN CHRONICLES: AN INTEGRATIVE APPROACH

1. *Introduction: The Davidic Covenant in Chronicles*

Any consideration of eschatology in Chronicles must begin with the central place of the Davidic covenant in the Chronicler's theology. In Samuel–Kings the covenant is concerned primarily with the promise to David of a perpetual dynasty (cf. 2 Sam. 7.12-16, 28-29; 1 Kgs 8.25-26). In Chronicles, on the other hand, the covenant has a more comprehensive significance. It undergirds Israel's identity as Yahweh's people, incorporating the earlier Abrahamic and Mosaic expressions of that relationship. The covenant also provides the possibility of Israel's future existence, through the promises of divine forgiveness, restoration and protection. The scope of these promises is the subject of this and the following chapter. It will be argued that the Chronicler, far from expressing an insular preoccupation with cultic affairs or a satisfaction with the *status quo* (whether from ideological or prudential reasons), looks instead to a transformation of his community's circumstances, including perhaps its political forms of life.

At the heart of this expectation is the Chronicler's belief that the Davidic covenant has constituted Israel as the earthly expression of Yahweh's kingdom. More explicitly and emphatically than anywhere else in the Old Testament tradition, the writer understands the Israelite kingdom of David and Solomon to be the concretized form of Yahweh's kingship, the theocracy in its fullest sense. Although 'theocracy' is often used interchangeably for 'hierocracy', the rule of cultic personnel, the Chronicler has a quite different understanding of how the divine kingship is exercised. The theocracy in Chronicles is really the union of two interests that have their origin in the Davidic covenant, the dynasty and the temple. Together these institutions are the principal expressions of Yahweh's kingdom. Although only the Jerusalem cult was a present reality for the Chronicler's community, the writer did not believe that the significance of the Davidic covenant was exhausted in the cultic arrangements of his day.[1] Instead, he demonstrated the mutual relationship of monarchy and temple, both in the first part of the work which describes how the kingdom is established, and in his account of the post-Solomonic period, where the faithful Davidide is the patron of the cult and experiences blessings on his realm.[2]

The Chronicler's form of the Davidic covenant must now be considered. The writer's conviction that Yahweh's kingdom was established in Israel through this covenant is conveyed by word-play and verbal and syntactic changes to the *Vorlage*. The word-play exploits the idea of בית, drawing on its different meanings as 'temple' and 'dynasty'. Such word-play is already present in the *Vorlage,* but the Chronicler draws these two senses more closely together. 2 Sam. 7.11b and 13a report the promise of a dynasty and Solomon's task as temple-builder as follows:

בית יעשׂה לך יהוה [...] הוא יבנה בית לשׁמי

In the parallel passage in 1 Chron. 17.10b, 12a verbal and pronominal changes create a more balanced chiastic effect:

ובית יבנה לך יהוה [...] הוא יבנה לי בית

Thus Yahweh will first 'build a house' for David, that is, establish a dynastic succession from Solomon, who in turn will build a 'house', the temple, for Yahweh. The significance of this word-play is extended in later verses. In 2 Sam. 7.16 Yahweh assures David that his dynasty will be perpetual: 'Your house and your kingdom (ביתך וממלכתך) will be made sure for ever before me;[3] your throne (כסא) will be established for ever'. In 1 Chron. 17.14 this is rewritten extensively to introduce the idea of the temple (ביתי; cf. 1 Chron. 28.6) and Yahweh's kingdom, in

---

1. Riley (1993: 224-25) emphasizes the continuing significance of the Davidic covenant for the Chronicler's community, but considers that it has lost its dynastic dimension and is now valid as it is expressed through the people. While this recognition of the central place of the Davidic covenant in the Chronicler's theology is salutary, Riley's understanding of the covenant (viz. that the supposed 'democratization' of the concept in Isa. 55.3 is the Chronicler's view as well; cf. 2 Chron. 6.42; contrast Williamson 1982: 221; Kaiser 1989) is contested in this chapter.

2. Cf. Chapter 8 for further treatment of this theme. Im (1985: 180-81) draws attention to the alternating step-parallels in the Davidic narrative between passages describing the advancement of the Davidic kingdom on the one hand (cf. 1 Chron. 11.12; 14; 17–20), and on the other hand, passages detailing the progressive establishment of the cult (1 Chron. 13; 15–16; 21–29).

3. 2 Sam. 7.16 MT reads 'before you' (לפניך); contrast LXX ἐνώπιόν μου.

which Solomon's own rule will participate: 'I will confirm him in my house and my kingdom (ובמלכותי בביתי) for ever, and his throne (וכסאו) will be established for ever'.

The closest links are thus forged between the two 'houses' of temple and dynasty, the twin foci of the Chronicler's work,[4] and it is emphasized that both are brought into existence through the Davidic covenant. It must be noted, too, that Yahweh's kingdom in Israel has material and corporate dimensions: as the Chronicler affirms through Abijah, the nation is 'Yahweh's kingdom in the hands of David's descendants' (2 Chron. 13.8; cf. v. 5). It will be seen that in the Chronicler's presentation Israel's national life is similarly constituted by the Davidic covenant, and so Yahweh's kingdom embraces the dynastic line, temple cult, people and land. In developing an integrative approach to the eschatological question in Chronicles, this chapter will examine the presentation of each of these elements for aspects of future expectation. A broader range of evidence must be considered than the traditional approaches which concentrate on the portrayal of the monarchy or cult. A common theme in this discussion will be the extent to which the Chronicler may be presenting an ideal that contrasts with the reality of his post-exilic community.

2. The Significance of the Dynastic Promise

This section will argue that the Chronicler holds the promise to David of a perpetual dynasty to be permanently valid for his community and a focus of its expectations. The dynastic line is, of course, personal, and yet Davidic rule had not been exercised since the early sixth century. Most recently, it has been argued that the Chronicler understood the Davidic kingship to be transmuted into and in some sense exercised through the temple.[5] However, it will be seen that the Davidic dynasty (and covenant) cannot be reduced to this one cultic concern. The principal

---

4.   Contrast von Rad's view (1930: 120): 'The Chronicler is not interested in the primal or the Mosaic history, and neither is the temple or the history of the people in itself the centre of his history writing. Rather his concern is with the throne of David under the judgment and grace of Yahweh in the changing conditions of the times' ('Nicht die Ur- und Mosesgeschichte interessiert den Chronisten, aber auch der Tempel und die Volksgeschichte an sich ist nicht das Zentrum seiner Geschichtsschreibung, sondern der Davidsthron unter Gericht und Gnade Jahwes im Wandel der Zeiten').

5.   Cf. Mason 1990: 32-33; Riley 1993: ch. 3 (see above).

questions here are: (i) the focus of the dynastic promise and its confirmation; (ii) its significance in the post-Solomonic narrative; and (iii) indications of its perdurance up to the Chronicler's time.

As was noted in the previous chapter, 'messianic' interpretations of Chronicles have understood the dynastic oracle in 1 Chron. 17.4-14 to refer to a distant and exalted descendant of David.[6] The principal reasons for this reading are the form of v. 11b (מבניך יהיה; contrast 2 Sam. 7.12b, יצא ממעיך), and the suppression of 2 Sam. 7.14b, 'When he commits iniquity, I will chastise him with the rod of men, with the stripes of the sons of men'. According to this line of interpretation, the Chronicler looks further ahead than Solomon (that is, his phrasing denotes '[one] who will come forth from one of your sons'), while the latter words were deemed inappropriate for a messianic figure and were therefore omitted.

The first point is sufficiently answered by Williamson (1983: 308-309). He notes that the phrase is ambiguous of itself, and so the immediate context and other passages amplifying the dynastic promise (e.g. 1 Chron. 17.12a; 22.9-10; 28.5-7) must determine exegesis. These passages make it plain that Solomon is the intended reference of the oracle. The second question, the omission of 2 Sam. 7.12b, has provoked a range of explanations that are connected with the wider question of how the Chronicler understands Solomon's reign. Mosis (1973: 90) argues that the Chronicler wished to avoid any suggestion that Solomon might sin. This is in keeping with his view that the Solomonic period is understood typologically as the time of eschatological rest. Japhet (1989: 463-67), on the other hand, believes that the question turns in part on the supposed conditional nature of the dynastic promise in Chronicles. She maintains that 2 Sam. 7.12b was omitted precisely because the Chronicler believed the continuance of the promise *was* conditional on the faithfulness and obedience of the Davidides. The continuation of the dynastic promise in the *Vorlage* (v. 15a, 'but my steadfast love [וחסדי] shall not depart from him') made it plain that the dynastic promise was unconditional: Solomon may be disciplined, but he will not be rejected.

---

6.   Cf. Keil 1966: 232-34; Rothstein and Hänel 1927: 326; von Rad 1930: 123-24; Galling 1954 on 1 Chron. 17.11; North 1963: 376-77. Im's discussion of 1 Chron. 17.11 (1985: 120-24) notes the ambiguity of the phrase (p. 122 n. 22) but does not interact with subsequent references in Chronicles to the oracle which specify Solomon. Similarly, Newsome rightly notes the stress on the eternity of the promise, but in associating it with Zerubbabel (1975: 213), he does not take into account the emphasis of later verses on Solomon as the recipient of the promise.

Japhet notes other verses in Kings (e.g. 1 Kgs 2.4; 8.25; 9.5) which appear to make the promise conditional on obedience, and she argues that the Chronicler aligned himself with this view (1989: 464):

> The prophecy in 2 Samuel raises the hypothetical question of the effect that a monarch's transgression would have on the promise and answers it in no uncertain terms: God's steadfast love is guaranteed no matter what the king does. In Chronicles [because of the omission of 2 Sam. 7.14b], this question remains unanswered. Moreover, other verses make it clear that the Chronistic answer would be very different: God's promise concerning the Davidic dynasty does depend on certain conditions.

Japhet mentions in this light 1 Chron. 28.6-7. In these verses David addresses the assembled leaders of Israel: '[Yahweh] said to me, "It is Solomon your son who shall build my house and my courts, for I have chosen him to be my son and I will be his father. I will establish his kingdom for ever if he continues resolute in keeping my commandments and my ordinances, as he is today"'. Japhet goes on to say (1989: 465, 467):

> The Chronicler expressly says that YHWH's promise to David is contingent upon the monarch's behaviour. It is clear that 2 Sam 7.14b must be deleted, given the view that the dynastic promise is conditional and may be annulled by the king's sinfulness. [...] In Chronicles, we are told that the monarchy came to an end because certain conditions, which were part of YHWH's promise to David, were not fulfilled.

However, Japhet's discussion fails to recognize that just as the oracle is focused on *Solomon*, so too is the condition of obedience. Further, her view does not explain why the end of Davidic rule occurred when it did, and not (for example) during the reign of a king as faithless as Ahaz.

Williamson (1983a) approaches the question of the conditional nature of the promise more specifically. He argues that the Chronicler understands Solomon as having an equal share with David in the establishment of the promise and makes him subject (in 1 Chron. 28.7, 10) to a twofold condition: to build the temple and to remain obedient to the Law throughout his reign. On this reasoning 2 Sam. 7.14b is omitted because that text could have no application for Solomon in the Chronicler's scheme. 'Either he was going to obey, in which case the dynasty would be established, or he would fail, and his house with him; the possibility was not foreseen that he would fail personally, but the dynasty nevertheless endure' (Williamson 1983a: 318). The Chronicler's account of Solomon's reign, with its omission of 1 Kings 1–2 and 11.1–40, is said to present him as one who did in fact keep both conditions in the most positive way, so that with Solomon's death, the Chronicler intends his readers to understand that the dynasty has been eternally established.

One difficulty with this interpretation, which is of course partly an inference from the narrative, is that it involves a certain tension between what the writer is said to be depicting of Solomon (an obedient reign from start to finish) and what he knows to be the case about him; note the critical indications in 2 Chron. 9.29; 10.4, 10-11, 14-15. As I argued in Chapter 4, the Chronicler is not concerned in 2 Chronicles 1–9 to present a 'Solomonic apologetic' (*contra* Braun 1973); the real interest of these chapters is the temple, and the covenant and divine kingdom to which it testifies. Solomon's obedience is an important matter to the Chronicler, but he sees this concentrated chiefly in temple-building, as 1 Chron. 28.9b-10 seems to imply:

> If you seek him, he will be found by you; but if you forsake him, he will reject you for ever. Take heed now, for Yahweh has chosen you to build a temple as a sanctuary. Be strong and do the work.

1 Chron. 28.7 (and 1 Chron. 22.13) show that the covenant has conditional aspects, but these do not override the unconditional way in which Solomon's election and the dynastic promise are presented in 1 Chron. 17.13-14.[7] The Chronicler is certainly aware of Solomon's later decline and his share in the division of the kingdom, but he appears more concerned to highlight the king's obedience in the matter of temple-building and Yahweh's covenant mercy toward his people. In these respects Solomon's reign, although marked by sin and inconsistency, signifies a complete break with the experience of Saul (cf. 1 Chron. 17.13).

The Chronicler further indicates that the dynastic promise is established *within* Solomon's lifetime, at the completion of the temple. The form of the Solomonic narrative indicates how these themes are interrelated. At the beginning of Solomon's reign mention of the dynastic promise is introduced in 2 Chron. 1.9a, in an addition to the *Vorlage*: 'Yahweh God, let your promise (דברך) to David my father be now confirmed (יאמן)'. This expression looks back to David's prayer for confirmation of the dynastic promise in 1 Chron. 17.23, and forward to Solomon's words at the completion of the temple in 2 Chron. 6.17: 'And now, Yahweh God of Israel, let your word be confirmed (יאמן) which you spoke to your servant David'. At the conclusion of his

---

7.   Cf. Selman 1994a: 180, 251.

dedicatory prayer Solomon again makes his plea that the dynastic promise (חסדי דויד) may be ratified (2 Chron. 6.42). This petition is immediately succeeded by a fire-theophany on the altar of burnt offerings (2 Chron. 7.1). This event is intended as a parallel to the revelation of Yahweh's glory on Mount Sinai (cf. Exod. 19.18-19; 20.18), and more specifically, the theophany that 'answers' (ויענהו) David's prayer in 1 Chron. 21.26. The miraculous event signifies that just as Solomon has completed Yahweh's 'house', the temple, so too Yahweh has granted Solomon's prayer and affirmed David's 'house', the dynastic line (cf. 1 Chron. 17.10, 12).

In the subsequent oracle (2 Chron. 7.12-22) the Chronicler introduces changes in v. 18 to express an intensified interest in the Davidic covenant. כרתי replaces דברתי (1 Kgs 9.5), and מושל בישראל, an echo of the messianic oracle in Mic. 5.1 (E v. 2), stands in place of מעל כסא ישראל. The Chronicler probably does not intend the use of this expression here in a specifically (exalted) messianic sense, but uses it rather to heighten the emphasis upon the promise of an eternal dynasty.[8]

The writer next provides indications in the post-Solomonic narrative that he understands the dynastic promise to be confirmed and of eternal validity, whatever the vicissitudes of Judah or the personal worthiness of individual Davidides. Explicit references to the Davidic covenant and dynastic promise are infrequent in this part of the work, but they are significant because they come from the Chronicler's own hand and feature at critical points in the narrative. Williamson (1977b) notes the circumstances in which these references are made. In 2 Chron. 13.5 Abijah affirms the perpetual validity of the covenant (ברית מלח) in the face of the military danger to Judah from the north. In 2 Chron. 21.7, in the midst of the fratricide that engulfs the Davidic house, the covenant is invoked as the reason for Jehoram's preservation. Finally, Jehoiada alludes to the dynastic promise in 2 Chron. 23.3, in his overthrow of the usurper Athaliah. Neither Jehoram nor Joash, for whom Jehoiada acts, is judged positively by the Chronicler, but both kings owe their standing to the divine promise.

De Vries (1987) makes a similar point in his discussion of the narrative form of this section. He discerns an imaginative 'schema of dynastic endangerment' superimposed on the work and especially evident from 2 Chron. 18.1 onward.[9] The Chronicler has reworked the material to

---

8. Cf. Williamson 1982: 226.
9. De Vries, in fact, finds evidence of this schema as early as 2 Chron. 11.22-23,

bring out a particular emphasis, that Jehoshaphat's marriage alliance with Ahab implicated the Davidic house in a spiral of corruption that extends over the next few reigns. 2 Chronicles 21–24 are specially modified to depict the threat of destruction standing over the dynasty, in the form of repeated catastrophes affecting the Davidic house.

First, the Chronicler notes that Jehoram, upon his accession, 'slew all his brothers with the sword' (2 Chron. 21.4, no parallel). In turn, Jehoram loses all his family to the Philistines and Arabs except Jehoahaz (Ahaziah), his youngest son (2 Chron. 21.17, no parallel). After Ahaziah's death, his family is virtually annihilated by Athaliah, but again, the youngest son, Joash, is preserved (2 Chron. 21.10-12 = 2 Kgs 11.1-3). The Chronicler has shown that by attaching itself to the Ahabites, the Davidic house has been brought under its control and practically extinguished. Nevertheless, as we have seen, it is in this darkest period of decline and apostasy that the Chronicler appeals to the dynastic promise as the ground for the preservation (2 Chron. 21.7) and restoration (2 Chron. 23.3) of the legitimate line. All this is asserted, even though Joash proved no better than his predecessors (cf. 2 Chron. 24.17-18). Across the generations, then, the Chronicler shows that the line is maintained, but only in the most tenuous form, through the survival of the youngest son. De Vries (1987: 73) interprets the significance of the author's reworking of these chapters as follows:

> There can be only one explanation for the development of this schema, superimposed by Chr on accounts drawn from Kgs. It has to be that, unlike Dtr, Chr retained a place for the Davidic promise in his model of the post-exilic community. Although no Davidide regained the throne following the Return, Chr cherished the concept of the Davidic kingship as a model of Yahweh's own perpetual rule.

with intimations of rivalry among Rehoboam's sons, but it is unlikely that the Chronicler intends us to understand the reigns from Rehoboam to Asa as overshadowed by danger (De Vries 1987: 65-67). De Vries further argues that Jehoshaphat's alliance with Ahab (2 Chron. 18.1-2) unleashed a destructive 'wrath' (קצף; cf. 2 Chron. 19.1) which finally found its mark in the reign of Joash (2 Chron. 24.18c): 'And they forsook the house of Yahweh the God of their fathers and served the Asherim and the idols. And wrath came upon Judah and Jerusalem *on that day* (LXX τῇ ἡμέρᾳ ταύτῃ)'. This aspect of De Vries's theory is also unconvincing. It is difficult to think of 2 Chron. 24.18 as the climax of the unit 2 Chron. 18–24, while De Vries's preferred reading is due to an internal corruption in the Greek (ἡμέρᾳ for ἁμαρτία; contrast MT באשמתם) which the Lucianic recension corrects.

Nevertheless, other interpreters dispute the view that the Chronicler saw lasting relevance for his own community in the promise of a perpetual dynasty. Japhet (1989: 467, 504) is unclear on this point, but Mosis (1973: 205-206) forthrightly denies that the Chronicler is interested in the future of the dynastic line. Commenting on the Chronicler's account of the last four kings of Judah (2 Chron. 36.1-21), which is highly compressed and omits most of the personal information given in 2 Kgs 23.30b–25.30, Mosis remarks (1973: 213):

> If [the Chronicler] was concerned with the problem of a legitimate, individual successor of the last kings, he would scarcely have paid so little attention to them, especially the last king, Zedekiah. This treatment of the last kings of Judah shows that he was not interested in a later successor in rule and his legitimation.[10]

Mosis's interpretation stems in part from seeing Ezra 1–2 as the sequel to the destruction, and thus a new episode in which the dynastic question does not feature. Begg (1987b), on the other hand, argues that the writer's sparse presentation in 2 Chronicles 36, in which he mentions the exile of these kings but not their deaths (contrast 2 Kgs 24–25), is a literary device which effectively leaves open the future of these kings, and the line which they represent, rather than treating the dynastic issue as a matter of indifference.

The question cannot be decided on the form (or silences) of the final chapter alone, any more than the concluding note of Jehoiachin's rehabilitation in 2 Kgs 25.27-30 may be taken as a clear affirmation of the Davidic promise in that work (see Chapter 9). Of greater significance is 1 Chron. 3.17-24, the line of Davidic descendants following the exile, beginning with 'Jehoiachin the captive'. This distinctive title is prospective: it anticipates the king's fate in 2 Chron. 36.10, but affirms that he did not die childless. These verses are one of the few portions of Chronicles to continue beyond the exile (possibly down to the writer's own time). This list is further confirmation that the Davidic line has been divinely maintained, and by virtue of its place within the genealogies (at the heart of the leading tribe, Judah), it affirms the continuing

---

10. 'Wenn ihn das Problem eines legitimen, individuellen Nachfolgers der letzten Könige bewegt hatte, hätte er kaum das Ende dieser Könige, insbesondere des letzten, Zidkija, so völlig außer acht gelassen. Diese Behandlung der letzten Könige von Juda zeigt, daß er nicht auf einen späteren Nachfolger in der Herrschaft und auf dessen Legitimation abzielt.'

significance and centrality of the Davidic promise in the life of the post-exilic community.[11]

In conclusion, we may say that the Chronicler demonstrates that a perpetual dynastic line for David was established through the Davidic covenant, and that the line continues as a personal expression of Yahweh's kingdom, alongside the temple, the other 'house' of the theocracy. The two 'houses' are, in fact, mutually related: Solomon's obedience in building the temple is understood as the means through which the covenant is accepted and confirmed, and henceforth the dynastic promise is presented as established and unconditional.

It remains to be asked, however, in what sense the Davidic covenant in its personal dimension continued to be relevant for the Chronicler. The earlier approaches to the Davidic interest in Chronicles (as an expression of messianism that was derived from the *Davidbild* or as a work composed in association with the Judean Restoration under the Davidide Zerubbabel) were reviewed in the previous chapter and were found to be unsubstantiated. Interpretation of this question continues to be disputed. It is useful to mention here the most recent studies which can be expected to influence future discussion of this subject. These works take account of, and usually accept, the newer views of the extent of the Chronicler's work (distinguishing it from Ezra–Nehemiah), and the dating this implies. They approach the Davidic question more tentatively, but with no more unanimity than their predecessors. Riley's study of royal ideology and cult in Chronicles rightly emphasizes that the Davidic covenant is of central and lasting importance to the Chronicler, but it concludes that the writer conceived the Davidic kingship to be

11. Although Rudolph (1955: 11, 26-27) disputed the originality of 1 Chron. 3, Williamson (1979) has demonstrated that the genealogy of Judah (1 Chron. 2.3–4.23) is presented in a chiastic structure which places the Davidic line (2.10-17; 3.1-24) at the centre. Williamson argues that these chapters were the conscious creation of one author working from four blocks of material. On this understanding, many of the tensions in the text (e.g. 2.18-24), which Rudolph took as evidence of its secondary nature, were already present in the sources before their incorporation by the Chronicler. Kartveit (1989: 37-38) rejects Williamson's analysis, but Willi (1991: 76-80) supports it and points out that Kartveit's approach reduces the Chronicler's authorial contribution to a bare minimum. I would suggest that Williamson's interpretation is supported by 1 Chron. 28.4-5, where the same 'concentric' picture of election is presented: Israel–Judah–David's בת אב–David–Solomon. The arrangement in the genealogies implies that, just as Judah is pre-eminent in Israel, so too is the Davidic line within Judah.

primarily cultic in its task and only provisional (1993: 201):

> By concentrating on the cultic vocation which the ancient ideology attributed to kings, the Chronicler placed the dynastic promise into the larger context of the Temple as the major effect of the Davidic covenant, and thus demonstrated through his narrative that the days of the dynasty had ended while the covenant with David remained. The Davidic covenant persisted for the Chronicler and his audience in the task (which the people had from the days of David himself) to worship at the Temple and to provide for its needs and the needs of the cultus in utter faithfulness.

The opposite extreme is represented by Wright's dissertation (1989) and related articles (1990; 1991), which propound the view that Chronicles is essentially a political work in support of the claims of a Davidide in a failed rebellion.[12] This supposed background is wholly hypothetical, and the reading misrepresents the Chronicler, whose activism is covenant- and cult-centred, not political.

A more balanced approach is taken by Oeming (1990), who interprets the genealogies in 1 Chronicles 1–9 as a 'proleptic summary' of the themes and *Tendenzen* of the rest of the work. In considering the likely significance of 1 Chron. 3.17-24, Oeming considers a number of rival opinions, but in the end he appears to align himself with Williamson's view (1990: 209):

> The growth and extension of the royal family of Davidides into the late post-exilic period demonstrates an interest in the continuation of the royal house. The door to autochthonous Israelite royal rule remains open, but the form of this is not messianic but in any case only 'royalist'.[13]

A complementary view is represented by Strübind (1991), who uses the Jehoshaphat narrative (2 Chron. 17–20) as a paradigm for interpreting the Chronicler's theology. Strübind does not consider the dynastic oracle, but he does discuss the role of the king in this extended pericope toward the cult personnel. He concludes that the picture of royal authority there gives no support to the antithesis drawn by Plöger between 'theocracy' and 'eschatology'.[14] Strübind remarks (1991: 201): 'In our

---

12. Wright 1989: ch. 6.

13. 'Die breite Entfaltung der Königsfamilie der Davididen bis in die spät-nachexilische Zeit zeigt ein Interesse am Weiterbestehen des Königshauses. Das Tor zur autochthonen israelitischen königlichen Herrschaft bleibt offen, ist aber nicht messianisch ausgestaltet, sondern allenfalls nur royalistisch.'

14. Strübind's conclusions provide independent confirmation of my discussion in the following chapter of the themes of war and the relation of king to cult in

opinion the question is not *whether* but *what kind of* eschatology the Chronicler represents.'[15]

We can only echo this statement. The 'royalist' interpretation is certainly possible, but unfortunately the Chronicler is not more precise or explicit at this point. He leaves us only with the remarkable insistence that Yahweh's kingdom is still expressed in *the personal line of David's descendants*, and the covenant is by no means absorbed wholly into the temple and cult. The Chronicler's emphasis on Yahweh's kingdom, mediated through the Davidic covenant, is a new and potentially transcendent element in the tradition. It may be that this fact relativizes the older political significance of the dynasty, at the same time as giving rise to hopes focused on David's line. If so, we may infer that the work, in the deeper structure of its ideas, harbours a restrained and implicit messianism.[16]

3. *The Hope of Redemption in the Depiction of the Cult*

This section argues that the Chronicler uses his presentation of the cult partly to give expression to his community's hope of deliverance, and indeed understands the cult as playing a central role in achieving this end. The point is evident, of course, on the general level of the Chronicler's thought, which correlates 'seeking Yahweh' (which is usually conceived cultically) with the salvation and prosperity of the

Chronicles. He rightly comments (1991: 201): 'Our analysis [*sc.* of 2 Chron. 17–20] found no indications for a justification of a *status quo* which would mark off "theocracy" from an "eschatology". Chronicles is evidently a "theocratic" work, in so far as theocracy denotes God's rule mediated through the king, worship and prophets. If, however, *theocracy* means *hierocracy* in the sense of rule by cult personnel—as we understand Plöger's meaning—then there are no clues for this theory in the portion of the text we have examined' ('Unsere Analyse brachte keine Indizien für die Rechtfertigung eines *status quo*, der als "Theokratie" von einer "Eschatologie" abzugrenzen wäre. Selbstverständlich ist die Chronik ein "theokratisches" Werk, sofern Theokratie die durch den König, Gottesdienst und Propheten mediierte Gottesherrschaft bedeutet. [...] Meint *Theokratie* aber *Hierokratie* im Sinne von Herrschaft des Kultpersonals—so meinen wir PLÖGER verstanden zu haben—so finden sich für diese Theorie keine Anhaltspunkte in dem von uns untersuchten Textabschnitt').

15. 'Fraglich ist u. E. nicht *ob*, sondern *welche* Eschatologie der Chronist vertritt.'

16. Cf. Selman 1994a: 181. Such an element of the Chronicler's outlook would allow of trajectories to other parts of biblical theology, especially the association made in the New Testament between the kingdom of God and the Davidic promise.

nation. There is, however, a more specific treatment of this question in the Chronistic theme of the choral rite, whose significance is examined below.

Consideration of worship must begin with the meaning of the temple, together with its services. For the writer this institution is important primarily as an expression of the Davidic covenant: the temple was established as a result of that covenant, and it testifies to its promises (1 Chron. 17.4-14; 2 Chron. 7.12-22). Moreover, just as the Chronicler presents the restored community as the legitimate successor of pre-exilic Israel (1 Chron. 9.2-3; 2 Chron. 36.22-23), the second temple is similarly a sign of continuity with the past. It stands as a focus of unity for 'all Israel',[17] and the means through which acceptable worship may be fostered according to divinely given ordinances (cf. 1 Chron. 6.34 [E 49]; 2 Chron. 8.13; 30.16; 35.6).

Beyond these questions of continuity and legitimacy, a few commentators have sought to define more closely the theological significance of the Chronicler's depiction of the cult. For Janowski (1982: 161-62, 241) the association of Chronicles with priestly theology and practice has suggested that the atoning rites were the author's primary interest and that he understood 'Kultgeschehen als Sühnegeschehen'. This interpretation is based on 2 Chron. 29.23, 24a, where Janowski believes the Chronicler has drawn a close connection between the blood rites of the altar and cultic atonement of the people.

Johnstone (1986) also thinks that sacrificial atonement is central, but he interprets this in a more typological way. Taking Israel's corporate guilt and its atonement to be the theme of the work, Johnstone finds this interest highlighted in the pivotal moments of 1 Chron. 21.26, where David offers sacrifice for his sin, and 2 Chron. 29.20-21, where Hezekiah arranges for national atonement after Ahaz's reign.

Sacrifice is clearly a matter of importance for the Chronicler. A significant passage which reveals his perspective is his designation of Solomon's temple as 'a house of sacrifice' (2 Chron. 7.12b), a phrase without parallel in his *Vorlage* (1 Kgs 9.3; cf. also 2 Chron. 2.3-5 [E 4-6]). However, the Chronicler generally presents ritual sacrifice in close association with intercession and praise (1 Chron. 16.40-41; 21.26; 2 Chron. 7.1-3; 23.18; 29.27-30). The continuation of Yahweh's reply to Solomon makes this connection plain and defines the nature of the cult as a complex of prayer and sacrifice: 'I have chosen this place for myself

---

17. Cf. Braun 1971; Williamson 1991.

as a house for sacrifice... Now my eyes will be open and my ears attentive to the prayer that is made in this place' (2 Chron. 7.12b, 15). The
writer gives no indication that he understands the atoning rites typologically, or that they have the primary significance for him that Janowski
and Johnstone suggest. The root כפר is found only in 1 Chron. 6.33
(E 49), 2 Chron. 29.24 and 30.18, although the uses are interesting. In
the last-named example Yahweh is the subject and the sense is not cultic
(Janowski 1982: 137). In 2 Chron. 29.21-24 the Chronicler does draw
attention to the specific purificatory rites, involving the manipulation of
the blood against the altar. However, this refers to a singular incident,
where the cult is reconstituted after its desecration and suspension by
Ahaz. The climax to this description is in fact the popular worship
involving the Levites and the assembly (vv. 25-36).

The Chronicler's principal cultic interest lies, in fact, in the regular
cycle of daily, weekly and seasonal offerings. Further, his concern with
these sacrifices focuses not on their expiatory role,[18] but rather on
the Levitical choral service and the popular worship that accompanies
the burning of the sacrifice. The Chronicler's interest in ritual music and
the Levitical singers has, of course, long been recognized,[19] but most
study has concentrated on the historical development of these offices.[20]
Comparatively little attention has been paid to the theological understanding of worship reflected in this presentation. The subject has now
been examined closely by Kleinig (1993), whose findings I follow and
develop to some extent. It will be seen that in the choral service in
particular the cult has a forward-looking character, as it expresses praise
for Yahweh's universal kingship, petition for the covenant people, and

---

18. Kiuchi argues from Lev. 17.11 that all blood sacrifices had an expiatory
character. However, the Chronicler's emphasis is on the Levitical ministry of praise
and intercession that accompanied the sacrifices (cf. 1 Chron. 16.4-5), and not this
specifically priestly concern. The עלה represents, of course, a broader range of
meaning; cf. de Vaux (1964: 37): 'The holocaust is above all an act of homage,
expressed by a gift.' The Chronicler's own understanding of the עלה may be gauged
from references in his *Sondergut*. Apart from association with the choral service (see
below), these references indicate that the Mosaic Law is faithfully upheld (1 Chron.
16.40; 2 Chron. 2.4; 4.6; 13.11; 23.18; 24.14; 29.7; 31.2, 3) as a regular aspect of
worship (1 Chron. 29.21; 2 Chron. 29.31-32; 30.15; 35.12, 14, 16).

19. Mention of liturgical music is made in 1 Chron. 6.16-32 (E 31-47); 9.14-16,
33; 15.1-16, 43; 23.2-5, 25-32; 25.1-31; 2 Chron. 5.11-14; 7.1-6; 8.12-15; 20.18-
30; 23.12-13, 18; 29.25-30; 30.21-22; 31.2; 34.12-13; 35.15.

20. See Kleinig 1993: 15, and the bibliography cited there.

the assurance of deliverance from enemies. The Chronicler is therefore concerned to recount the institution and development of this rite, and to demonstrate in a number of instances its significance for his age.

1. *The Origin of the Choral Rite*

The Chronicler first describes the foundation of the service by David, on the occasion of the transferral of the ark to Jerusalem (1 Chron. 16.4). It was no doubt important for the writer to demonstrate divine sanction for this major innovation in the central rite of Israel's regular worship, the presentation of the burnt offerings. The Chronicler repeatedly stresses that the nation's cultic life should be properly authorized (1 Chron. 15.13; 22.13; 2 Chron. 8.13; 13.11; 30.16; 35.6, 12), and yet the choral rite is not stipulated in the Mosaic Law. At a later point, therefore, he remarks that the service was commanded by Yahweh through David and his prophets Gad and Nathan (2 Chron. 29.25). It therefore possessed the same authoritative status as the cultic requirements of the Pentateuch and should be accepted as such.

At the institution of the service the Asaphites are appointed 'to proclaim,[21] thank and praise Yahweh' as they minister before the ark (1 Chron. 16.4, 37). At the same time, David appoints the Hemanites and Jeduthunites to offer a service of sacred song (v. 7) to accompany the presentation of the burnt offerings on the Mosaic altar at Gibeon (vv. 39-42). The services in Jerusalem and Gibeon are synchronized (vv. 37, 40-41).

David next organizes the times (1 Chron. 23.30-31),[22] personnel and instruments (1 Chron. 25.1-6) for the choral rite in the future temple. Each detail of the rite is therefore shown to be properly authorized. The completion of the temple and the installation therein of the ark and the Solomonic altar of burnt offering are also marked by the union of the Gibeon and Jerusalem services, as 2 Chron. 5.12-13 indicate (cf. 1 Chron. 6.16-17 [E 31–32]). Thus the service of praise commanded by David is fully enacted by Solomon (2 Chron. 8.14). The interest

---

21. On the meaning and traditio-historical background of להזכיר, see Kleinig 1993: 35-37.

22. 1 Chron. 23.25-32 has been considered a secondary expansion (Williamson 1979a). On the other hand, the holy times mentioned for the choral service are identical with the information in 2 Chron. 2.3; 31.3 (cf. 2 Chron. 8.12), which is unique to Chronicles. On the tension between vv. 2-6a and vv. 28-31, Selman (1994a: 226) argues that the Chronicler is drawing a distinction between the Levites in general who led the nation in praise and the special group responsible for musical accompaniment.

in the choral rite is purely Chronistic, since none of these or later references (2 Chron. 23.18; 29.25-30. 31.2; 35.15; cf. 20.18-20) is paralleled in the *Vorlage*.

2. *The Theological Significance of the Choral Rite*

The Chronicler does not describe the choral service simply out of epideictic interest. Rather the rite is linked in his understanding with the meaning of sacrifice, the evocation of the divine glory, intercession and the proclamation of Yahweh's presence on his people's behalf.

First, the synchronization of the service with the daily offerings (1 Chron. 16.6, 37, 40-41; 2 Chron. 8.14; 23.18; 29.27; 31.2) indicates that the performance of sacred song was an integral part of the total sacrificial ritual. More specifically, the rite was co-ordinated with the presentation of the public burnt offerings in the presence of the congregation, whom it addressed with a summons to praise and thanksgiving (see below on 1 Chron. 16.8-36). It thus served as a stimulus to popular participation in worship (1 Chron. 16.36b; 2 Chron. 7.3, 6; 29.27-30). Like the temple, the rite was Davidic in origin and divinely authorized (1 Chron. 16.4; 2 Chron. 8.14; 29.25; 35.15). Further, it was understood in some sense to be 'prophecy' (1 Chron. 25.1-6).[23] Kleinig (1993: 155-56) takes this to mean the prophetic proclamation of Yahweh's name and benefits, his judgment on the gods of the nations and his salvation (cf. 1 Chron. 16.23-27).

Secondly, the Chronicler forges a link between Yahweh's appearing or advent in power and the performance of sacred song by the Levites. This is suggested first in the account of the temple dedicatory rituals (2 Chron. 5.2–7.10 = 1 Kgs. 8.1-66). A synoptic comparison of these accounts brings out this emphasis:

> 5.2-11a = 1 Kgs 8.1-10a, Solomon assembles the people to install the ark in the temple.
> 5.11b-13b (no par.), the Levites' musical service begins.
> 5.13c-14 = 1 Kgs 8.10b-11, the glory cloud fills the temple.
> 6.1–7.1a = 1 Kgs 8.11-54a, Solomon's dedicatory prayer (Rudolph 1955: 211).[24]
> 7.1b-3, 6 (no par.), theophany on altar and over temple; worship and singing before the altar.

---

23. See Kleinig 1993: 148-56 for a review of the interpretation of 1 Chron. 25.1-6.

24. See Chapter 9 on the Chronicler's different conclusion to this prayer.

1 Kgs 8.54b-61 (no par.), other prayers.
7.4-5, 7-10 = 1 Kgs 8.62-66, other ceremonies.

It appears that, whereas both Kings and Chronicles understand the installation of the ark to be the precondition of the appearance of the glory cloud, the Chronicler makes that event depend on an actual invocation through the choral rite (Rudolph 1955: 211).

A further description of the manifestation of the divine glory is given in 2 Chron. 7.1b-3. The relationship between this passage and 2 Chron. 5.13c-14 is disputed, principally because both accounts speak of Yahweh's glory 'filling' the temple.[25] However, we should not think of an additional act of divine 'filling' here. Verses 1b-2 are best taken as a disjunctive circumstantial description, indicating that the fire-theophany and the 'filling' of the temple occurred simultaneously (Williamson 1982: 222). The thought of Yahweh's glory is extended in v. 3 where (in an allusion to Lev. 9.23-24) it is stated additionally that Yahweh's glory appeared 'over the temple', in the sight of the Israelites. Their response is to prostrate themselves in worship, using the refrain of the choral rite (cf. 1 Chron. 16.34). It appears that in both cases, in the holy place and above the temple, the manifestation of Yahweh's glory has been evoked by the service of song. These foundational events give ritual significance to the performance of this service in the Chronicler's own day, declaring Yahweh's presence at the time of sacrifice to receive the praise and prayers of his people.[26]

Finally, we must consider the content of the sacred song as it is presented in 1 Chron. 16.8-36,[27] and its redemptive focus. Although this hymn is a composite derived from Psalms 105.1-15 (= vv. 8-22), 96.1-13 (= vv. 23-33) and 106.1, 47-48 (= vv. 34-36), it has been modified and formed into a unity through catchwords and the repetition of imperatives.[28]

In its original context the hymn celebrates the successful arrival of the ark, which denotes God's presence and power (2 Chron. 6.41) and anticipates the temple, where the ark will be kept. As such, the hymn is

25. Rudolph (1955) argued that the earlier reference to the glory cloud was secondary, while Welten (1979) takes that reference to be an 'anticipatory description' ('Vorwegnahme') of a single event.

26. Cf. Kleinig 1993: 168.

27. See Hill 1983: 99 for arguments that the Chronicler is responsible for the insertion of vv. 7-36.

28. See Hill 1983: 97-101 for details of the psalm's structure.

a fitting climax to this stage of the narrative. However, it may also be rightly seen as a vehicle for concerns affecting the Chronicler's own community. The different components are unified by the common theme of Israel's relationship to the surrounding nations. This remained a matter of urgent concern throughout the post-exilic period, when the loss of statehood had made the validity of the ancient promises of land and dynasty, and the identity of Israel itself, problematic. The Chronicler approached this question in a characteristic way, simultaneously affirming Yahweh's *particular* election of Israel, where his kingdom is concretized, and his *universal* kingship, which embraces both the nations and the cosmos. Together these principles become, in this hymn, a basis for worshipful response in the present and hopeful petition for a decisive deliverance from adverse circumstances (vv. 35-36).

The hymn is marked by a clear progression of thought in which first Israel (vv. 9-22), then the nations (vv. 23-30), and finally the cosmos (vv. 31-33) are summoned to praise Yahweh. Israel is admonished in vv. 15-22 to remember the promise to the patriarchs and the attendant divine protection. The modifications from the form of their *Vorlage* in the Psalms in vv. 15, 19 (זכרו ;בהיותכם)[29] are intended to contemporize the historical review, in effect identifying the post-exilic community with the patriarchs and so applying the Abrahamic covenant to them, especially the promise of land (v. 18). Verse 22 also assures protection for 'my anointed ones'. In its original context this is an exalted reference to the patriarchs, but in his *relecture* of this psalm material the Chronicler may have in mind the Davidic descendants, whose line has been protected through the vicissitudes of history.[30] Yahweh's universal kingship (v. 31) is next declared to the nations (vv. 23-34), whose gods are mere idols (v. 26). The nations are themselves summoned to acknowledge Yahweh, whose advent in judgment is declared (v. 33). The concluding portion of the hymn resumes its particularist focus, with a petition for Israel's deliverance and regathering to the land for Yahweh's praise (vv. 35-36). To underline this point, the Chronicler adds ישענו and והצילנו to v. 35. This hope awaits consummation in the

---

29. These details are obscured in the RSV and NIV, which wrongly correct Chronicles MT toward Psalms MT, and are partly clarified in the NRSV (v. 15).

30. משיח is found only here and in 2 Chron. 6.42, where it refers to kings (plural in MT; but contrast LXX and Ps. 132.10). The verb משׁח is used exclusively of kings in 1 Chron. 11.3; 14.8; 22.7; 2 Chron. 22.7; 23.11; but in 1 Chron. 29.22 it is used of Zadok as well as Solomon.

Chronicler's day and is mediated through worship. As Williamson comments (1982: 129), 'In the reality of worship, Israel's eschatological role in the world is upheld, but in the harsh actuality of life as a minor province of a vast empire, it is recognised that such a role can only be introduced by God's intervention.'

The idea of divine activity on Israel's behalf informs a later allusion to the choral rite in 2 Chron. 20.1-30. Here, Jehoshaphat summons the people to the temple in the face of an invasion by an eastern coalition. The Levite Jahaziel declares that Yahweh will fight on Israel's behalf (vv. 14-17), and in response to his words there is an outburst of popular worship and Levitical praise (vv. 18-19). The following day a choir is appointed at the vanguard of the army, and at the beginning of their song, Yahweh intervenes against Judah's enemies (vv. 21-22). I would suggest that this remarkable narrative is intended to give concrete expression to what is anticipated in 1 Chron. 16.8-36, the triumph of Israel's heavenly king and the vindication of his people. The following parallels in language and thought should be noted:

1. Yahweh is declared to be universal judge (1 Chron. 16.14, 33; 2 Chron. 20.12) and king (1 Chron. 16.31; 2 Chron. 20.6).
2. The promise to Abraham (1 Chron. 16.16; 2 Chron. 20.7) and the gift of the land (1 Chron. 16.18; 2 Chron. 20.7, 11) are affirmed as the basis of Israel's appeal for its help in its weakness before the nations (1 Chron. 16.19-20; 2 Chron. 20.12).
3. Yahweh is praised 'in holy array' (קדש בהדרת, 1 Chron. 16.29; 2 Chron. 20.21).

It may also be remarked that the refrain from the service (1 Chron. 16.34) is echoed in 2 Chron. 20.21[31] and that Yahweh's advent in power is evoked by singing (v. 22). The allusions to the choral rite in this narrative indicate that the Chronicler understood the performance of Israel's worship as a veritable means of defence, and that it was focused on the deliverance and gathering of the people for Yahweh's praise (1 Chron. 16.35; 2 Chron. 20.28).

3. *Conclusion*

The Chronicler's special interest in the cult centres not so much on atonement, which was the task of the Aaronides, as on the Levitical choral rite, which was authorized by David and formed part of a

---

31. Cf. its use in other allusions to the choral rite in 2 Chron. 5.13; 7.3.

complex of sacrifice, praise and petition that involved the whole assembly (קְהַל). The Chronicler emphasized the popular character of the cult, and there can be little doubt that he sought to make worshippers of the people through their participation in the rite (cf. 1 Chron. 16.35a, 36b; 2 Chron. 7.3b). Sacred song was understood as evoking Yahweh's protective presence and declaring his universal kingship, which was exercised on Israel's behalf. This dimension of the cult is anticipatory and forward-looking, and may be fairly seen as a vehicle for expressing the hope of redemption.

4. *Israel in Future Perspective*

This section argues that the Chronicler does not treat Israel as he knew it, viz. the land and people of the post-exilic community, as a completed entity but instead projects a larger ideal that awaits future realization. It will be seen that the Chronicler retains a particular interest in Israel's relationship to the world of nations and, contrary to Rudolph (1955: xxiv) and Plöger (1968: 39-40), cannot be said to be indifferent to the future destiny of the Gentiles.

My approach in this section depends in large measure on the nature and form of 1 Chronicles 1–9, the so-called 'genealogische Vorhalle' (Wellhausen). The widest diversity of views has been maintained on the historical accuracy, originality and significance of these materials. They have been seen variously as fictitious, a reflection of post-exilic settlement patterns, and the product of successive expansions.[32]

A number of considerations have moderated these judgments in recent years. First, careful source-critical work has uncovered various earlier materials, many of them pre-exilic and of a military nature, that have been combined with canonical sources. This is a particular emphasis in Johnson's study (1988: 62-68) and Williamson's commentary (1982: 45-92; cf. Williamson 1979b).

Secondly, there is a growing recognition that these chapters have a theological character, that their literary form has been shaped to give expression to the *Tendenzen* and characteristic interests of the Chronicler. This has long been evident, for example, in the significance accorded Judah in the extensive tables that head the genealogies of Israel (1 Chron. 2.3–4.23) and the interest in the Levites (1 Chron. 5.27–6.66

---

32. See Oeming 1990: ch. 2 for a survey of research in the nineteenth and twentieth centuries.

[E 6.1-81]), but more recent work has interpreted these chapters as in some sense programmatic or 'kerygmatic' (Oeming). This approach draws on the perceived structure of 1 Chronicles 1–9 and its coherence with the themes of the narrative. As I have noted to some extent already in Chapter 4, a number of literary features comes into play here, such as the use of chiasmus, word-play, historical notices, and the significance of breadth of detail, especially for Judah.[33]

A third factor in the reassessment of these chapters has been the perspectives on their literary form supplied by analogy with the ancient Near East and more contemporary comparative anthropological studies. Wilson's researches here (1975; 1977; 1979; 1984) have contributed towards clarifying some of the interpretational problems posed by these texts. Wilson notes that earlier study of Old Testament genealogies concentrated on their historical problems and used them as a resource for reconstructing early Israelite history. The rejection of the Old Testament chronology and the problems posed by parallel and contradictory genealogies led to scepticism over this approach, and in some cases the attempt to reconstruct a supposed 'original' form of the text, out of which the present assumed variant arose (see below on 1 Chron. 7.12). Wilson argues that this approach fails to consider the *function* of genealogies within ancient societies (1979: 19):

> In many cases the question of genealogical accuracy may not be a fruitful one because the genealogies involved express a perceived reality which is not open to outside observation. The genealogies express the way in which the writer *viewed* domestic, political or religious relationships.

Thus the relative status of individuals and tribes, their powers, prerogatives and rights, along with matters of ideological and theological concern, can all be mediated in the form of genealogies. Wilson further distinguishes two types of genealogy, segmented and linear. The former group is used to express kinship relationships and may justify claims to land or inheritance. Segmented genealogies may also function in the religious sphere, 'serv[ing] to define the boundaries of the religious community and indicate the persons who may legitimately participate in the lineage's religious life' (1984: 59). By contrast, linear genealogies have essentially only one function: 'They serve to support an individual's claim to status, power or property by linking the individual with an early ancestor' (1984: 60).

---

33. See especially the studies of Johnson, Kartveit and Oeming.

None of these approaches to 1 Chronicles 1–9 is exclusive, and the interpretation of these chapters is best served by combining the perspectives of source criticism, exegesis of their theological ideas, and sociology. The particular value of the more recent source and literary criticism is that it confirms that the Chronicler did not compose these chapters out of whole cloth. It says nothing, of course, about their historical value, but it suggests that they are (substantially, at least) a unitary composition depending on earlier materials. A special place in interpretation must be given to the structure and organization of these chapters, since it is here that the writer's hand and purpose may be most readily discerned.

1. *The Ideal of the Land*
Two related questions are considered here that are reflected in the genealogies and elsewhere in the narrative: the place of Israel in the world, and the theological understanding of the land.

(i) *The place of Israel in the world.* It is initially surprising that a work which concentrates so intensively on Israel should begin by enumerating the nations of the world (1 Chron. 1.5-23) according to the traditional pattern in Gen. 10.2-31.[34] However, while the Chronicler retains the order of his *Vorlage,* he abbreviates it considerably, so giving it a different function. Willi (1991: 23) observes that Genesis 10 depicts a historical *development* in the pre-Israelite world that leads to Israel, whereas the interest in 1 Chron. 1.5-23 is geographical rather than historical. The Chronicler depicts a *condition,* 'the total intertwining of the nations', stressing the essential unity of humanity and describing the *co-Israelite world* of the nations in which Israel has its place.

This diverse yet essentially unitary depiction of humanity is the presupposition for the Chronicler's portrayal of Israel. The significance of this opening description should not be overlooked. Here, post-exilic Israel, a small, stateless community within the Achaemenid empire, sets forth a picture of its place within humanity. Israel is at once implicated with the rest of humanity, with which it shares a common origin, and yet at the same time it possesses a heightened self-consciousness. First, a linear genealogy connects Israel (v. 34) with Adam (v. 1), suggesting

---

34. Oeming (1990: 75-78) surveys the textual and versional problems and rejects the earlier view that this passage is secondary (Benzinger, Galling, Rudolph). Willi (1991) supports Oeming's conclusion.

that Israel is the goal of God's purposes from creation. The geographical details support this interpretation.[35] The nations are enumerated in a counter-clockwise direction from the perspective of Judah or Jerusalem: vv. 5-7 list the Japhetites, to the north and west; vv. 8-16, the Hamites, mainly to the south and southwest; and vv. 17-23, the Shemites, to the east and southeast.

The same pattern is followed in enumerating the southern neighbours of Israel. Taking up in vv. 24-27 a linear genealogy of the Shemites which culminates in Abraham, the Chronicler describes a semi-circle from west to east from the perspective of Jerusalem: the Ishmaelites of northern Sinai (vv. 29-31), the Keturites in the southeast (vv. 32-33), and the descendants of Esau and the Edomites further to the east (vv. 35-42). Kartveit comments on the significance of this presentation (1989: 116):

> 1 Chronicles 1 is not only genealogy but also a *mappa mundi*, perhaps even the expression of an *imago mundi*, in which Israel lies in the middle. It is the only place in the OT where the genealogies of the primal history are connected with the table of nations and the particulars of the southern neighbouring nations, and from this a unique conception arises. Admittedly there is no word of a *tabbur ha'araes* here. However, is the chapter not dominated by the idea that Israel is the people in the midst of the peoples and in a land in the midst of the lands?[36]

More specifically, Oeming argues that the opening chapter is intended to express the idea of Israel's election (1990: 91); further, he holds that the distinction here between Israel and the world is continued in the geographical arrangement of 1 Chronicles 2–9, which follows the order 'world–Israel–Jerusalem–temple', and may be represented by a series of concentric circles (p. 210):

---

35. The order of 1 Chron. 1.5-23 is derived from Gen. 10, but the same pattern is found in vv. 24-27 (see below), and so is probably part of the Chronicler's intended picture.

36. '[1 Chronicles 1] ist nicht nur Genealogie, sondern auch eine *mappa mundi*, vielleicht sogar ein Ausdruck einer *imago mundi,* wo Israel in der Mitte liegt. Es ist die einzige Stelle des ATs, wo die Genealogien der Urgeschichte mit der Völkertafel und den Angaben zu den südlichen Nachbarvölkern verbunden werden, und dadurch entsteht eine einzigartige Konzeption. Hier ist zwar kein *Wort* von einer *tabbur ha'araes*. Ist aber das Kapitel nicht von der Vorstellung beherrscht, daß Israel das Volk inmitten der Völker ist und in einem Land inmitten der Länder wohnt?'

The world of nations forms the first, external circle, with Israel as the centre; the tribes of Israel form the second centre, in which Judah, Benjamin and Levi form definite 'centres of gravity', with Levi in the middle; the third circle is Jerusalem with its inhabitants, in which the temple, the dwelling of Yahweh and his personnel, stands in the centre.[37]

Oeming thus sees the whole geographical arrangement marked by 'a well-thought out model of concentric holiness'.[38] The sacral character of the land, as this is reflected in 1 Chronicles 2–9, is considered below. It appears, in any case, that the opening chapter sets the land and people of Israel as the centre of the world of nations and the focus of the divine purpose. This is, of course, in sharp contrast to how the political realities of the day must have appeared to the Chronicler's community. The writer's response is to affirm that Israel stands in distinction to its neighbours, 'the kingdoms of the countries' (1 Chron. 29.30; 2 Chron. 12.8; 17.10; 20.29), and yet both are of the same origin and subject to Yahweh's lordship (2 Chron. 20.6). The implication of the opening chapter is that Israel may take confidence from its election and continuing divine protection.

(ii) *The land in theological perspective and expectation.* The land is intrinsic to the Chronicler's concept of Israel and the subject of continuing theological interest. Willi (1991: 54-55) observes that the opening chapters portray Israel as 'the people of its land', characterized both by patriarchal descent and connection with particular tribal territories. The genealogies of the tribes in 1 Chronicles 2–8, though in some cases very fragmentary, are intended to give expression to the social and geographical aspects of Israel's identity. The conclusion to these chapters is found in 1 Chron. 9.1a: 'And all Israel was listed in the genealogies in the book of the kings of Israel'. This statement summarizes the

---

37. 'Den ersten, äußeren Kreis bildet die Völkerwelt mit dem Zentrum Israel; den zweiten Kreis bilden die Stämme Israels mit den eindeutigen Schwerpünkten Juda, Levi, Benjamin, wobei Levi in der Mitte steht; der dritte Kreis ist Jerusalem mit seinen Bewohnern, wobei im Zentrum der Tempel, die Wohnung Jahwes, und sein Personal steht.'

38. '...ein wohldurchdachtes Modell konzentrischer Heiligkeit.' This is, of course, an inference drawn from the order of the material, but it may be correct. The notion of degrees of holiness in Erez Israel is clearly expressed in the later biblical and post-biblical literature: note the description of Judah in Zech. 2.16 (E 12) as the 'holy land' and the sacral division of the land in Ezek. 45, 47–48; cf. also *m. Kelim*; *m. Tanhuma Kedoshim*; *1 En.* 36.1-2; *Jub.* 8.12, 19; *b. Yom.* 54b.

significance of these chapters as an inclusive description of Israel in its totality. It affirms that the tribes and lands enumerated there, often through the use of eponyms and accounts of settlements, are part of Israel.

The meaning of this affirmation must be set against the fact that the territories for the most part were no longer Israelite and some of the tribes were extinct. Although these chapters are modelled mainly on pre-exilic records, the Chronicler's concern is not so much historical as the expression of an ideal. Johnson (1988: 47-57) finds in these tribal and territorial data a projection of the Davidic kingdom, when Israel was united and at its greatest extent. More recent writers argue that the geographical notes in the genealogies are an implicit claim to the Israelite status of these lands, upon which the writer focuses his expectations. Thus Oeming (1990: 209-10) concludes that this data is programmatic: the genealogical section '(outlines) an Erez Israel which is modelled in the past and is still expected for the future',[39] while Kartveit (1989: 166-67), rather more tentatively, suggests that the details of settlements and tribal boundaries are theologically coloured and intended to awaken hopes of the restoration of lost lands.

If the Chronicler's intention has been rightly discerned here, a parallel may be proposed with Neh. 11.25-35, a list of settlements which could in no way be considered a part of the Jewish province in the Persian period. Stern (1982: 85) argues that the list was added 'not as a realistic rendering of the *status quo* but as a utopian ideal of the area where the returned exiles *should* settle', in the historical territory belonging to Judah.[40] Of course, the Chronicler gives no explicit statement of his purpose in including these geographical details, but it is unlikely to have been simply historical. It is probable that the Chronicler is affirming here that the land, no less than the people (see below), is the subject of a continuing promise, and he expresses here and more openly elsewhere the hope that this promise may yet be fulfilled.

Confirmation of this suggestion is found in the way in which the Chronicler understands the bond to have been established between the land and the descendants of Jacob/Israel. *Contra* Japhet (1979; 1989:

---

39. 'Die "Vorhalle" (umreißt) ein Erez Israel, das in der Vergangenheit vorgebildet ist und für die Zukunft zu erwarten steht.'

40. Williamson (1985: 350) broadly supports this interpretation but also notes other possibilities (e.g. that it may be an interpolation reflecting Maccabean conditions).

363-93), the Chronicler *does* depict Israel's occupation of the land as the fulfilment of promise and a historical act, but in a way that differs significantly from the Pentateuch and Deuteronomistic History. References from the *Vorlage* to the patriarchal promise of land are reproduced in 2 Chron. 6.25, 31; 7.20; 33.8. It is also clear that the writer does not deny the exodus and conquest traditions (cf. 1 Chron. 17.5, 21; 2 Chron. 5.10; 6.25; 7.22). Instead he subsumes them, and more particularly the tradition relating to the Abrahamic covenant, as a stage toward the fulfilment that took place in the Davidic–Solomonic kingdom (cf. Johnson 1988: 74-75). Once more, then, the Chronicler's outlook is determined by the central place of the Davidic covenant in his theology.

The writer makes this point through typological allusion and direct statement. In 1 Chron. 21.22-25 David's purchase of the temple site is patterned after Abraham's purchase of the cave of Machpelah in Genesis 23, as the expression בכסף מלא and other allusions indicate (Williamson 1982: 149). David thus acts as the patriarch in acquiring this site, in fulfilment of the divine promise. A further allusion to Abraham is found in 2 Chron. 3.1, which identifies the temple site with Mount Moriah (cf. Gen. 22.2, 14). In the Chronicler's view the Abrahamic covenant promising the land to Israel for ever (1 Chron. 16.15-18) finds its fulfilment, just as the Sinaitic covenant does, in the temple established through David and Solomon. We find the same conjunction of ideas in Jehoshaphat's prayer for help against those who would dispossess Israel of the promised land (2 Chron. 20.7-8; cf. v. 11):

> Surely you, our God, drove out the inhabitants of this land before your people Israel, and gave it for ever to the descendants of Abraham your friend. And they have dwelt in it, and built in it for you a sanctuary for your name...

The connection between obedience and possession of the land is also made in David's charge to the leaders of Israel at the time of Solomon's accession (1 Chron. 28.8): 'Observe and seek all the commandments of Yahweh your God so that you may possess this good land and leave it as an inheritance for your sons after you for ever.' Japhet understands these words as contemporizing the original tradition into a challenge that is presented afresh to each generation.[41]

---

41. Japhet 1993: 491. In a similar way, in a slight addition to the *Vorlage*, Solomon prays for exiles that God would 'bring them again to the land which you gave *to them* and to their fathers' (2 Chron. 6.25). The Chronicler's generation would recognize that they too had been 'given' the land.

This is in fact what we should expect in a work that presupposes the resettlement of the exiles in their old possessions (1 Chron. 9.2). The Chronicler is not so much concerned, as the Deuteronomist was, with accounting for the exile and loss of land, as he is with stressing the fact of the resumption of Yahweh's saving activity towards Israel, and what the people's appropriate response should be. The land which is intrinsic to Israel's identity may also share in this restoration. Significantly, the land occupies a central place in the oracle to Solomon (2 Chron. 7.14), where Yahweh confirms the establishment of the Davidic covenant, and in the conclusion to the work (2 Chron. 36.21). In this way the writer indicates that the divine promises relating to the land, ratified fully in the time of David and Solomon, retain their validity and await their fulfilment. There is no suggestion that the concept of Israel has been reduced simply to a cultic community. We find instead a heightened theological (priestly?) interest in the land, which may be 'healed' (2 Chron. 7.14), 'purified' like the temple (2 Chron. 34.3, 8), and 'enjoy its sabbaths' (2 Chron. 36.21; cf. Lev. 26.43). In short, in a more positive way than his predecessors (compare the laments over the state of the land in Neh. 9.36-37 and Ezra 9.7-8), the Chronicler indicates how Israel may continue to possess its inheritance, through careful attention to the Law, and he holds out the possibility of a more extensive fulfilment.

2. *The Ideal of the Community*

The Chronicler's understanding of Israel has received renewed attention of late, from which it appears that he defined the community in somewhat different terms from Ezra–Nehemiah.[42] This reappraisal of the Chronicler's view centres largely on his attitude toward the north. As was noted in Chapter 1, Japhet (1989: 278-309) argues that Chronicles depicts Israel throughout as a functioning tribal unity, while Williamson (1977a) has examined the book's use of יׂשראל and its narrative structure. He concludes that in the Chronicler's view the northern tribes, though in rebellion, did not forfeit their status as descendants of Israel. The work contains an appeal to them to return to the legitimate institutions, while redressing exclusivist tendencies in the Jerusalem community (1977a: 140).

---

42. Cf. Japhet 1989: 267-334; Braun 1979; 1986: xxxv-xxxvii; Williamson 1977a; see Chapter 1 above, but contrast Pohlmann 1991. Oeming represents a partly dissenting view, attributing some features of 1 Chron. 2–9 to a presumed anti-Samaritan *Tendenz*.

In expressing such a conciliatory purpose, Chronicles also indicates that the future of the people is as yet open and awaits a greater fulfilment. The post-exilic community is far from being gathered, yet the restoration has begun. The reality of this beginning is signalled by the statement in 1 Chron. 9.3 that the new Jerusalemites included 'those from Judah, Benjamin, Ephraim and Manasseh'. Significantly, in the parallel to this text in Neh. 11.4 there is no mention of Ephraim and Manasseh. Williamson sees in Chronicles an appeal to set about regathering all who have a legitimate claim to participate in Israel's life, finding this particularly in the portrayal of Hezekiah in 2 Chronicles 29–30 (1977a: 119-31). Hezekiah's appeal to the north affirms that the repentance of those remaining in the land (in the sense of submitting to the authority of the Jerusalem temple) will lead to the return of exiles (2 Chron. 30.6-9). This speech reflects a concern of the post-exilic period to see the growing diaspora returned to the land (cf. Zech. 8.20-23; Isa. 56.8; 66.20).

The Chronicler's position may be defined, then, as the hope that Israel will once more be an integrated people in the land. Just as with his treatment of the land, there is no suggestion that his own community in Jerusalem and Yehud represented the totality of Israel. However, the writer is equally concerned with the spiritual dimensions of 'return'. In 1 Chronicles 2–9 he combines pre-exilic and more contemporary records to set out an ideal presentation of Israel. While there is no full agreement on the significance of the arrangement of these chapters,[43] it is generally accepted that they affirm the primacy of Judah, and the central place of the Davidic line (1 Chron. 3) and the temple with its Levitical institutions (cf. 1 Chron. 6). The two 'houses' of the theocracy remain, then, as constitutive of the community.

More recent writers have attempted to refine our understanding of the significance of some of the details relating to the tribes in these chapters. Johnstone (1986: 130-31) argues that the omission of Dan (cf. 1 Chron. 6.46, 54 [E 61, 69]; 7.12)[44] is intentional because this tribe

---

43. Cf. Williamson 1982: 46-47; Japhet 1989: 352-55; Willi 1991. The inclusion of an additional Benjaminite genealogy (1 Chron. 8.1-40; cf. 1 Chron. 7.6-12) has proved problematic to interpreters and is variously explained: cf. Williamson 1982; Oeming 1990; Johnstone 1986; Walters 1991.

44. On the original form of 1 Chron. 7.12, and whether it once contained a reference to Dan, see Oeming 1990: 163-64 who reviews the range of proposed reconstructions and concludes: 'Dan und Sebulon fehlen jedenfalls ganz und nur ein

signified apostasy and schism in the earlier traditions (cf. Judg. 17–19). Kartveit (1989: 166-67) hints at a similar motive, but does not develop the point. According to Johnstone, the genealogies should be seen as an ideal of Israel, purged of its idolatry and with the Levites dispersed throughout the tribes to sanctify its life. Oeming offers the most thoroughgoing interpretation of these tables. He believes they are intended to indicate who belongs to 'the true Israel' ('das wahre Israel') and finds a polemical motive in the paucity of information (genealogical and geographical) given about the northern tribes, as if to say that their attachment to Israel is tenuous (1990: 166). However, he grants that these chapters affirm the Israelite status of the north, and he interprets them as an invitation to recognize the primacy of Judah and Jerusalem (1990: 217-18).

Final certainty about some of these points is probably impossible. Nevertheless, as most writers recognize, it is likely that 1 Chronicles 2–9 are in some sense an ideal or programmatic presentation of the community. By gathering together past and present the Chronicler portrays an inclusive picture of 'all Israel', organized around the central institutions of the theocracy. This may be understood as an indication of what Israel may yet become, and it corresponds to the message of the narrative.

To conclude, the Chronicler depicts the concept of Israel as a covenantal bond of land and people, which was at its most extensive and united in the time of David and Solomon (cf. 1 Chron. 11.1-3; 13.5; 28.1; 2 Chron. 1.2). The status of the people as Yahweh's possession and the object of his love is affirmed in the Davidic covenant (1 Chron. 17.9; 2 Chron. 7.14, 'my people who are called by my name'), and the Chronicler is concerned to stress through a number of direct and indirect means that these promises remain valid and capable of increasing fulfilment through obedience to the demands of the covenant.

Vorurteil über die angeblich zu fordernde Struktur der Vorhalle hat zu den zahlreichen Hypthesen [sic] geführt, ihre Stammbäume an verschiedenen anderen Stellen entdecken zu wollen.' There is, however, a reference to Levitical cities in Zebulon in 1 Chron. 6.48 [E 63], whereas mention of Dan has probably been suppressed in vv. 46, 54 [E 61, 69].

5. *Summary and Conclusion*

This chapter has addressed the question of eschatology in Chronicles by connecting it with the writer's central theological ideas and tracing its expression in a number of significant themes. It was seen first that the Davidic covenant is not a marginal concern (*contra* Japhet) but is in fact foundational to the Chronicler's conception of Israel. Through these promises Israel is constituted as the earthly form of Yahweh's kingdom (1 Chron. 17.14; 28.5; 2 Chron. 9.8; 13.8). The covenant and kingdom have a twofold expression in the Davidic line and the temple. The dynastic promise to David was fulfilled by Solomon's obedience, and the preservation of that line down into the writer's time, despite the disobedience of most of its members, is shown to be due to God's irrevocable promise. The Davidic line is not provisional or solely cultic in its purpose (*contra* Caquot and Riley). Thus Yahweh's kingdom in the personal form of the Davidic family continues to be the focus of the community's hopes, but the Chronicler does not specify more exactly in what sense this is so. The temple also testifies to the covenant, and the two 'houses' of the theocracy are shown to be mutually related.

Secondly, the Chronicler's primary interest in the cult was seen to centre on the Levitical choral service established by David. Here the worship of Israel becomes the vehicle for expressing the hope and assurance of deliverance from enemies. The choral service (as it is interpreted in 1 Chron. 16.8-36) proclaims Yahweh's universal kingship and his choice of Israel, and invokes his presence and protection. The cult reflects not a satisfaction with the status quo (*contra* Plöger and Hanson) but a longing for and hopeful expectation of salvation (cf. 1 Chron. 16.35) which embraces land, people and Davidic line.

Thirdly, the Chronicler holds out an ideal of Israel in its land and population which is inclusive and seems to reflect the conditions of the Davidic–Solomonic kingdom. The picture may be programmatic in its intent (note the leading place of Judah and the centrality of the Levites in 1 Chron. 2–8), and it confirms that the earlier promises relating to the land and the people contained in the Abrahamic and Sinaitic covenants have found their confirmation and continuing validity in the covenant with David.[45]

---

45. For a contrasting discussion of how the land and people are related in the Davidic covenant, see Riley 1993: 230-35 (although I cannot agree with his 'democratizing' interpretation of 2 Chron. 6.42).

Chapter 8

SUBSIDIARY THEMES AND MOTIFS IN
THE CHRONICLER'S PRESENTATION

1. *Introduction*

The major themes that constitute Israel as the 'kingdom of Yahweh' in
the Chronicler's conception (that is, the Davidic covenant, reflected in
the dynasty and temple cult, and Israel as a bond of land and people)
were examined in the previous chapter for evidence of their futurist perspective. While the outlook reflected in this presentation was not found
to be evidently 'messianic' or 'eschatological' in a historically consummatory sense, it was concluded that the Chronicler's expectation
exceeded the post-exilic status quo in a number of ways:

1. the writer affirmed a continuing significance for the Davidic
    covenant in its personal focus;
2. he looked for a regathering in the land of the covenant people
    (understood in the widest traditional sense of the twelve tribes)
    with the temple as their cultic centre; and
3. in his special emphasis on cultic song the Chronicler anticipated
    the acknowledgment of Yahweh's universal lordship by the
    nations.

This viewpoint is not always *explicitly* expressed, but is inferred in
part from the structure and content of the genealogies and the literary
patterns discerned in the narrative.[1] The expression of such a hope is in
any case necessarily indirect, given the historiographical form of the
work. However, if we have correctly discerned the contours of the
Chronicler's outlook in these larger, more general themes, we should

1.   On the significance of literary structure for interpretation, see especially
Williamson 1977a: 119-30; Williamson 1979a; Begg 1987b; De Vries 1987; Oeming
1990.

expect to see this reflected in the more specific subsidiary themes and motifs that belong either to the work's *Sondergut* or to its redaction of traditional materials. Five features in particular stand out for comment:

1. the significance of the paraenetic style of the work (reflected especially in the Chronistic addresses) and the concluding notice (2 Chron. 36.22-23);
2. the Chronicler's special presentation of war and peace;
3. his portrayal of the relationship between king and high priest;
4. the attitude in Chronicles toward foreign alliances; and
5. the Chronistic expression 'kingdom of Yahweh' or its equivalent.

This chapter seeks to determine whether the conclusions of the previous chapters can be corroborated by examining these subsidiary Chronistic motifs for the light they cast on the writer's eschatological outlook, as well as his retributive theology.

2. *Paraenesis in the Speeches: Motifs of Appeal and Consultation; the Function of the Concluding Notice*

The homiletic style of Chronicles has long been recognized. Already Keil (1966 [1872]: 39) commented on the 'hortatory-sermonic' character of the narrative, and numerous writers continue to approach the work from a paraenetic or kerygmatic angle.[2] Much of this effect is derived from the numerous Chronistic addresses, which are ascribed to various royal, prophetic or priestly figures, but have for the most part uniform thematic concerns and style.[3] The form-critical implications of this fact were examined in von Rad's study of the 'Levitical sermon' (1934; ET 1966: 267-80). It is doubtful whether so precise a *Gattung* as von Rad suggested actually existed, or whether 'sermon' is an adequate description for such a diverse range of speeches.[4] Nevertheless, as von Rad recognized, the addresses have a number of features in common: they appeal to an agreed 'scriptural' authority (usually through an allusion to the writing prophets); they enunciate some theological teaching about God; and they call for a response.

The predominant themes of the speeches are: the Davidic covenant,

2. Cf. Williamson 1982; Begg 1982.
3. See the summaries in Throntveit 1987: 127-28 and Mason 1990: 137-44.
4. Cf. Matthias 1984; Mason 1990: 133-37.

which is central to the Chronicler's understanding of election; the presence and help of God, which are available to king and people; conversely, God's judgment on disobedience; and the summons to an appropriate response of faith with the promise of reward. David's charge to Solomon and the leaders (1 Chron. 22.6-19; 28.2-10), Abijah's warning to Jeroboam (2 Chron. 13.4-12), and Hezekiah's summons to the Levites (2 Chron. 29.5-11) exemplify this stock of ideas. The hortatory note is sounded repeatedly in the imperatival summons to 'seek' Yahweh and his commandments, to be active in cultic obedience (cf. 1 Chron. 22.19; 28.8, 20; 2 Chron. 29.11, 31; 30.6-8; 35.3-6), and to trust in Yahweh and his prophets (2 Chron. 20.20; 32.7). To judge from their grammar and language, the speeches are evidently the Chronicler's own compositions, and although they are narratologically set in the past, their primary concern appears to be with the present: no less than the Chronistic prayers and prophecies, these speeches convey the author's theological concerns and effectively address the post-exilic cultic community as the successor of the pre-exilic kingdom. They seek to elicit from the קהל a similar expectant faith, diligent support for the cult and active performance of the cultic duties prescribed by the Law. This paraenetic use of the speeches has an analogy with the way in which the historical material of 2 Chronicles 10–36 has been arranged homiletically as paradigms of faith and apostasy.

Closely related to this motif of summons is what Japhet (1989: 417-27) calls 'the "democratizing" trend in Chronicles'. This is more accurately a motif of consultation and collaboration in questions affecting national and cultic life. Over against Samuel–Kings, the Chronicler represents the monarch as seeking popular advice and consent before such undertakings (cf. 1 Chron. 13.1-4; 2 Chron. 1.2; 20.21; 30.2; 32.3), often in speeches laden with cohortatives and appeals which seek to encourage such participation (cf. 1 Chron. 13.3; 29.5; 2 Chron. 14.6 [E 7]), with the leaders, people and Levites duly responding.[5] This transformation of the *Vorlage* may reflect the writer's ideal of leadership and community life for the post-exilic period.

In connection with this emphasis, we should note the significance of the conclusion, Cyrus's edict permitting the rebuilding of the temple and

5.   Contrast 2 Sam. 6.12 with 1 Chron. 15.25, where the Chronicler shows the participation of all Israel in fetching the ark; cf. also the involvement of the people or קהל in 1 Chron. 11.4 (contrast 2 Sam. 5.6); 2 Chron. 23.8, 10 (contrast 2 Kgs 11.9, 11); 29.20, 23.

inviting the exiles to return to Jerusalem (2 Chron. 36.22-23). The view that these words are an original part of the Chronicler's work was defended in the introductory chapter. The precise significance of this conclusion is disputed, but it is clear that these words are not cited simply to give Chronicles a positive ending (the announcement of the end of exile in 2 Chron. 36.20-21 would be positive enough in itself). Neither are they intended to indicate where the narrative is continued, according to the older view that reads Ezra–Nehemiah as the narrative continuation of Chronicles.[6] The Chronicler wishes to emphasize that the conditions for achieving a fuller measure of restoration now exist. Significantly, the concluding word of the book is the jussive ויעל, 'and let him go up', an invitation that evokes the sense both of return to the land and cultic participation. Again, this functions as an appeal to the Chronicler's own community, which stands typologically in the same situation as the original returnees (cf. 1 Chron. 9.2-3).[7] By concluding his work with this (modified) citation the Chronicler indicates that the history of his community is not 'realized' or complete but rather is on

6. In the view which I develop in the following chapter, Chronicles does not so much look *forward* to Ezra–Nehemiah as hold that work (theologically, at least) *in retrospect*: the concluding verses resume the message of Ezra–Nehemiah (where they serve as introduction) and place the event of the return in a different, more positive light. The Chronicler may also have slightly re-interpreted his *Vorlage*. Ezra 1.3b makes Cyrus's edict the expression of a wish or permission: יהי אלהיו עמו ויעל; whereas the MT of 2 Chron. 36.23b reads: יהוה אלהיו עמו ויעל. The reading יהוה may, of course, represent the Chronicler's own rewording, in the same way that v. 22 (= Ezra 1.1), בפי ירמיהו, has been assimilated to the form of v. 21. However, the majority Greek text of Chronicles reads ἔσται instead of κυρίος in v. 23b (Allen 1974: 121), suggesting that the original text of Chronicles read יהיה (which is reflected in the final ה of יהוה in Chronicles MT). If this emendation is correct, the indicative verbal form 'is/will be' represents a recasting of the optative יהי into an emphatic statement assuring the returnees of God's presence with them; cf. the reformulation of the dynastic petition of 2 Sam. 7.29, 'Now be pleased to bless the house of your servant, so that it may continue forever before you', into the greater definiteness of 1 Chron. 17.27, 'Now you have been pleased to bless the house of your servant, so that it may continue forever before you'. However, even without emendation 2 Chron. 36.23b could bear an indicative meaning as a nominal clause + *wayyqtl* verb (cf. Waltke and O'Connor 1990: 560).

7. Cf. (with some exaggeration) Johnstone (1986: 115) on 1 Chron. 9.2-17: 'The Chronicler is not now interested in the historian's discriminations of time and epoch; rather, his purpose is to gather together in a global manner the fulness of Israel past and present in timeless contemporaneity.'

the threshold of a new period, awaiting fulfilment. The significance of this conclusion is well expressed by Walters (1991: 68):

> [ויעל] is a word which, in the Chronicler's typological understanding, opens expansively towards the future in many ways: ויעל intimates the great pilgrim festivals at which devout Israelites go up to Jerusalem; it expresses the wistful longing of God's people in diaspora for Jerusalem; it asserts in every age the divine presence with God's people, and calls for them to participate in 'building the LORD's house'. Above all, it links God's gift of hope for the future with divine worship, and with human participation in it.

As in the above examples of paraenesis, then, the conclusion of the work is really an invitation, grounded in Yahweh's redemptive activity, to which the community is exhorted to respond in the appropriate faithful way.

3. *The Presentation of War and Peace in Chronicles*

The importance of this subject to the Chronicler is evident from the large proportion of the work devoted to it. Chronicles describes or mentions some forty military engagements, of which nineteen have no parallel in the *Vorlage*.[8] The writer's *Sondergut* also contains many sections that detail army organization or installations. Whatever historical basis these sections may have,[9] these portions are intended as tangible signs of Yahweh's blessing on obedient kings. There is also a special Chronistic interest in peace, which must be considered alongside the presentation of war.

1. *War as Retribution*
Most of the Chronicler's references to war have an obvious function within his schema of reward and punishment. Whether he is dealing with

---

8. See Weinberg 1985 (esp. pp. 122-23) for a summary of the data relating to war and military themes in Chronicles. Weinberg's statistically based study is very thorough, but it is overly lexical rather than contextual-semantic in its approach and its conclusions about the Chronicler's outlook are doubtful. It depends on over-schematic anthropological perspectives (as well as a confessedly Marxist-materialist view of history) and seems too rigid in its categories. Weinberg argues that the Chronicler 'demythologizes' and 'desacralizes' war from a supposed general conception of war in the ancient Near East and sees it primarily as a social phenomenon, but he ignores the writer's theological treatment of war and his evident interest in miracle (see below on 'Yahweh war').

9. Cf. Chapter 5 above for a discussion of this question.

his own material or parallel accounts, the author loses no opportunity to insert comments or details which explain a defeat as punishment for apostasy or lack of faith (e.g. 2 Chron. 12.1b, 2b, 5; 21.10b; 21.16-17; 24.23-24; 28.5). The final judgment, of course, comes in the form of a decisive conquest and destruction (2 Chron. 36.17-20).

Conversely, as Williamson (1981: 166-67) notes, the king who 'seeks Yahweh' or 'does what is right in his eyes' receives divine 'help' (עזר√) in his military endeavours.[10] The root עזר is also found with reference to the victory of the Transjordanian tribes in 1 Chron. 5.20; in 1 Chron. 12.19 to denote the growing military support for David leading to his coronation; in 2 Chron. 18.31 to signify Jehoshaphat's rescue from battle, following prayer; in 2 Chron. 26.7, 15, God's military assistance for Uzziah; and in 2 Chron. 32.8, Hezekiah's exhortation of the people, in the face of Sennacherib's threat. By contrast, to seek the help of others or to help the ungodly will lead to disaster (cf. 2 Chron. 19.2; 28.16, 23 [2×]). All these uses are peculiar to the Chronicler, featuring either in his *Sondergut* or as editorial additions to Kings.

Chronicles thus witnesses to a heightened theological understanding of war: *contra* Weinberg (1985), the writer has no concept of a 'profane' war, but invariably sees Yahweh as involved in the conflicts of Judah and Israel, punishing unfaithfulness and rewarding faith. This point is amplified in the following section and in the later discussion of alliances.

2. *'Yahweh War' in Chronicles*

The Chronicler's re-use of the 'Yahweh war' motif is a distinctive feature of his presentation, with important implications for delineating his eschatological outlook. It is important first to distinguish the different examples. Some accounts which bear features of the old conception of the divine warrior assisting Israel are basically reproduced from the *Vorlage* and may contribute little to a specifically Chronistic understanding (e.g. 1 Chron. 14.8-16 = 2 Sam. 5.17-25; 1 Chron. 18.1-13 = 2 Sam. 8.1-14; cf. the reference to the oracle and the ascription of victory to Yahweh in 1 Chron. 14.10, 14-15; 18.6, 13). However, the addition of the formula

ויהוה נתן את פחדו על כל הגוים

---

10. Asa, 2 Chron. 14.10 [E 11; 2×]; Amaziah, 25.2, 8, 11-12; Uzziah, 26.4, 6-7; Jotham, 27.2, 5, 7.

in 1 Chron. 14.17 to the report of David's initial victories over the Philistines (vv. 8-16) does accentuate the link between this passage and the 'Yahweh war' tradition. The parallels to this expression in Chronicles (2 Chron. 14.13 [E 14]; 17.10; 20.29) suggest that the reference here is to the fear of Yahweh rather than David. The formula is used only of kings favourably assessed (David, Asa, Jehoshaphat) and refers to an incapacitating terror placed on Israel's enemies by Yahweh, which deters them from attack. Such a fear arises either through Yahweh's intervention in war on Judah's behalf or, significantly, through the Levitical instruction of the people in Torah (2 Chron. 17.10).[11]

This last measure would have had a particular significance for the Chronicler's generation. Although subject to foreign control, it enjoyed the free exercise of its religious life within the Achaemenid polity.[12] It is understandable that the cult should become an avenue for expressing the aspirations of the community. Thus the popular teaching mission of the Levites (cf. Neh. 8.7-15) is presented as a means of obtaining the peace and security of the land in the face of hostile neighbours. The 'law of Yahweh' (2 Chron. 17.9; 19.8) which governs the community's life is a concrete expression of the theocracy. As it is disseminated, a divine fear restrains Judah's enemies. This presentation is in keeping with the other aspects of the Chronicler's religiously focused activism.

Complementing this emphasis on Torah, the writer also depicts aspects of the cult in overtones of spiritualized warfare. The most extreme development of this tendency is found in 2 Chron. 20.1-30 (discussed further below), the account of Jehoshaphat's prayer and Judah's deliverance from the invading coalition. The pericope is framed by a temple setting. In vv. 4-5 Judah and the king assemble there for urgent intercession, which is duly answered with a *Heilsorakel* from the Levite Jahaziel (vv. 14-17). The Levitical choir which heads the force on the following day invokes Yahweh by his song (v. 21; cf. 1 Chron. 16.7-8; 2 Chron. 5.13; 29.27), so leading to the defeat of the invading coalition by the agency of 'ambushers' (מארבים). Japhet (1993: 798) holds that this expression denotes human agents (cf. Judg. 9.25), but more probably supernatural beings are intended (cf. Williamson 1982: 300).

---

11. De Vries (1989: 310) links 17.10 with vv. 11-19 as a statement of Jehoshaphat's military might, but it seems better to follow Gabriel (1990: 134) in connecting it with the teaching mission in vv. 7-9; cf. also 2 Chron. 19.9, where the motifs of instruction and the fear of Yahweh also occur.

12. See Smith 1984: 233-34.

The victory is capped by a further liturgical gathering in the temple (v. 28), while the 'fear of God' (פחד אלהים, v. 29) befalls the surrounding kingdoms.

Von Rad (1951: 6-14) identified the tradition-critical background of this and other motifs in the 'institution' of 'Yahweh war' (or 'holy war' in his terminology). He deduced the concept form-critically from passages relating to the conquest in Exodus, Deuteronomy and Joshua. The Chronicler's own 'Yahweh war' narratives are themselves stylized descriptions of an evidently literary nature which reflect the traditional motifs. Three of these accounts belong to the *Sondergut* (2 Chron. 13.3-18; 14.8-14 [E 9-15]; 20.1-30), while a fourth (2 Chron. 32.21) summarizes the *Vorlage* (= 2 Kgs 19.35-37). The content of this special material is quite homogeneous. Among its common features the following details stand out:

1. In each case the attacking force greatly outnumbers Judah (13.3; 14.8-9 [E 9-10]; 20.2; 32.7; cf. Deut. 20.1).
2. Speeches before the battle give the assurance of Yahweh's presence and victory (13.5-13; 20.5-17; 32.7-8; cf. Deut. 20.1-4).
3. The battle is designated as Yahweh's, who fights on Judah's behalf (13.12, 16; 14.11 [E 12]; 20.15, 17; 32.8; cf. Exod. 14.14; Deut. 1.30).
4. Judah is encouraged not to fear but to believe (14.10 [E 11]; 20.15; 32.7; cf. Exod. 14.13; Deut. 20.3).
5. The battle may be opened with a war cry (תרועה) and the sounding of trumpets by priests (13.12, 15; cf. Num. 10.8-9; 31.6; Josh. 6.16; in 20.22 the cry has been 'spiritualized' into a hymn of praise [von Rad 1951: 80]).
6. There is no *herem* in the Chronistic accounts but the emphasis placed on the booty suggests the dedication of this plunder to Yahweh (14.12-13 [E 13-14]; 20.25; cf. 15.18; 32.23) in keeping with earlier practice (cf. Josh. 6.18-19).

These details point to the literary and schematic character of the Chronicler's accounts. In considering the writer's purpose in including these highly coloured narratives we should note the following features.

The first is the defensive nature of these wars. Cross argued from his analysis of the earliest poetry in the Old Testament that 'the normal locus of holy warfare is discovered in the Exodus-Conquest' (1973: 100). According to Cross, this literature is marked by a ubiquitous motif, the march of Yahweh, the divine warrior, from the southern mountains (or from Egypt) to the land (cf. Deut. 33.2; Judg. 5.4-5; Ps. 68.18). Later applications of the image of the divine warrior, such as Isa. 51.9-11 and 63.1-6, preserve this motif in depicting the Return according to Exodus-Conquest typology. However, there is a further development of the motif which is centred on Zion, in which the activity of the divine warrior is clearly defensive. This is notably associated with kingship psalms, in which Yahweh is petitioned in his sanctuary on behalf of Zion against the attacking nations (Pss. 9; 20; 24; 46; 48; 76). Psalm 20 is of particular interest because it reflects a temple liturgy before battle in which intercession is made for the king. The structure of this psalm is as follows:

a. vv. 2-6, prayer for God's help for the king 'on the day of distress' (ביום צרה);

b. v. 7, a declaration (presumably from a cultic personage) marking a turning point in the ritual and promising deliverance;

c. vv. 8-9, the concluding praise of the whole congregation in its new-found confidence.

This corresponds closely to the structure of the liturgy that precedes the battle with the eastern coalition (2 Chron. 20). Standing in the temple precincts 'in the assembly of Judah and Jerusalem', Jehoshaphat prays 'in our distress' (מצרתנו, v. 9) for deliverance. He is answered by an oracle from a Levite (vv. 15-17), and the whole assembly concludes with praise (vv. 18-19). It seems likely, then, that some such cultic source as those kingship psalms reflecting the motif of the divine warrior acting in defence of his sanctuary has shaped this presentation. The Chronicler's special interest in the Psalms is well known. This is reflected in the 'Yahweh war' narratives not only in 2 Chron. 20.21 but also in 2 Chron. 32.21, where the writer comments that Sennacherib withdrew 'with shame of face'. Williamson (1982: 385) suggests the influence here of such sources as Pss. 31.17, 83.16-17 and 97.7, while Selman (1994b: 514) draws attention to Psalms 34.4-6 and 35.4-6, where Yahweh's enemies are repulsed by his angel and put to shame. The entire pericope of 2 Chronicles 20 is, of course, cultically conceived, as singing replaces warfare and the religious rather than national character of the community is emphasized. At the same time, as I note below, the geopolitical question of the security of the community from military attack remains an important concern.

Two other features of the Chronicler's 'Yahweh war' narratives should be noted:

1. The attacks all occur *following* reform according to the Mosaic Law or a statement affirming the legitimacy of Judah's institutions (13.10-11; 14.2-4 [E 3-5]; 19.4-11; 32.1). There is therefore nothing punitive about them, in contrast to the Chronicler's outlook elsewhere which correlates invasion with apostasy (cf. 2 Chron. 12.2-9; 25.22-24; 28.5-7; 33.11; 36.17-18). Rather they are opportunities for Judah to express faith in Yahweh (13.18; 14.10 [E 11]; 20.12, 17; 32.7-8) and experience his salvation.[13]

2. In each case it is Yahweh who deals the decisive or only blow. Judah may have sizeable forces (2 Chron. 13.3; 14.8 [E 9]; 20.21), but their role is confined for the most part to harrying the enemy or gathering the spoil. In 2 Chron. 20.15-17 the military passivity of Judah is taken to its furthest degree as the people are admonished (in a citation from Exod. 14.13-14) to 'stand still and see the victory of Yahweh'.

This material has an evidently paraenetic character. It aims to encourage the Chronicler's small and demilitarized community to project its hope upon an intervention by Yahweh, 'in [whose] hand are power and might' (כח וגבורה, 2 Chron. 20.6; 1 Chron. 29.12).[14] Such a presentation belies the picture sometimes urged of a generally sedate era or a satisfaction with the status quo.[15] A fairer assessment is offered by Welten's general view of the writer's purpose in the special *topoi* of 2 Chronicles 10–36 (1973: 204):

> According to those passages which have been inserted as 'topoi' into 2 Chronicles 10–36, the Books of Chronicles have a contemporary role in the Judah of their time. They exhort the cult community to adopt a certain attitude and conduct, and at the same time they convey the hope of a fundamental improvement in the threatening external political situation.[16]

13. 2 Chron. 24.23-24 is an instance of the writer using a 'reverse Yahweh war' motif to indicate divine punishment on Judah.

14. כח and גבורה are traditional attributes of God in the Psalms; cf. Pss. 65.7; 66.7; 89.14; 111.6; 145.11; 147.5.

15. Thus Bickerman, Caquot, Hanson; cf. Chapter 6.

16. 'Nach den als Topoi bezeichneten Einsatzstücken in 2 Chr 10–36 haben die Chronikbücher eine aktuelle Funktion gegenüber dem Juda ihrer Zeit. Sie sind

A clear indication of this view is found in Jehoshaphat's prayer in 2 Chron. 20.5-12. The point of this petition is to affirm Israel's claim to the land and to plead for the vindication of that right against the incursion of hostile neighbours. Good (1985: 393) comments on this section:

> It reaches its climax when Jehoshaphat calls for Yahweh to judge Israel's enemies, and it includes the sorts of information and rhetorical flourishes one might expect in legal argument. Thus, Jehoshaphat produces title to Judah's territory and shows that Israel has held the land properly and with due regard for the honor and authority of Yahweh. [...] War, for the Chronicler, is a jural affair.

The passage is a further indication that the possession and integrity of the land remains an important concern for the Chronicler (cf. 1 Chron. 28.8; 2 Chron. 7.14; 36.21) and the object of continuing expectation.

Finally, and most significantly, the contrast drawn by Plöger and Hanson between Chronicles, seen as a product of priestly-theocratic circles content with the status quo, and the viewpoint of apocalyptic (or proto-apocalyptic) groups, is difficult to square with the presence in this work of the motifs these writers associate more readily with apocalyptists. It is in any case overly schematic to oppose hierocracy with eschatological perspectives. Dillard (1987: 161) plausibly suggests instead that the Chronicler's inclusion of 'Yahweh war' narratives is in fact a reflection of 'eschatological hope, a longing for the Day of Yahweh, when the divine warrior would conquer in behalf of his people as he had done so often so long ago'. It is important to note that the Chronicler's treatment of this theme appears to be temple-centred and defensive in character, and so reaches back to the pre-exilic Zion traditions. We may conclude that the 'Yahweh war' passages have a special importance in the Chronicler's hope of redemption. Recourse to the temple in prayer (cf. 2 Chron. 6.34; 20.9) and the diligent pursuit of reform according to the Law are the community's guarantee of defence and vindication. This conclusion is closely related to the following section.

3. *The Theme of Peace in Chronicles*
Despite his interest in military matters, it may be said that the Chronicler's real concern is with peace, as the conclusion to one 'Yahweh war' narrative indicates (2 Chron. 20.30). The Chronicler

Ermahnung zu einem bestimmten Verhalten und Handeln im Rahmen der Kultgemeinschaft, sie geben damit zugleich Hoffnung auf eine grundsätzliche Verbesserung der so bedrohlichen außenpolitischen Lage.'

evinces a special interest in this subject. He shows how peace is established definitively in Israel and how, by implication, it may again be the people's experience.

The concept of peace in Chronicles belongs clearly to the sociopolitical realm. It refers to 'rest' for the land, that is, its freedom from the disturbance of enemies and its enjoyment by the people. However, this concept is understood in explicitly theological terms: it is presented as a gift of Yahweh's salvation to Israel and, as is the case with all of the Chronicler's theological themes, is connected in the closest terms with the temple.

The writer draws in part on Deuteronomy and the Deuteronomistic History but develops the theme in a distinctive way.[17] Briefly, Deuteronomy 12 and the Deuteronomistic History connect Israel's enjoyment of 'rest from enemies round about' with the demand for the centralization of the cult and other associated motifs (including the ark of the covenant), as Carlson has shown.[18] Josh. 18.1 and 23.1 are early instances of this theme, while in 2 Sam. 7.1-2 (see below) rest of a more permanent character is granted to David, in virtue of which he proposes to build a temple for the ark. The Chronicler's contribution to the development of this theme is to cast the promise and its fulfilment forward on to the time of Solomon. The terms שלום and שקט and the root נוח have a particular importance here, which is reflected in their use in the *Sondergut* and the Chronicler's omission of the root נוח from parallel passages.

The latter point is demonstrated in the Davidic narrative. In 1 Chronicles 11–16 David is shown to reverse the effects of Saul's disobedience, the dispossession of Israel by the Philistines (1 Chron. 10.7). The Nathan oracle which follows (1 Chron. 17.4-5) is prefaced in the *Vorlage* (2 Sam. 7.5-6) with the statement 'Yahweh had given him [David] rest (הניח) from all his enemies about him' (2 Sam. 7.1), and includes the promise (v. 11) 'I will give you rest (והניחתי) from all your enemies'. The Chronicler omits the first statement and rewords the second to read 'I will subdue (והכנעתי) all your enemies' (1 Chronicles 17.10). This promise is fulfilled in the account of David's wars in 1 Chronicles 18–20 (cf. 1 Chron. 18.1, ויכניעם), which create the conditions of peace necessary for temple-building. Rest comes only at the end of David's reign (1 Chron. 22.18). The Chronicler further

17. Cf. von Rad 1966: 94-98; Gabriel 1990: ch. 2.
18. Carlson 1964: 100-102.

revises the tradition to present Solomon as an איש מנוחה (1 Chron. 22.9). Besides word-play on Solomon's name, the writer makes this king instead of David the recipient of the promise of 2 Sam. 7.11 and affirms that in his reign Yahweh will grant Israel 'peace and quiet' (שלום ושקט).

The fulfilment of this promise is connected with the completion of Solomon's task as temple-builder. It is thus fitting that Solomon concludes his dedicatory prayer by installing the ark with the invocation 'And now arise, Yahweh God, to your resting place (לנוחך), you and the ark of your might (וארון עזך)' (2 Chron. 6.41 = Ps. 132.8; cf. 1 Chron. 28.2). The implication seems to be that as Yahweh takes his 'rest' among his people, they will experience 'rest' in turn.[19] Rest is thus the distinguishing mark of Solomon's reign. It may be significant that the Chronicler makes no mention of Solomon's later military problems recounted in 1 Kgs 11.14-25, although he does note his capture of Hamath Zobah (2 Chron. 8.3, no parallel).[20]

In the post-Solomonic narrative the theme of rest is closely connected with reform, 'seeking' Yahweh and obedience to the Law. This point is made repeatedly in the description of the opening years of Asa's reign (2 Chron. 13.23; 14.4, 5, 6 [E 14.1, 5, 6, 7]; 15.15), which is virtually a homily on the means of securing peace. As we have noted, rest also marks the apogee of Jehoshaphat's reign (20.30). Two other references are found: the quiet that befalls Jerusalem after Athaliah's overthrow (2 Chron. 23.21 = 2 Kgs 11.20); and Yahweh's gift of rest to Jerusalem after its delivery from Sennacherib (2 Chron. 32.22, following LXX and Vulgate). These examples show that the Chronicler understands rest to be a recurrent experience in Israel's history. The possibility was established definitively by the temple, the place of Yahweh's 'rest', and it may be actualized afresh by covenant loyalty.[21] All the references (except 2 Chron. 23.21) are without parallel in the *Vorlage*, suggesting strongly that the matter was one of urgent interest to the writer's own time.

19. Cf. Gabriel 1990: 97.

20. Thus Gabriel's statement that 'under Solomon Israel does not conduct any wars' ('unter Salomo führt Israel keine Kriege') (1990: 193) is not quite accurate. Gabriel's judgment (p. 108) that Solomon is presented 'a type of an awaited ruler of peace' and that 'all Israel is promised for the future a life in freedom and peace under a *Solomon redivivus*' ('als Typos eines erwarteten Friedenherrschers'; 'Ganz Israel wird ein Leben in Freiheit und Frieden unter einen *Salomo redivivus* durch Jahwe für die Zukunft verheißen') has affinities with Mosis's view and is unlikely.

21. Thus, rightly, Japhet (1989: 392), against Mosis.

Both war and peace, then, stand out as matters of special emphasis for the Chronicler. Through his treatment of this theme he conveys to the politically subject and vulnerable community of the post-exilic period the hope of deliverance and secure existence in the land, an expectation to which the temple as the vehicle of the divine promises to David testifies.

4. *The Relationship between King and High Priest*

Theocratic interpretations of Chronicles usually hold that it reflects a development in post-exilic times away from a political-geographical understanding of Israel toward a conception of a community centred on cult and law. According to this view no continuing role was foreseen for the Davidic king. Rather, in his special material the Chronicler indicated that David's primary significance was as a founder of the cult, especially in his provision of a site and material for the temple and his organization of the Levites (cf. 1 Chron. 15.4-24; 16.4, 37-38; 22; 25.1-2; 28.1–29.9). Associated with this interpretation is the fact that the office of high priest grew in status during the post-exilic period, increasingly assuming the functions that had formerly been reserved for the Davidic king. This development probably began early in the Restoration period, since Zechariah 4 and 6 appear to place the high priest on par with the governor Zerubbabel. Clear evidence of the ascendancy of the high priest is provided much later by Sir. 50.1-4, which eulogizes Simon the high priest (c. 200 BCE) for his work in repairing the temple and fortifying Jerusalem, tasks which otherwise would have been the responsibility of the local governor.

The course of this development in the intervening period is uncertain. Part of the argument turns on the dating and interpretation of P. In Wellhausen's view (1885: 148-49) the depiction of Aaron in that corpus was of a figure of incomparable importance and sanctity, such as was not to be found elsewhere in the Old Testament. P represented the high priest as sovereign in the temple, contrary to his true pre-exilic status as servant of the king. The high priest appeared as head of the theocracy and representative of the nation, anointed and attired like the king (cf. Lev. 4.3; 6.20, 22), yet possessing few real political attributes. This presentation reflected a time when civil power had been withdrawn from the nation, leaving the community to occupy itself unhampered with its cultic life (1885: 151):

> Thus the temple became the sole centre of life, and the prince of the temple
> the head of the spiritual commonwealth, to which also the control of polit-
> ical affairs, so far as these were still left to the nation, naturally fell, there
> being no other head.

This view has been generally endorsed by scholarship, with some
modifications. De Vaux (1961: 398-401) suggests that the royal anointing was transferred to the high priest once the monarchy had disap-
peared. Cody (1969: 176) also argued that the title הכהן הגדול for Joshua
in Haggai and Zechariah reflected the reduced status of the Davidic civil
governor and the new independence of the high priest from the
monarch.[22]

It must be asked how the Chronicler, standing at the midpoint historically of this period, understood this development, whether he appeared
to support it or presented an alternative view. Following de Vaux and
Cody, we may consider first whether the titles used of the high priest
help determine this question, and secondly, the way in which the
Chronicler characterizes the relation of high priest to king.

**1. *The Titles of the High Priest in Chronicles; the Purpose of the
Genealogical Notes***
The high priests are first mentioned in 1 Chron. 5.29-41 and 6.34-38
(E 6.3-15, 49-53) as the בני אהרן. These passages point to the Mosaic
origin of the institution and affirm through a schematic arrangement the
pre-eminence and centrality of the Aaronides within the Levites
(Williamson 1982: 69). Two points from this genealogical material are of
particular interest. First, the Chronicler concludes the list with the
mention of Jehozadak's exile (1 Chron. 5.41 [E 6.15]). This note shows
not only the degree to which unfaithfulness infected Israel (Oeming
1990: 153), but also establishes a parallel with the similarly exiled
Davidic line (1 Chron. 3.1-16). Secondly, it is emphasized that the
Aaronides are charged with 'making atonement for Israel, according to
all that Moses the servant of God had commanded' (1 Chron. 6.34
[E 49]). Despite serious sin, divine provision for atonement is made
in the temple, the seat of the Aaronides. The point is underlined by
repeated references to Solomon's time (1 Chron. 5.36; 6.17, 38 [E 6.10,
32, 53]). Selman (1994a: 108) remarks that, alone among the

---

22. Of course, the significance of the description of Aaron in P is interpreted
differently by those who assign a pre-exilic date to this material; cf. Haran 1978:
210-11.

genealogies, the Davidic and Aaronide lines are presented in a parallel way (from the patriarchs to the exile), thus presenting them jointly as the focus of Israel's survival and future hope. Together they represent the Chronicler's conception of the theocracy.

The other titles for the high priest reflect his function in the temple. In 1 Chron. 9.11 and 2 Chron. 31.13 he is called the נגיד בית האלהים (cf. Neh. 11.11). De Vaux (1961: 398) suggests that this title denotes 'a leader appointed by God', but this overpresses its significance. In 2 Chron. 35.8 the high priest Hilkiah and his colleagues Zechariah and Jehiel are collectively termed נגידי בית האלהים, suggesting that the title denotes a chief officer in a sphere of service. In parallel passages the Chronicler usually retains the usage of the *Vorlage*. In 2 Chron. 23.8, 9 and 24.2 Jehoiada is called simply הכהן, following 2 Kgs 11.9, 10; 12.2. Hilkiah is called הכהן הגדול in 2 Chron. 34.9 (cf. 2 Chron. 22.4) but הכהן in v. 14 (contrast 2 Kgs 22.8, הכהן הגדול).

A characteristic expression from the Chronicler's *Sondergut* is כהן הראש (2 Chron. 19.11; 26.20; 31.10; also 24.11; contrast 2 Kgs 12.10, הכהן הגדול).[23] Bartlett suggests that this title refers to the judicial function of the leading priest rather than his status *qua* leading priest. Certainly each of its uses appears to be related to the Mosaic Law. It may be that the title reflects the underlying sources of these passages.

No overall pattern emerges from the Chronicler's use of titles for the high priest. If in his own material the writer appears to highlight the high priest's judicial role or his function in the sanctuary, yet his other references do not reflect an exaltation of this office over against the king's. *Contra* de Vaux, the titles themselves give no clear indication how the author understood the relative power and status of these offices.

2. *The Interaction between King and High Priest*

A clearer indication of the Chronicler's view may be determined from those passages, both synoptic and non-synoptic, which recount contact between king and high priest. The synoptic passages are reviewed here for signs of any systematic redaction, and if so, in what direction. Similarly, the *Tendenz* of the non-synoptic passages is examined.

---

23. A variant to this title is found in 2 Chron. 24.6, where Jehoiada is designated הראש, contrary to the Chronicler's usual practice. Williamson (1982: 320) presents thematic and stylistic arguments for treating vv. 5b-6 as secondary.

(i) *2 Chronicles 22.10–24.14 (= 2 Kings 11.1–12.16), Jehoiada and Joash.* The Chronicler adds the note (v. 11) that Jehoshabeath is 'wife of Jehoiada the priest'. The text of Kings may be disturbed at this point (v. 2), or the Chronicler may be indicating the involvement of the high priestly family from the start in preserving the dynasty. The coup itself which restores Joash is thoroughly sacralized by the Chronicler, who emphasizes the role of the clergy and the קהל instead of the Carites and the guard. Thus the personal agreement which Jehoiada makes with the officers (2 Kgs 11.4; cf. 2 Chron. 23.1) gives way instead to a covenant between the קהל and the king (v. 3a). The significance of Jehoiada's words in v. 3 for the author's understanding of the future of the monarchy ('Here is the king's son! Let him reign, as Yahweh promised concerning David's descendants') was noted in Chapter 7. Dillard (1987: 181) comments: 'in the Chronicler's portrayal, the temple is not the seat of a satisfied theocratic status quo, but rather is the guardian and promoter of the Davidic succession.'

The account of Joash's coronation has been altered in a number of small ways. 2 Kgs 11.12 reads: '[Jehoiada] brought out (ויצא) the king's son and set (ויתן) on him the crown and the testimony; and they made him king and anointed him'. In 2 Chron. 23.10 the first two verbs are pluralized, presumably making them refer to 'the people' (v. 10). The Chronicler further supplies the subject 'Jehoiada and his sons' to וימשחהו to make the priests the ministers of the royal anointing. The sense here is probably durative ('while'). It distinguishes between the actions of the people and the priesthood (acting collegially). Willi (1972: 127) observes that these changes can hardly be intended to reinforce the status of the high priest: 'The fact that in Chronicles above all the high priest remains conspicuously in the background can only cause astonishment for those who, contrary to close inspection, attribute to Chronicles an extreme, unhistorical hierocratic standpoint.'[24]

Other changes in the Joash narrative appear to increase the king's status, particularly as patron of the cult. In 2 Chron. 24.8 the collection chest for the temple repairs is made 'at the king's command', whereas 2 Kgs 12.9 attributes the initiative to Jehoiada. In the matter of administration, 2 Chron. 24.12 and 14 specify the king's personal role alongside Jehoiada.

---

24. 'Daß in der Chronik v. a. der Hohepriester auffällig im Hintergrund bleibt, kann nur den in Verwunderung setzen, der der Chronik wider allen Augenschein einen extrem unhistorischen, hierokratischen Standpunkt vindiziert.'

Finally, Jehoiada's burial among the kings (v. 16), unique for a high priest, is in virtue of his service in restoring the dynasty and the temple services, as the continuation of that verse makes clear: 'because he had done good in Israel and toward God and his house'. This singular honour certainly does not suggest that the Chronicler favoured the tendency in the post-exilic period to merge the roles of king and high priest, since Jehoiada works to see the legitimate Davidic line reinstated and continued (cf. 2 Chron. 24.3).

(ii) *2 Chronicles 26.16-20 (no parallel), Azariah and Uzziah.* Azariah is mentioned here first as 'the priest' (v. 17) and then as 'the chief priest' (v. 20) in this incident in which the Aaronides oppose Uzziah's attempt to usurp their cultic prerogatives. The question in view here is the priestly law of offering incense (cf. Exod. 30.7-8; Num. 18.1-2) and the authority of the sanctuary (v. 18). The passage reflects a clear demarcation between royal and priestly functions, where the latter are stipulated in the Mosaic Law. It should be noted further that the priesthood is shown as acting collectively in defying and ejecting Uzziah (vv. 17-18, 20), and so the passage does not appear to elevate the status of the high priesthood itself.

(iii) *2 Chronicles 31.2-21 (no parallel), Azariah and Hezekiah.* The question of the king's support for the cult and his authority in religious matters is addressed especially in the Chronicler's Hezekiah and Josiah narratives. Hezekiah acts like David and Solomon in appointing the divisions of priests and Levites (v. 2) and in making provision for the burnt offerings (vv. 3-7). He also commands the priesthood in the matter of preparing storerooms in the temple (v. 11), while v. 13 states that the Levites charged with the collection hold their appointment 'from Hezekiah the king and Azariah the chief officer of the house of God'. Both this account and Josiah's measures (2 Chron. 35.2-6) point to a continuing royal authority in some cultic matters at least, following the united monarchy.

(iv) *2 Chronicles 34.8-22 (= 2 Kings 22.3-14), Hilkiah and Josiah.* There are stylistic differences between the accounts (cf. v. 9 and 2 Kgs 22.4) but no particular significance attaches to them. As in the *Vorlage*, Hilkiah is shown to be subject to the king's command (vv. 20-21).

3. *Conclusion*

Not all the passages surveyed are of equal weight, but it is clear that the Chronicler does not exalt the high priest over the Davidic king or treat him in any sense as his successor. Overall, the Chronicler pays little attention to the high priest, for all that he affirms his central role in the cult (1 Chron. 6.34 [E 49]). The high priest's function appears to be circumscribed to certain rituals, although 2 Chron. 19.11 suggests a judicial authority in religious matters. The Davidic king is presented as having a continuing role in areas relating to the organization and support of the cult. In a number of passages the Chronicler also heightens the standing of the king over against the high priest. Furthermore, as Williamson (1982: 29) emphasizes, the most distinguished of the high priests, Jehoiada, is singled out for his efforts to preserve and restore the Davidic monarchy from the threat of destruction. From these details it is concluded that the Chronicler reflects an ideal of the relationship between the two offices that differs markedly from the hierocratic model that may well have been developing during his period.

5. *The Presentation of Alliances in Chronicles*

The importance of this *topos* for the Chronicler is widely recognized. Drawing for the most part on Kings, the author depicts Judah as participating in a variety of alliances with its neighbours. These include military and maritime ventures, and a marriage pact involving the royal house. Through his redaction of this material, the author indicates the consequences of these alliances and his own attitude towards them. Because they generally entail some kind of divine chastisement, these alliances have a special role within the work's retributive outlook. This is in keeping with the writer's practice of patterning the history of Judah according to periods of fidelity and unfaithfulness, which alliances characterize. The Chronicler inserts interpretative comments, in which the treaties of the post-Solomonic period are condemned as expressions of disloyalty or lack of faith in Yahweh's power to defend his people. Whereas the Deuteronomist refrains from explicit comment on the alliances, and allows the inference that in some cases they brought short-term benefit, the Chronicler considers them throughout as baneful for the nation.

The rhetorical shaping of this *topos* (particularly through prophetic speeches of warning, encouragement and judgment) indicates that its primary concern is not historiographic but a pragmatic matter facing the

Chronicler's own community. The following discussion considers the form and significance of the Chronicler's treatment of this theme, the possible traditio-historical background to his reflection, and whether the *topos* contributes to an understanding of the Chronicler's hope. In particular, it must be asked whether such a treatment coheres with a hierocratic, non-eschatological outlook. Alliances in Chronicles fall into two groups: military pacts made with foreign powers, and treaties between Judah and Israel. These are examined in turn.

1. Military Pacts with Foreign Powers
(i) *Asa's pact with Ben-Hadad against Israel (2 Chronicles 16.2-6 = 1 Kings 15.18-22).* The Chronicler largely reproduces his *Vorlage* but recontextualizes it so that it bears a different significance. In Kings the alliance is not condemned and appears to have brought some measure of relief for Judah, whereas in Chronicles it is framed by an account of Yahweh's help during Asa's faithful period (2 Chron. 14.8-14 [E 9-15]) and a prophetic condemnation afterwards (2 Chron. 16.7-9). The contrast between the periods is reinforced through the catchword שען. In the first episode Asa triumphed because he 'relied' (2 Chron. 14.10 [E 11]) on Yahweh; on the second occasion he 'relied' on the king of Aram (2 Chron. 16.7; cf. v. 8).[25] Hanani condemns Asa in an allusion to Samuel's rebuke to Saul (v. 9; cf. 1 Sam. 13.13) and predicts that war rather than security will be his lot. The nature of Hanani's criticism must be understood. The focus is upon Asa's attitude or disposition. In 2 Chron. 15.17-18 (= 2 Kgs 15.14-15) the Chronicler notes that Asa's heart was 'blameless' (שלם) in fulfilling the covenant and that he brought into the temple votive gifts (קדשים) of silver and gold. The implication of 2 Chron. 16.9 is that Asa's heart is no longer 'blameless', as is indicated by his plundering of these gifts to finance the treaty (contrast the slightly different wording in 1 Kgs 15.18).

(ii) *Ahaz's Appeal to the 'Kings of Assyria' (2 Chronicles 28.16-17; cf. 2 Kings 16.6-7).* The Chronicler's account of the Syro-Ephraimite war differs in important respects from Kings, including his explicit assessment of the role of Tiglath-Pileser. Whereas 2 Kgs 16.9 notes that the

---

25. Many commentators have followed the Lucianic version of 2 Chron. 16.7, which refers to victory over the king of Israel rather than the king of Aram, but the MT probably conveys the Chronicler's sense (cf. Curtis and Madsen 1910, Williamson 1982, Dillard 1987).

king of Assyria responded to Ahaz's financial inducement by attacking Damascus, the Chronicler reworks the narrative to preach a message on the theme of false help. The catchword עזר, which is significant elsewhere for describing true help from Yahweh,[26] is used here to designate Ahaz's recourse to a pagan power (vv. 16, 21, 23). Kings allows that the treaty brought short-term benefit to Judah, and it records Ahaz's subsequent cultic innovations (2 Kgs 16.10-18) factually, without evident praise or condemnation. By contrast, the Chronicler treats the alliance as destructive rather than helpful (vv. 20-21), since it induced Ahaz into deepening apostasy (vv. 22-25). Once more, the root question is Ahaz's disposition of unfaithfulness and his failure to repent 'in his time of distress' (contrast Manasseh in 2 Chron. 33.12).

(iii) *Hezekiah against Sennacherib (2 Chronicles 32.2-3)*. This example treats the theme of alliances by omitting details from the *Vorlage* that pointed to Hezekiah's less than exemplary behaviour. It appears from the Rabshakeh's speech in 2 Kgs 18.21, 24 that Hezekiah had opened negotiations with Egypt for help, a recourse that was criticized by Isaiah (Isa. 30.1-5; 31.1-3). The Chronicler suppresses these references in Kings and instead presents Hezekiah (in words echoing Isa. 31.1, 3) as urging trust in Yahweh's help alone. The people 'lean' (ויסמכו) on these words (rather than Egypt; cf. the use of יסמך, 2 Kgs 18.21), and their faith is duly vindicated (v. 22).

2. Treaties between Judah and Israel
The account of Judah's contacts with its northern neighbour must be distinguished from its associations with foreign powers. In the Chronicler's view the northern tribes retained their status as 'Israel', despite their rebellion (Williamson 1977a). Moreover, the author recounts every contact between the two states reported in his *Vorlage* (with the exception of 2 Kgs 3.4-27, whose omission is discussed below). Nevertheless, the cult of the northern kingdom is rejected as illegitimate (cf. 2 Chron. 13.5-9), and treaties with this kingdom are consistently condemned. Again, this fact arises from redaction of the material which clarifies the author's outlook. Whereas Kings seems content for the most part simply to report these alliances, once more the Chronicler reorders the material or inserts interpretative comments to bring out the

26. Cf. 1 Chron. 5.20; 12.17, 18, 22; 15.26; 2 Chron. 14.10 [E 11]; 18.31; 25.8; 26.7; 32.8.

significance of these treaties. These concern marriage and economic ventures, as well as military matters.

(i) *Jehoshaphat's alliances (2 Chronicles 18.1-2; 20.35-37)*. The paratactic structure of the Chronicler's Jehoshaphat narrative was discussed in Chapter 4, where it was noted that it consists of alternating tableaux of periods of fidelity and compromising alliances with the north. The significance of the latter involvement is now examined more closely.

After describing Jehoshaphat's exemplary start (2 Chron. 17.1-19), when the king rejected Baalism and the practices of Israel (vv. 3-4) and so received 'riches and honour' (v. 5), the author repeats this latter notice in 2 Chron. 18.1, suggesting perhaps that pride induced the king to enter a marriage alliance with the House of Ahab (cf. v. 3). In the Chronicler's eyes there could be no justification for such an association with the north. Kings has a different focus, the judgment on Ahab (cf. 1 Kgs 22.36-40, no parallel). It makes no mention at this point of the marriage alliance,[27] nor does it comment on Jehoshaphat's involvement with Ahab in the battle at Ramoth-gilead. By contrast, the Chronicler remarks that Ahab 'enticed' (ויסיתהו, v. 2) Jehoshaphat, an expression with undertones of apostasy (cf. Deut. 13.7 [E 6]). Jehu's rebuke on the king's return from battle (2 Chron. 19.2, 'Should you help the wicked and love those who hate Yahweh?') is directed against the alliance with the north. The expressions 'love' (אהב) and 'hate' (שׂנא) have a political (and covenantal) connotation here, denoting actions within a treaty relationship.[28] The Chronicler also uses 'help' to designate formal military support (1 Chron. 18.5; 2 Chron. 28.16).

Jehoshaphat's second alliance with the north is the failed maritime venture with Ahaziah (2 Chron. 20.35-37). This account differs significantly from 1 Kgs 22.48-49 and has given rise to the charge that the Chronicler rewrote his *Vorlage* to explain why disaster befell an otherwise good king.[29] The divergences in the Greek witnesses[30] do not

27. Although the Chronicler bases his account here on inferences from passages such as 2 Kgs. 8.18. Jehoshaphat's reply in 1 Kgs 22.4 also implies an alliance (Gray 1964: 399).

28. Cf. Thompson 1979: 203-204.

29. Cf. Curtis and Madsen 1910: 412.

30. These are the parallel passage in 2 Chron. 20 (LXX); 1 Kgs 22.41-42 (LXX); and the insertion 1 Kgs 16.28c-g (LXX). OL has its own divergences from the MT and LXX.

permit us to state with confidence the exact nature of the Chronicler's *Vorlage* at this point, but it is clear from the style of this passage that it has been reworked by the author.[31] This is most evident in the insertion of prophetic censure for alliance with 'Ahaziah king of Israel, who acted wickedly' (v. 35).

(ii) *Dynastic association with the Ahabites (2 Chronicles 21–23)*. The importance of this theme was discussed in Chapter 7, where it was seen that as a result of Jehoshaphat's marriage pact the Davidic house was brought to the brink of destruction and yet was preserved because of Yahweh's commitment to the Davidic covenant. The Chronicler lays stress upon the evil counsel that such association brings, particularly as it may induce the nation into apostasy (cf. 2 Chron. 21.13; 22.4-5, no parallel).

(iii) *Amaziah's Mercenaries (2 Chronicles 25.6-10)*. The prophetic repudiation of Amaziah's attempt to use Israelite mercenaries is based on familiar themes: these soldiers are considered apostates, and God's power and help are sufficient for his people (vv. 7-8). The clear implication of the unit is that Amaziah should be wholehearted in trusting Yahweh alone (cf. v. 2).

The remaining question from this survey concerns the Chronicler's omission of 2 Kgs 3.4-27. In this account Jehoshaphat responds to Joram's appeal to join forces with him and the king of Edom against Moab. The mission receives (qualified) prophetic endorsement by Elisha (vv. 16-19) and is apparently successful, though it ends on an ambiguous note (v. 27). The Chronicler's omission of this narrative has been much discussed; however, the older view that posited a midrashic literary connection with 2 Chron. 20.1-30 is now generally rejected (cf. Williamson 1982: 279). The probable reason for omission is the element of prophetic endorsement in the *Vorlage*. Such an act runs counter to the Chronicler's presentation, in which prophets consistently condemn such alliances.

31. Willi (1972: 219) explains the Chronicler's version as a natural interpretation of 1 Kgs 22.50, taking אמר as pluperfect and אז as 'at that time'. Yet, as Knoppers observes (1991: 521), this does not explain why Jehoshaphat in 1 Kgs 22 refuses Ahaziah's offer, whereas in 2 Chron. 20.36 he acts in alliance with him. Must the possibility be rejected that the two works record different aspects of the tradition?

3. *Conclusion*

All the above examples have shown that the Chronicler has redacted his *Vorlage* to express consistent opposition to alliances with the ungodly. This view is certainly no innovation in the biblical tradition. Rather it has a clear traditio-historical background, and we may well see here a (proto-)midrashic application on a theme reflected in two corpora of particular importance to the Chronicler, the Law and the classical prophets. In Exod. 23.32, 34.12-16, and Deut. 7.2, each from passages in 'Yahweh war' tradition relating to the conquest, Israel is forbidden from making a treaty (ברית) with the inhabitants of the land. Recourse to foreign powers is also widely condemned as futile and unfaithful in the prophetic writings.[32] The Chronicler stands within this prophetic tradition, closely reflecting its ideas and language.[33]

The immediate significance of the motif of opposition to alliances is not clear, but it is possible that in the vulnerable circumstances of the Chronicler's own time, when Judah's borders were threatened by the encroachment of hostile neighbours, some circles may have sought an accommodation with their neighbours and Samaria. If so, the Chronicler rejected such a line. Dillard (1987: 144) suggests that the writer's 'frequent introduction of this theme into his history must have had rhetorical relevance for the post-exilic community: though facing opposition and afforded many opportunities to trust in foreign powers and alliances, Judah in the restoration period was urged to trust in her God alone.'

However, closer examination of these cases shows that the Chronicler's objection is not to alliances *per se*, but rather to those associations that express disloyalty to Yahweh and foster religious corruption in his covenant people. The evidence of 2 Kgs 17.24-41 and Ezra 4.2-3 points to a considerable amount of syncretistic Yahwism in the post-exilic period, elements of which sought some association with the leadership of the *Galut*. Perhaps the Chronicler echoes such controversies in his treatment of this theme. In any case, he perceived the issue as one of priorities: faith in God must always take precedence over political convenience, and there was no place for the kind of religious compromise that had brought destruction upon the pre-exilic state. However, while the writer rejects military and other pacts for the period of post-schism Judah, it must be recalled that he also depicts the time of David and

---

32. Cf. e.g. Hos. 7.11-12; 8.9-10; Isa. 20.5-6; 30.1-14; Jer. 2.14-19, 36-37.
33. Cf. Chapter 3 above on the 'vocabulary of retribution'.

Solomon as one of economic collaboration with Hiram, including maritime ventures (1 Chron. 14.1; 2 Chron. 2.3-16; 8.17-18; 9.21; contrast 2 Chron. 20.35-37).[34] Furthermore, both Hiram and the queen of Sheba recognize Yahweh's choice of Solomon as king over Israel, and both bear witness to the fulfilment of the divine promises made to David's son (2 Chron. 2.11-16; 9.1-9). By the same token Cyrus's action in facilitating the Return evidently contributes to the furtherance of those promises (2 Chron. 36.22-23).

What may be said, then, about the Chronicler's own attitude to the political arrangements of his day? It will be recalled that the circles from which this work emanated depended to some extent on Achaemenid patronage. The temple had been built at the behest of the Persian emperor and with the subvention of imperial revenue (Ezra 1.1-6; 4.3; 6.3-12). Hanson (1975: 274-75) argues from these facts that 'the Chronicler's work' (i.e. Chronicles–Ezra–Nehemiah) is marked by 'pro-Persian proclivities' and supported a policy of collaboration with the Persians because the restoration depended on the active support of the Persian emperor. Hanson draws the further inference that '[t]he price paid for this Persian support was absolute fidelity to the Persian emperor, with the resulting necessity that hopes for regained national autonomy be eschewed. The Chronicler stands in whole-hearted support for this Persian-Israelite alliance.'

However, Hanson's evidence for this interpretation is deduced only from Ezra–Nehemiah and the supposition is projected on to Chronicles.[35] 'Alliance' is, of course, used in this case in a different sense from the above examples, where it connotes arrangements between approximate equals; here, Persia is clearly the ruling authority, and had

---

34. Williamson (1982: 200) and Japhet (1993: 629-30) hold that Hiram is presented as a vassal in these arrangements, while Selman (1994b: 298-99) maintains that a parity treaty is intended.

35. It may be questioned, however, whether Hanson's claim does justice to Ezra–Nehemiah either, considered as a separate work from Chronicles. Cf. McConville (1986), who argues that the attitude toward Persia in these books, so far from being favourable (so also Rudolph), is at best equivocal: the parallel of the return with the exodus likens Babylon to Egypt; Ezra 6.22 ('the king of *Assyria*') links Darius with Sennacherib and Shalmaneser; and the prayers of Ezra 9 and Neh. 9 reveal that the relationship with Persia was essentially burdensome and incompatible with the true realization of the community's hopes. Ezra 9.8-9 does reflect a more positive experience of Persian rule, but this is understood as Yahweh's doing rather than Persia's.

been so for perhaps two hundred years. Even if the Chronicler took a basically positive view of Persian rule (and the evidence is equivocal, for all that he understands Yahweh to be working through Cyrus; cf. 2 Chron. 36.22-23), nevertheless the writer was keenly aware that such a subject condition was a consequence of sin (which might be reversed by repentance), and that there remained a great difference between '(Yahweh's) service and the service of the kingdoms of the countries' (2 Chron. 12.8).

6. *The 'Kingdom of Yahweh' in Chronicles*

The theme of Yahweh's kingship is a common one in the Old Testament, but the Chronicler deals with it in a distinctive way that has implications for determining his future hope. There are two main strands to the writer's presentation here. In the first case, he explicitly represents Israel and Judah under the Davidic dynasty as the earthly expression of Yahweh's kingdom. This understanding of Israel was discussed in general thematic terms in the previous chapter. Secondly, the Chronicler reflects the broader Old Testament conception of Yahweh's universal kingship, which is eternal, and embraces the nations and the cosmos. The two notions are not naively equated in his work, but the reality of Yahweh's rule in the former case is strongly affirmed.[36]

This discussion concentrates on the language employed by the Chronicler to convey these concepts. The expression 'kingdom of Yahweh' (or its semantic equivalent) is neither widespread nor frequent in the Old Testament,[37] but there is a marked emphasis in Chronicles, which features at significant points in the narrative.

First, there is the manifestation of Yahweh's kingdom in Israel. The first implied reference is found in 1 Chron. 10.14, with the account of Saul's death: 'Yahweh turned the kingdom (את המלוכה) over to David' (cf. 1 Chron. 12.24 [E 23]). The explicit association of Yahweh's kingdom and the earthly kingdom of Israel under the Davidic house is made in the account of the dynastic promise. Whereas 2 Sam. 7.16 reads:

> Your house and your kingdom (ביתך וממלכתך) will be established for ever before me; your throne (כסאך) will be established for ever,

36. Cf. Japhet 1989: 397 n. 9; Selman 1989: 166.

37. Yahweh's 'kingdom' is represented by מלוכה, ממלכה, מלכה, מלכות and Aram. מלכו. Cf. Pss. 45.6; 103.19; 145.11-13; Obad. 21; Dan. 2.44; 3.33 [E 4.3]; 6.27 [E 26]; 7.14, 18, 27; 1 Chron. 17.14; 28.5; 29.11; 2 Chron. 13.8.

in 1 Chron. 17.14 this is altered to:

> I will confirm him in my house and in my kingdom (בביתי ובמלכותי) for
> ever, and his throne (וכסאו) will be established for ever.

Next, at the transition of rule, David declares that Yahweh 'has
chosen Solomon my son to sit upon *the throne of the kingdom of
Yahweh over Israel*' (1 Chron. 28.5). This striking expression is given
added force by the description of Solomon's accession: 'Then Solomon
sat on *the throne of Yahweh as king* in place of David his father'
(1 Chron. 29.23); and by the recognition of this fact by the queen of
Sheba (2 Chron. 9.8a):

> Blessed be Yahweh your God, who has delighted in you and set you on
> *his throne as king for Yahweh your God* (contrast 1 Kgs 10.9a, 'and set
> you on the throne of Israel').

Japhet (1989: 400) comments: '"The throne of the LORD" constitutes
an abstract expression referring to YHWH's dominion over Israel, which
is put into concrete political practice by means of David and Solomon.'
In the Chronicler's view theocracy in Israel is properly (and inalienably)
exercised through the legitimate Davidic line, a point emphasized in
Abijah's address to the north (2 Chron. 13.5, 8):

> Ought you not to know that Yahweh God of Israel gave the *kingdom over
> Israel* to David and his descendants by a covenant of salt? [. . .] And now
> you think to withstand *the kingdom of Yahweh in the hands of David's
> descendants*.

The above references are all taken from the Chronicler's *Sondergut* or
redaction. Complementing this specific, localized understanding of
Yahweh's kingdom are several passages which stress its universal and
eternal character.

The substantive ממלכה and equivalent expressions denoting kingly rule
are of particular importance here. The thought of Yahweh's universal
rule comes to the fore especially in connection with worship and the
temple, where, not surprisingly, the influence of the Psalter may be discerned. Thus, the installation of the ark in Jerusalem, prefiguring the
temple, evokes the confession, 'Let the heavens rejoice, let the earth be
glad, and let them say among the nations, "Yahweh reigns!"' (יהוה מלך)
(1 Chron. 16.31 = Ps. 96.10). In the great paean that marks the climax
of David's reign (1 Chron. 29.10-19), the king extols Yahweh's universal rule as offerings are made for the construction of the temple (vv. 11-
12a):

> To you, Yahweh, belong the greatness, the power, the glory, the majesty
> and the splendour; for all that is in the heavens and earth is yours. Yours,
> Yahweh, is the kingdom (הממלכה); you are exalted as head over all.
> Wealth and honour come from you, and you rule over all (מושל בכל).

Selman (1994a: 259-60) points to the influence here of Psalm 145,
which has several references to Yahweh's kingdom (vv. 11-13) and has
in other respects shaped the thought and language of this prayer.[38] A
further allusion in Chronicles to Yahweh's universal kingly rule is found
in 2 Chron. 20.6 by Jehoshaphat, again in the context of worship in the
temple:

> Yahweh, God of our fathers, are you not God in heaven? You rule (מושל)
> over the kingdoms of the nations, and in your hand are power and might
> (ובידך כח וגבורה).

The latter phrase, stressing Yahweh's omnipotence, appears to be a
direct citation from the continuation of David's prayer (1 Chron.
29.12b).

To conclude, the Chronicler combines two distinct senses of Yahweh's
kingdom: its earthly, specific manifestation in the Davidic dynasty; and
its eternal, universal character, which is particularly recognized in the
cult. Each aspect would have given the Chronicler's original readers
grounds for hope and assurance. Although the dynasty had long since
ceased to function, because Israel's kingdom was irrevocably connected
with Yahweh's kingdom, it was secure and everlasting, whatever the
post-exilic community's experience of political subservience indicated
(cf. Williamson 1982: 26). Worship in the temple would also remind the
community of Yahweh's universal rule and his omnipotence exercised
on Israel's behalf. The 'kingdom of Yahweh' in Chronicles is not a
(consummatory) eschatological concept as in later Jewish and Christian
thought, but a present, immanent reality as well as a fact of Israel's past
that may be realized afresh, as and when Yahweh wills.

7. *Summary and Conclusion*

This chapter has examined five features of the work, including its style
and subsidiary motifs, to determine whether they corroborate the
general lines identified in the previous chapter. These elements are all
expressions of the Chronicler's own outlook, although they have their

---

38. E.g. v. 11, which is reminiscent of Ps. 145.3-6. Cf. also Selman 1989.

traditio-historical background in a wide range of earlier biblical materials. The following conclusions have emerged.

1. The passages of direct speech are exhortative and paraenetic in character; at the rhetorical level they address the Chronicler's own community with the aim of fostering an expectant faith in Yahweh and diligent support of the cult. The conclusion (2 Chron. 36.22-23) also functions on the same level of inviting a proper response to Yahweh's continuing purposes in the restoration. It does not speak of the present experience as fulfilment but points instead to a wider horizon of expectation.

2. The Chronicler's depiction of war and peace was seen to have an important role in both his retributive and eschatological outlook. War is the punishment of apostasy, while 'rest for the land' is the blessing for faithfulness to the covenant. The 'Yahweh war' narratives in the *Sondergut* are especially significant for conveying the hope of deliverance. The use of this theme in a work emanating from temple circles is also notable, and it indicates that an institutionalized hierocracy and the lively hope of national redemption ('spiritualized' in this traditional literary-ideological form) are not necessarily opposed to each other.

3. The relationship between king and high priest was examined next. It was concluded that a trend associated with post-exilic hierocracy, the exaltation of the office and status of the high priest at the expense of the monarchy, was not supported by the Chronicler. Instead, the writer appeared to heighten the standing of the king over against the high priest. He also affirmed the importance of the king in leading and providing for the temple cult, though not participating in specifically priestly rituals. These details suggest that the Chronicler understood there to be a continuing role for the Davidic king in cultic matters, rather than agreeing with the supersession of the king by the hierocracy. Moreover, the king is plainly the representative of the nation.

4. The writer takes a nuanced view of alliances, rejecting associations with pagans and apostates that would undermine Judah's covenantal loyalty, but not rejecting alliances *per se*. The Chronicler's position is fundamentally religious: loyal faith in Yahweh alone must take priority over the commitments of international politics, and in this way, the community may be assured of divine protection from its hostile neighbours. Furthermore, although the Chronicler understood Yahweh's

purposes to be continued through Cyrus, in no sense is Cyrus to be understood as a 'successor' of David.[39]

5. The Chronicler's distinctive understanding of Israelite kingship (whereby it is linked with Yahweh's eternal kingdom) similarly witnesses to a hope for the transformation of the present circumstances of the community. Yahweh's kingship over Israel is given inalienably to David's descendants, so Israel cannot be finally subject to a different order. The emphasis on Yahweh's transcendence and universal kingly power is also striking, and it serves to some extent to reduce the significance (and seeming permanence) of the world powers to which the Chronicler's community was subject.

It is concluded, then, that the force and tendency of these subsidiary motifs are very much in line with the interpretation offered in the previous chapters of the broader themes that make up the Chronicler's presentation.

39. As Riley (1993: 193, 197) asserts.

Chapter 9

CHRONICLES AS THE DEVELOPMENT OF TRADITION

1. *Introduction: Chronicles and the Deuteronomistic History*

The previous two chapters have argued that the Chronicler's outlook is marked by a forward movement of thought and expectation, a pervasive sense of what Israel's circumstances may yet be, rather than a static, 'ecclesiastical' conception of 'theocracy'. Thus, it was argued in Chapter 7 that the different elements that constitute Israel as the kingdom of Yahweh (the Davidic covenant as this is expressed in the dynastic line and the temple, and the land and the people that make up the covenant nation) all anticipate a greater fulfilment than is presently the case. The subsidiary motifs discussed in Chapter 8 were found to support this conclusion. This point must now be considered at the comparative level, in order to put the Chronicler's work in its religious and historical context and to grasp more clearly his purpose in writing.

Comparative work naturally focuses upon the relationship of Chronicles to the Deuteronomistic History, especially Samuel–Kings, since by far the greatest proportion of the Chronicler's work is dependent on that corpus. In fact, the writer's canvas is much wider, embracing as it does Pentateuchal sources in the genealogies, citations from the Prophets in his 'Levitical sermons', and excerpts from (or allusions to) the Psalms in his cultic descriptions and prayers.[1] Ezra–Nehemiah also comes into the writer's purview. However, it is in comparison with the

---

1.   Cf. Willi 1972: 137, 176-77 on the Chronicler's anthological style and biblicism. Willi sees the Chronicler's procedures as evidence of an underlying concept of canon (1972: 133-34). Whether or not this is correct, it is evident that these writings had normative and authoritative status in the post-exilic community; cf. Williamson 1988: 35. Selman (1994a: 26) makes the persuasive suggestion that 'the Chronicler's overall aim was to offer an interpretation of the Bible as he knew it', and he presents an extensive survey of the Chronicler's 'inner-biblical exegesis'.

Deuteronomist's[2] understanding of judgment, retribution and hope that
the clearest perspective on the Chronicler's view of these topics emerges.
Ezra–Nehemiah provides an additional, intermediate stage of comparison, and is similarly considered, although more briefly, for its theological relationship to Chronicles. This chapter focuses strictly on these
ideological questions, among the numerous points of difference, and is
not intended as a full-scale comparison. Nonetheless, these issues, being
central to the concerns of both Chronicles and the Deuteronomistic
History, and to Old Testament theology in general, are among the most
important for comparison and interpretation. Taking the Chronicler's
retributive and eschatological doctrines as test cases, and setting them
against earlier reflection on these questions, this chapter will argue that
the Chronicler intended his work as a conscious continuation and
authoritative *development* of those traditions.

The relation of Chronicles to the Deuteronomistic History is one of
the oldest and most perennial issues in Chronicles studies,[3] in which
probably more attention has been focused on historical and textual
problems than on questions of theological difference.[4] In speaking of the
Deuteronomistic History, it will be clear that the final form of that work
is meant. The composition of this work is a complex matter on which
there is little consensus, and new hypotheses continue to be proposed on
this question.[5] Put simply, however, these views fall into three main
groups.

2. The singular is used for convenience throughout, whether we are to think of
an individual author/compiler or a pre-exilic 'Deuteronomistic school' of traditionists
(Nicholson, Weinfeld), whose work was incorporated in the final form of the book.
On theories of multiple redaction of the Deuteronomistic History, see below.

3. For a survey of this question see Willi 1972: 12-47. The LXX title
ΠΑΡΑΛΕΙΠΟΜΕΝΩΝ may reflect one of the earliest understandings of the
relationship of this work to Samuel–Kings; cf. Strübind 1991: 10-12.

4. On the historical problems raised by Chronicles in relation to Kings see
especially Graham (1990) on nineteenth-century criticism, and Japhet (1985) for a
survey of twentieth-century views. The textual questions have been studied
especially by Lemke (1965), Ulrich (1978) and McKenzie (1985). Interest in
theological differences has concentrated largely on the question of the Priestly Law in
the respective works, as classically expressed by Wellhausen (1885: ch. 6). Von Rad
(1930) and Noth (1967 [1943]) compared the retributive doctrines of the works, a
procedure carried out more extensively by Japhet (1989: 153-54). These views were
criticized in Chapter 4 above, and further points of difference will arise in this
discussion.

5. For a survey of this question see McKenzie 1991: 1-19.

The oldest position, which stems from Noth (1967 [1943]), holds that the Deuteronomistic History is essentially a unified exilic composition which may contain some secondary passages from the post-exilic period.[6] The second view maintains that an exilic Deuteronomistic *Grundschrift* was supplemented by other hands to make possession of the land or the perdurance of the dynasty contingent on obedience to the law.[7] The other major alternative holds that the original form of the work ('Dtr 1') dates from Josiah's reign and was intended to support his reforms. These expectations were, however, confounded by events, and other passages (principally the pericope blaming Manasseh for the exile in 2 Kgs 21.2-15 and the section from 23.25b to the end) were added by the exilic 'Dtr 2'. This reshaped the work into a document relevant to exiles, for whom the bright hopes of the Josianic era were past.[8] These different recensional theories have been proposed to account for tensions perceived in the overall presentation. They imply conflicting understandings of the community's history and expectation at different periods, but it is not necessary to engage with that question here. Only McKenzie (1985) has maintained that the Chronicler used a pre-exilic version of the Deuteronomistic History, but his arguments for the dating of Chronicles and indications of the use of 'Dtr 1' are unconvincing.[9] Like the rest of

6. Noth 1967: 1-110. There is a tendency in recent work to draw upon literary features such as irony or other narrative indications to reassert the unity of the Deuteronomistic History; cf. Hoffmann 1980; Long 1984; Hobbs 1985; McConville 1989; 1992.

7. Cf. Dietrich 1972; Veijola 1975.

8. Cross 1973: 274-89. Cross's view is accepted with modifications to the extent of the Dtr 2's work by Levenson (1980), Nelson (1981) and McKenzie (1991).

9. For reviews of McKenzie (1985), see R.W. Klein, *CBQ* 49 (1987): 478-79; J.G. McConville, *JTS* 38 (1987): 137-39; M.A. Throntveit, *JBL* 106 (1987): 319-20; H.G.M. Williamson, *VT* 37 (1987): 107-114. McKenzie agrees with Cross on multiple editions or expansions of Chronicles, and so assigns 'Chr 1' to the early Restoration period. He suggests that the account of Manasseh's repentance (2 Chron. 33.11-17) may have originally stood in the Chronicler's *Vorlage* (1985: 163), but this is very unlikely on stylistic and ideological grounds; see below on the role of Manasseh in the respective works. McKenzie's strongest point has to do with the differences between Chronicles and Kings in 2 Chron. 35.20–36.23, which he thinks must be attributed to the Chronicler's use of another source (1985: 187). A different hypothesis was proposed earlier by Williamson (1982: 408-411; 1982a), who suggested that the additional details in the Chronicler's account of Josiah's confrontation with Neco (2 Chron. 33.21-25) were already found in his *Vorlage* of

his later (fourth century) post-exilic community, the Chronicler knew the Deuteronomistic History essentially in its present form. Our first task, then, is to outline the understanding of history and what expectation (if any) the Deuteronomist held out for his community, as the backdrop against which the shape of the Chronicler's thought is more readily appreciated.

2. *Judgment in the Deuteronomistic History and Chronicles*

Retribution is one of the fundamental themes of the Deuteronomistic History. Noth begins his discussion of the central theological ideas of the work by stating that the author composed his work to show the true meaning of Israel's history from the occupation to the destruction of the old order, namely (1967: 100) 'that God had acted recognizably in this history, responding to the steadily increasing decline with warnings and punishments, and finally, when these had proved fruitless, with complete annihilation'.[10]

How 'complete' or definitive this destruction was in the Deuteronomist's eyes has occasioned considerable debate. It is clear, however, that the Deuteronomist wrote to confirm the justice of God's acts in the destruction and exile, and to convince his readers of that fact.[11] The

---

Kings and represent a further stage in the development of the Deuteronomistic History beyond its canonical shape. Begg (1987a) has contested this suggestion, while Williamson has reaffirmed it in a rejoinder (1987a). If Williamson's suggestion is correct, it would point to the Chronicler's use of a (Palestinian) version of Kings which ended in the destruction, leaving the people in the land, rather than their transportation into exile. However, notwithstanding the different endings of Chronicles and Kings, it remains more likely that the Chronicler worked from a recension of the Deuteronomistic History much like the canonical form. 2 Chron. 30.9 picks up the exilic reference in 1 Kgs 8.50 (see below), while 2 Chron. 36, although different in many respects from 2 Kgs 23.30-31, still has verbal affinities with that chapter that suggest dependence on it (cf. Chapters 1 and 4 above). The Chronicler has adapted it to express his own schema of 'exile and restoration'.

10. '... daß Gott in dieser Geschichte erkennbar gehandelt hat, indem er auf den ständig wachsenden Abfall mit Warnungen und Strafen und schließlich, als diese sich als fruchtlos erwiesen hatten, mit der völligen Vernichtung geantwortet hat.'

11. Cf. Patrick and Scult on the rhetoric of the Deuteronomistic History as 'forensic narrative' (1990: 76): '[The Deuteronomist] had foreshadowed the course of things to come in Deut. 29.1–30.10 and the poetic prophecy in Deuteronomy 32, and again in the last words of Joshua (Josh. 23; 24); he drove home the tenor of his theme in his assessment of each king's performance, his interpolations into the

Deuteronomist, no less than the Chronicler, understood Yahweh to be presiding over the course of history and recompensing the deeds of his covenant people.[12] The Deuteronomic law of worship was the touchstone of fidelity, and because Israel and Judah had failed to follow that law, their histories had ended in destruction. The thought is expressed clearly in Deuteronomy 4 and 28, where it is emphasized that obedience to the Sinaitic covenant will bring prosperity and the secure possession of the land, but apostasy will lead to judgment and the exile of the people. These ideas underlie Solomon's temple dedication prayer (1 Kgs 8.23-53) and the description of Josiah's reforms (2 Kgs 22–23).[13] Chronicles tells much the same story, and in places even strengthens the allusion to the Sinaitic covenant.[14]

The usual contrasts that are drawn between Chronicles and the Deuteronomistic History on cumulative guilt, collective punishment, and the deferment of punishment,[15] have been examined at some length above, where it was concluded that the differences were more a matter of degree and relative emphasis than of conflicting understandings of retribution and human responsibility. The Chronicler also treats the exile as an inevitable outcome from 2 Chronicles 28 onward (the point is conveyed through the repeated literary motif of exile), an indication that he most probably understood this event as the result of repeated disobedience to which numerous acts contributed, rather than purely the fault of Zedekiah and his generation.[16] It is true, however, that the Chronicler emphasizes the short-term nature of retribution and its 'individual or 'generational' character.[17]

The Deuteronomist, on the other hand, reflects a more varied picture

words of the prophets, and his selection and arrangement of incidents. [...] The reader cannot escape the conclusion that YHWH was justified in his judgment, his people were amply prepared for it, and they should now accept the blame.'

12. See Gammie 1970 for a refutation of Koch's influential view that retribution in the Old Testament is really an impersonal process, and for a useful discussion of the relation between recompense and covenant in Deuteronomy.

13. Already Keil (1966 [1872]: 125-33) showed in detail that 1 Kgs 8.23-53 reflects the covenant curses in Lev. 26.14-45 and especially Deut. 28.15-68.

14. Cf. 2 Chron. 7.14 and Deut. 28.10; 2 Chron. 7.20 and Deut. 29.27 [E v. 28]; 2 Chron. 34.24.

15. Cf. von Rad 1930: 12-13; Noth 1967; Japhet 1989: 156-60; cf. Chapter 2 above.

16. *Contra* Japhet 1989: 156-65; 1993: 1069.

17. See Chapter 4 on the paraenetic significance of this particular emphasis.

of the workings of retribution. It seems from a number of narratives that punishment may be meted out relatively quickly or else deferred until a much later time.[18] But whatever may pertain in individual cases, there seems to be a consistent underlying pattern to the Deuteronomistic History. Throughout it demonstrates Israel's repeated propensity to violate the covenant and therefore undermine its possession of the land. The book of Judges is sometimes contrasted at this point with Kings: the former work is said to reflect recurring cycles of apostasy, judgment, repentance and deliverance (cf. Judg. 2.6–16.31), whereas Kings seems to show an inexorable downward spiral.[19] However, as Webb (1987: 112) notes on Judg. 2.19a, 'the turning back of each generation is to a *worse* state of apostasy than that which characterizes the one before it', and Judges concludes on a note suggesting that Israel's hold on the land is increasingly tenuous and marked by chronic failures.

Similarly, the capacity of the Davidic monarchy itself to bring salvation to Israel is called into question in Kings. Among recent writers who have commented on the narrative tendency of the work,[20] it is argued that even reform according to the Law promoted by faithful Davidides such as Hezekiah and Josiah proves to be ineffectual in the face of Judah's mounting disobedience.[21] Such evil reaches its zenith during the

---

18. Thus, punishment soon befalls Jeroboam's family (1 Kgs 14.18), Baasha's house (1 Kgs 11.10-13), Ahab (1 Kgs 22.34), Ahaziah (2 Kgs 1.15-17) and Jezebel (2 Kgs 9.30-37), in each case according to the prophetic word. Other acts of punishment are postponed or extended. Eli's line will be cut off with the deaths of Phinehas and Hophni (1 Sam. 2.34). The people's request for a king and Samuel's reply (1 Sam. 8.4-22) may reflect Solomon's period. The condemnation of Jeroboam's house also extends for some generations (1 Kgs 14.10-18), while 2 Kgs 10.32 intimates the beginning for Israel of the covenant curses of exile and loss of land. These will reach their full realization in 2 Kgs 17 (cf. vv. 7-23). Against this, 2 Kgs 13.23 speaks of the divine compassion that forestalled the exile, presumably to give Israel the opportunity to heed the prophetic call to repentance (2 Kgs 17.13; cf. Wolff 1961). On divine forbearance, cf. also 1 Kgs 11.12-13, 34-36; 21.29; 2 Kgs 22.18-20.

19. Cf. von Rad 1962: 347. Proponents of the 'double redaction' theory believe that Josiah's reign initially represented a decisive reversal of that trend, which is certainly evident at least from Solomon's time (1 Kgs 11).

20. Cf. Hoffmann 1980; Hobbs 1985: 185-86, 296-97, 343; McConville 1989. For contrasting interpretations of Hezekiah and Josiah which presuppose pre-exilic editions of the Deuteronomistic History, cf. Provan 1988; Cross 1973; Nelson 1981; McKenzie 1991.

21. Since Hezekiah is succeeded by the faithless Manasseh, who precipitates the

reign of Manasseh (2 Kgs 21). It is here, too, as is frequently remarked, that the most striking differences appear between the Deuteronomistic History and Chronicles. This fact bears directly on the understanding of judgment reflected in the respective works.

Long (1991: 248-50) describes the Deuteronomistic Manasseh as 'a pivotal figure in the history of the monarchs', because he is presented as an antitype to both Hezekiah and Josiah. Manasseh undoes the work of his father and reintroduces the apostasies of the north into Judah (v. 3). These are the practices of Ahab for which the northern kingdom was finally destroyed (1 Kgs 16.32-33; 2 Kgs 17.10, 16). The list of offences is terrible: it includes idolatry, desecration of the temple, necromancy and human sacrifice (vv. 3-9). Josiah will rectify each of these sins (cf. 2 Kgs 23.4-8, 10, 12) and his own piety will be commended and rewarded, but he cannot finally avert judgment (2 Kgs 22.18-20; 23.26-27). For the Deuteronomist Manasseh precipitates an end that has been long foreshadowed in a history of covenant-breaking (cf. 2 Kgs 21.15). The oracle in 2 Kgs 21.10-15 now states that the sentence on Judah is irrevocable. Alluding to Ahab in v. 13 and the judgment against Samaria in 2 Kgs 17.7-23, it declares that Yahweh's 'inheritance' (נחלה), Israel as an entity of people, land and covenantal bond (cf. Deut. 9.26, 29; 1 Kgs 8.53), will be cast off and given into the hands of enemies.[22]

An altogether different function is served by the Chronicler's presentation of Manasseh's reign (2 Chron. 33.1-20). It is important first to note that the writer not only shares the negative evaluation of Manasseh reflected in his *Vorlage*, but in some respects even intensifies it.[23] The addition of הוא in v. 6 and the pluralizing of 'Baal', 'Asherah' and 'son' in vv. 3 and 6 give added emphasis to Manasseh's wrongdoing. The Chronicler has also included the phrase 'in the valley of the son of Hinnom' and omitted the Deuteronomist's comparison with Ahab (2 Kgs 21.3). Together these changes suggest that the Chronicler's Manasseh is modelled more directly on the arch-apostate Davidic king Ahaz, rather than on the northern king Ahab (cf. 2 Chron. 28.2-4).

exile (in which Hezekiah has his own share; cf. 2 Kgs 20.16-17), and Josiah's reform is carried out in the shadow of Huldah's oracle (2 Kgs 22.15-20).

22. According to the 'double redaction' theory, this unit and others which blame Manasseh for the exile (2 Kgs 23.26-27; 24.2-3) are secondary expansions ('Dtr 2'); cf. Cross 1973. For differing views on the unity of 2 Kgs 21 see Nelson 1981: 65-69; Lowery 1991: 65-69; Long 1991: 246-50.

23. *Contra* Wellhausen 1885: 207-209; Lowery 1991: 185-86.

Since the fall of the northern kingdom is not described *expressis verbis* in Chronicles, the comparison in the *Vorlage* would not be appropriate in the later work. This fact may also explain in part the omission of the judgment oracle against Jerusalem and Judah,[24] although a more compelling reason for this omission is suggested below. 2 Chron. 33.9-10 make it clear that the people followed Manasseh in doing evil, so that his own exile has typological significance: it adumbrates the people's own experience and may also suggest that, in the Chronicler's view, this king and his generation shared joint responsibility for the fall of judgment.

Thus far, the two historical pictures of Manasseh are basically in agreement. However, as we have noted before, the Chronicler's purpose is often more theological and homiletical than simply historical, and the writer's additions (vv. 11-17, 19) indicate how he understood the primary significance of this individual king. These verses recount how Manasseh is personally taken to Babylon at the hands of the Assyrians, where he repents and is restored to his throne. His return is followed by building work and partial reform of the cult. There are a number of historical problems about this additional material,[25] but its theological and rhetorical intention is clear. Whereas the Deuteronomist maintained that Manasseh's guilt had precipitated the fall of judgment, the Chronicler presents him instead as the most outstanding paradigm of the efficacy of repentance. This striking difference is explained by the controlling interests and outlooks of the works: the Deuteronomist was providing a historical theodicy for the exile, while the post-exilic Chronicler's aim was to address and encourage a community that had experienced (at least in historical memory) its own Babylonian exile and restoration. It was no doubt conscious of living in the shadow of that event and feeling its many practical strictures. The Chronicler's homiletic response in this instance was to depict Manasseh, the epitome of unfaithfulness who precipitated judgment in the received tradition, as the outstanding sign of Yahweh's mercy and restoration.

24. 2 Kgs 21.11-15; cf. v. 13, 'the measuring line of Samaria and the plumb line of the house of Ahab'.

25. A range of views is represented in the most recent discussion of the historical problems raised by this passage. Williamson (1982: 391-92) is cautious about the historicity of Manasseh's captivity, while Lowery (1991: 185-89) rejects the account as ideologically motivated invention. Schniedewind (1991: 455-61) argues instead that the source citation in 2 Chron. 33.18b reflects original archival information which the Chronicler incorporated and reinterpreted in his message of 'exile and restoration'.

Once more, the possibility of repentance signified by the temple is the key to the writer's purpose. The language of the additions in 2 Chron. 33.12-13, 19 (ויכנע, ויתפלל, וישמע; cf. וישיבהו and ומעלו) is clearly intended to call to mind the promises of 2 Chron. 7.12b-16a. In this case, the most instructive point lies in Manasseh's response to his circumstances. Having established a comparison with Ahaz in vv. 3 and 6, the Chronicler now contrasts these two: 'in the time of his distress this king Ahaz increased his unfaithfulness against Yahweh' (למעול ביהוה, 2 Chron. 28.22), but 'in his distress [Manasseh] entreated Yahweh his God and humbled himself greatly before the God of his fathers' (2 Chron. 33.12). The Chronicler teaches, therefore, through the example of Manasseh that God is disposed to hear his people and restore their lost blessings, if they will emulate his penitent response and make obedient use of the cult (cf. 2 Chron. 33.15-16).

Although this point has been foreshadowed earlier in the narrative,[26] it must be underlined that Manasseh is the *supreme* example of restoration in Chronicles. This perception of Manasseh is not, of course, in opposition to the historical understanding of his role in Kings, but rather reflects the Chronicler's emphatic belief in restoration *out of* judgment, more so than the alternatives of being preserved from harm or the sad reality of punishment for rebellion. For the Chronicler, Manasseh is the darkest foil against which the merciful, restorative will of God appears all the brighter.

This distinction is brought out additionally by the differing perspectives on the destruction and exile. For the Deuteronomist the catastrophe of 587 is evidently the climax of the work. The events and dates of the final collapse of Judah and Jerusalem are recounted with unusual precision (cf. 2 Kgs 25.1, 3, 8), while the concluding note of Jehoiachin's rehabilitation (vv. 27-30) probably takes us down to the writer's own situation and time (Long 1991: 288). The Deuteronomist is thus keenly aware of living in the aftermath of the loss of statehood, with the attendant exile and dispersion of his people.

The Chronicler, on the other hand, has a wholly different historical

---

26. The same pattern of (partial) restoration to the penitent has been depicted already in the case of Rehoboam and Judah following Shishak's invasion (2 Chron. 12.6-8, 12), and in Hezekiah's appeal to the north after the Assyrian destruction (2 Chron. 30.6-9). Both passages use the term פליטה 'escapee', which took on a more specialized meaning in the post-exilic period for the returnees for Babylon (Ezra 9.8, 13-15; Neh. 1.2; cf. Williamson 1985: 135).

(and geographical) perspective. Writing in Jerusalem, where the restoration is a partial reality, he looks on the exile as an episode from the past whose end was effected by the prophetic word that controls history (2 Chron. 36.21). Moreover, the citation of Lev. 26.43 in 2 Chron. 36.21 shows that the Chronicler considered the exile as an essentially positive period when the land 'enjoyed (רצתה) its sabbaths'. Ackroyd (1991: 242) takes this to mean 'a period of enforced fallowness, comparable with the sabbath years of the law (cf. Lev. 25)', which makes the land once more acceptable to God: 'The exile is not viewed by him [the Chronicler] simply in terms of punishment—though this is evident enough in the context—but also in terms of the recuperation needed for the new life of the post-exilic period'.[27] It should be noted, too, that Cyrus's decree (vv. 22-23) is also the fulfilment of prophecy. This edict reverses two of the effects of the disaster, the destruction of the temple and the exile of the people. For the Chronicler, then, the consequences of past wrongdoing are fully requited, and his community now enjoys a new dispensation of opportunity.

3. *Hope in the Deuteronomistic History and Chronicles*

The nature of the 'Deuteronomistic hope' has provoked a long and continuing debate, which has itself become more complex as different redactional theories have been proposed.[28] Again, however, our concern must be with the final form of the text as the Chronicler would have known and interpreted it. Two sharply divergent positions are represented in research. The first minimizes the elements of hope in the work, while the second lays great stress on the promise to David of an eternal dynasty (2 Sam. 7.11-16).

The earliest—and most pessimistic—interpretation of this question

27. Cf. similarly Japhet 1993: 1075-76.
28. From a redactional perspective, the main issue concerns the promissory covenant with David. As I discuss below, von Rad identified in the Deuteronomistic History a theme of grace centring on Nathan's oracle (2 Sam. 7.11-16). Cross (1973: 285-87) argued that this theme of an indefectible promise (cf. 1 Kgs 11.12-13, 32, 34, 36; 2 Kgs 8.19; 19.34; 20.6) belonged to the Josianic Dtr. 1 and had no place in the thinking of the exilic Dtr. 2. Support for this view is found in those passages which make perdurance of the promise conditional on obedience (1 Kgs 2.2-4; 6.11-13; 8.25; 9.1-9); cf. Levenson 1981: 145-46. By contrast, McConville (1989; 1992) criticizes redactional approaches for being overly schematic and failing to understand literary features of the work.

was stated by Noth. In his view the Deuteronomist had demonstrated that the judgment on Israel was definitive and final. The work did not express any hope for an exiled and scattered people; instead, it treated their destruction as an accomplished fact. The report of Jehoiachin's rehabilitation (2 Kgs 25.27-30) was simply the last information available to the historian and was not intended to herald a new age (1967: 108).

Not surprisingly, few have followed Noth in his precise understanding of the work's purpose or future outlook.[29] Von Rad (1948; ET 1953) countered Noth's interpretation by arguing that the real concern of the Deuteronomistic History was with the operation of Yahweh's word in history. The schema of prophecy and fulfilment in the work showed that this had a double capacity, judging and destroying as well as saving and forgiving. Thus, alongside the Deuteronomic curses and the prophetic threats stood 'a note of grace' in the promise to David (1953: 89): 'It is the Nathan promise which runs through the history like a κατέχων and wards off the long merited judgment from the kingdom "for the sake of David".'

Von Rad found in those passages throughout 1 and 2 Kings alluding to the Davidic promise[30] a series of 'Messianic conceptions' which, in his view, provided the basis of hope on the part of the Deuteronomist for the restoration of the Davidic monarchy. In this light, the reference to Jehoiachin's release was seen to have special theological significance. While the judgment component of Yahweh's word dominated, at least for the time being in the reality of the exile, and the Deuteronomist could not minimize the severity of God's punishment, neither could he concede that Yahweh's promise to David had failed. The Deuteronomist resolved this dilemma by recounting Jehoiachin's release from prison. In this way he indicated that the Davidic line had continued despite judgment and that it provided an opportunity for Yahweh to begin anew with his people.

Again, few have been fully persuaded by this argument. It has been rightly objected that no mention is made at the end of 2 Kings of the Nathan oracle, nor indeed of Yahweh's hand in this episode, as we might expect if the Deuteronomist was signalling the resumption of

29. But cf. Schmidt 1983: 112, and Würthwein 1984: 481-84, who have reaffirmed Noth's interpretation. Van Seters sees the Deuteronomist's purpose as historiographic: he wrote 'as the first known historian in Western civilization' (1983: 362) to render an account of his nation's past for posterity.

30. Cf. 1 Kgs 8.20, 25; 9.5; 11.12-13, 32, 36; 15.4; 2 Kgs 8.19; 19.34; 20.6.

saving history. The most this passage allows, together with the Gedaliah incident (cf. 2 Kgs 25.24), is the possibility of good treatment of the Judean survivors at the hands of the Babylonians.[31] To this extent, the work does end on a positive note, but it is muted and falls far short of fuelling expectations of restoration.[32]

The Deuteronomist demonstrated both the failure of the dynasty (the defection from the Davidic ideal is evident from the time of Solomon, 1 Kings 11) and the persistent sinfulness of the people that resulted in their dispossession. Nevertheless, the Deuteronomist affirms that even in exile Israel is still Yahweh's people, and as such, has the possibility of a new existence. Wolff (1961) has argued that the purpose of the work is to be found in its repeated pattern of apostasy, punishment, repentance (√שוב) and deliverance, which is reflected particularly in Judges and the people's request for a king (1 Sam. 12; cf. vv. 19-22). According to Wolff, the Deuteronomist's intention was to show the exiles that they were in the second stage of that cycle and therefore needed to cry out to Yahweh in repentance. For Wolff, then, the Deuteronomist's purpose was not wholly negative as it was for Noth, nor did it offer a Davidic hope, as von Rad claimed. Rather, the writer raised only the possibility of hope by demonstrating the pattern of Yahweh's previous dealings with his people; the essential task of the exiles was to respond to the invitation to repent.

This interpretation seems basically correct. The most significant use of the motif of repentance (√שוב), as Wolff recognized, is found in Solomon's temple dedication prayer (1 Kgs 8.23-53). The composition of this chapter is disputed, but it is generally agreed that the concluding verses (vv. 46-53) at least are of exilic origin.[33] These verses specifically

---

31. Thus Begg 1986: 54.

32. Levenson (1984) has sought to give modified support to von Rad's interpretation of the last verses of Kings. He argues that 2 Kgs 25.28 (וידבר אתו טובות) connotes a treaty with Evil-Merodach, a form of 'conditional messianism in the diaspora' in which the original covenant with David is brought 'into line with the new historical reality'. Begg (1986) questions the likelihood of this interpretation, pointing out that nothing is said about Jehoiachin's sons. Deut. 4.29-31 speaks of exilic repentance and 30.1-10 of a return to the land. Wolff (1961: 182) considered these passages secondary; cf. Noth 1967: 109 n. 3; Cross 1973: 278 n. 3; Nelson 1981: 94. An alternative approach is suggested by McConville (1992). He argues from a linguistic comparison of Deut. 29.17-27 and 1 Kgs 8.46-53 that the writer of Kings is consciously distancing himself from Deuteronomy and its hope of return.

33. Cf. Levenson 1981: 152-59.

address the question of what Israel should do in the event of exile for disobedience. The Deuteronomist's answer is precise: the people must acknowledge the justice of Yahweh's act, repent [34] and beseech Yahweh for forgiveness. In the conclusion to the prayer (vv. 50b-52) the fullest statement of the writer's hope may be found:

> Grant them compassion in the sight of their captors, so that they may have compassion on them. For they are your people and your inheritance, whom you brought out of Egypt, from the midst of the iron furnace. Let your eyes be open to the supplication of your servant and to the supplication of your people Israel, hearing them whenever they call to you. For you separated them from all the peoples of the earth to be your inheritance, as you declared through Moses your servant, when you brought our fathers out of Egypt, Lord Yahweh.

Two aspects of this prayer call for comment. First, it is significant that its final specific petition is a plea for merciful treatment at the hands of Israel's captors.[35] Nothing is said at this point either about the dynastic promise or a return to the land; instead, the focus is on the survival of Israel as a community in exile (McConville 1992: 76). Secondly, the prayer is grounded on Yahweh's election of Israel in the exodus and Sinaitic covenant. Judgment has resulted in the loss of those centres which gave cohesion and identity to Israel: the land, city, temple and functioning kingship; and yet the people remain Yahweh's special possession (נחלה). Exile has apparently returned Israel to the pre-monarchic status ante quo, in which the ancient deliverance and election take on a new salvific significance. For the Deuteronomist Yahweh's presence is not restricted to the land or temple, so the possibility of renewed blessing, dependent on repentance, is left open.

The Chronicler's use and modification of this material is striking, particularly in the new ending he assigns to the prayer. First, the Deuteronomist's petition for mercy for the exiles (1 Kgs 8.50) is omitted, presumably because it would not be so relevant to a community that had been restored to the land. That petition is, however, echoed by the Chronicler's Hezekiah in 2 Chron. 30.9: 'If you return to Yahweh, your brothers and your sons will find mercy from their captors and

---

34. Note the repeated word-play on captivity and repentance in vv. 46-48: ושבום, שביהם, נשבו, ושבו, שביהם, שבו, ושבו, והשיבו, שביהם.

35. This, incidentally, accords with Begg's view (1986), noted above, of what the Deuteronomist intends through Gedaliah's words and Jehoiachin's release.

return to their land'. This verse witnesses to a concern with the continuing diaspora in the Chronicler's day, that it too would be restored to the land.

Secondly, the petition that Yahweh would hear his people 'whenever they call to you' is reformulated and connected explicitly with the temple as 'the prayer of this place' (2 Chron. 6.40; 7.15). The temple, being restored after the destruction and exile, is now presented as an impetus to expectant prayer.

Thirdly, and most significantly, the Chronicler has replaced the reference to the exodus with an appeal on the basis of the Davidic covenant: 'Remember your steadfast love for David (חסדי דויד) your servant' (2 Chron. 6.42).[36] These changes signify more than a mere updating of earlier material in the light of the Return: they reflect a *development* (and to some extent, *transformation*) of these traditions and theological motifs in terms of the Chronicler's beliefs, as the following section argues.

4. *Chronicles as Resumption and Development*

We are now in a position to consider the message of Chronicles in relation to its immediate literary-theological predecessors. So far the work has been examined in comparison only with the Deuteronomistic History, but there is in my view an additional, intermediate stage which Chronicles presupposes and implicitly comments upon, the programme of community restoration reflected in Ezra–Nehemiah. While the themes of judgment and hope are perhaps less pronounced here for the purpose of comparison,[37] it does appear that Chronicles and Ezra–Nehemiah have a special literary relationship with each other. This should not be characterized as 'continuation' (according to the older critical view of unitary composition), especially if the view is correct which sees them as separate works by different authors, with Chronicles post-dating Ezra–Nehemiah. But neither are the two works wholly disjunct, with their similarities to be explained by the mere fact that both are (most probably) the products of temple circles with overlapping interests and

36. Cf. Chapter 7 on the meaning of חסדי דויד and its possible messianic or 'royalist' significance for the Chronicler.

37. But note the use of exodus typology for the return in Ezra 1.5-8, 11 (Williamson 1985: 15-19) and the 'Deuteronomistic' understanding of judgment in Ezra 9; Neh. 1, 9.

outlooks. Although the *narrative* of Chronicles precedes that of Ezra–
Nehemiah, it is written from the perspective of the Return, in part as this
is described in Ezra–Nehemiah, and it appears, to some extent, to draw
upon the language and themes of that work. In terms of its message,
Chronicles offers a *resumption and development* of the thought not only
of the Deuteronomistic History but also of Ezra–Nehemiah.[38] Taking the
works, then, in the order Deuteronomistic History–Ezra–Nehemiah–
Chronicles, it may be suggested that the Chronicler understood his own
composition as setting forth the *third* stage, as it were, in the restoration
of Israel from the catastrophe of judgment and exile.

To begin with, the Chronicler develops two themes in particular from
the Deuteronomistic History, repentance and the Davidic covenant, and
gives them a more comprehensive and central place in his own presentation. It will be recalled that the exilic Deuteronomist writes for a
chastened people to counsel repentance for their age-long violation of
the covenant. As a theodicy for Yahweh's judgment and a summons to
cry out to him in penitence, the Deuteronomistic History makes coherent, rhetorical sense, but as that situation passed, the work would have
lost its immediate relevance for the community.[39] The Chronicler may
assume that this exilic repentance (the first stage in restoration in his
work [cf. 2 Chron. 7.14], as indeed it is for the Deuteronomist) has in
fact taken place, for Yahweh has forgiven his people and facilitated their
return. This fact goes beyond the clearest expectation of the
Deuteronomist.[40] Over against the Deuteronomistic History, Chronicles
must appear a much more hopeful and positive work, as well as more
specific in the character of its hope.[41]

Next, the theme of the Davidic covenant is developed considerably
from the earlier history, and is in fact made the basis whereby such
restoration is possible. The promises to David in 2 Sam. 7.11-16 are
taken up first in 1 Chron. 17.10-14, and are echoed next in several

38. Indeed this very relationship is suggested by the literary *Wiederaufnahme* of
Ezra 1.1-3 in 2 Chron. 36.22-23. See Chapter 1 for arguments that the ending is an
original part of the Chronicler's work, though derived from Ezra, and Chapter 8 for a
discussion of its paraenetic significance in the Chronicler's use.

39. Cf. Patrick and Scult 1990: 77-78.

40. Cf. 1 Kgs 8.50 and its re-use in 2 Chron. 30.9.

41. Similarly, we have seen repeatedly how its doctrine of retribution is really to
do with the possibility of repentance and restoration, a point dramatically underlined
through its portrayal of Manasseh that diverges radically in its significance from the
Deuteronomist.

Chronistic passages: David's speeches in 1 Chron. 22.7-19, 28.2-10 and 29.1-5, and his prayer in 1 Chron. 29.10-19. These passages draw a close connection between the dynastic promise and the building of the temple, and indicate that in that activity the promises find their initial fulfilment. The conclusion to Solomon's temple prayer (2 Chron. 6.42) is in the same vein and looks to a continuing fulfilment thereafter on the same basis (cf. 2 Chron. 6.10). Those in the Chronicler's time who made use of the temple as Solomon's prayer envisaged would be reminded of the Davidic covenant which that building, in its complete functioning, signified.[42] This promise, which in the Deuteronomistic History was presented so brightly in 2 Samuel 7 as a charter of hope for Israel (cf. vv. 18-29), but which became problematic from Solomon's reign onward and is effectively absent from the Deuteronomist's hope,[43] is once more reasserted at the very heart of the Chronicler's presentation and programme.[44]

The second stage of the restoration is the return of the exiles and the

42. Selman (1994b: 551) makes the persuasive suggestion that the expression 'to build him a house' in the conclusion of the work in 2 Chron. 36.23 (= Ezra 1.2) is not simply fortuitous but 'a deliberate echo of the central promise of the Davidic covenant' (cf. 1 Chron. 17.11-12 [contrast 2 Sam. 7.11, 'Yahweh will *make* you a house']; 22.10; 28.6; 2 Chron. 6.9-10). David Gunn, in a discussion that is orientated to the poetics and the intertextual relationships of these works, remarks (1989: 147): 'The end of Kings is a gaping hole which, when we peer into it, loops us back to Deuteronomy, to where we stand "today" before Moses, "outside" pondering the invitation to enter and participate in a new gift. The ending of Chronicles bridges that gulf surely, converts desolation into a sabbath (2 Chron. 36.21), and marches us resolutely toward an unambiguous goal—to build YHWH a house. Cyrus' decree (36.23) strikingly resumes David's charge to Solomon (1 Chron. 22.6, 18-19).'

43. Thus Wolff, rightly, against von Rad; cf. Veijola. It must be stressed, however, that as a *promissory* covenant, the Davidic covenant is eternal (cf. 2 Sam. 7.13b; 23.5). It is not presented in the Deuteronomistic History as having been abrogated, as proponents of multiple redactions have asserted, and *a fortiori* this is certainly not the case with the Chronicler (*contra* Japhet 1989: 460-67). Cf. McCarthy 1972: 45-52. The conditions of obedience reflected in passages such as 1 Kgs 2.4, 8.25 and 9.4-5 have to do with the benefits of individuals within the line, rather than the validity of the promise as such. There can be no doubt that the events of 587 dealt a severe blow to this faith (cf. Ps. 89.20-46 [E 19-45]), but it was the genius of the Chronicler to pick up again this central theme and affirm its eternal validity for his community.

44. The central place of the Davidic covenant in the Chronicler's thought is affirmed most recently by Riley (1993: 168-85) although he denies that this ideology has any dynastic overtones or a personal focus.

232   *Retribution and Eschatology in Chronicles*

re-establishment of the community's cultic life. As this period is presented in Ezra–Nehemiah, it has its positive features but it is still ambiguous and far from ideal: sin persists in the community (Ezra 10; Neh. 13), and Judah's subject status is perceived as continuing punishment (Ezra 9.6-15; Neh. 1.5-11; 9.32-37). The temple is now functioning again, but it is not associated in this work with the ideology of the Davidic covenant.

The Chronicler's work should be understood as presupposing and building upon the account in Ezra–Nehemiah.[45] This concerns the structure of the work as well as its thought.

First, Selman (1994a: 38) notes that two of the three main sections of Chronicles (1 Chron. 1–9; 2 Chron. 10–36) conclude with citations from Ezra-Nehemiah, both of which have to do with the temple and the Return to the land (1 Chron. 9.2-17 = Neh. 11.3-19; 2 Chron. 36.22-23 = Ezra 1.1-2). The first-mentioned passage goes on to depict (in 1 Chron. 9.10-34) the temple cult being faithfully performed through the Levitical offices. This was the ideal round of activities to which the Return in 2 Chron. 36.22-23 was directed, and the description indicates the successful fulfilment in the post-exilic period of God's purposes for the temple.

Secondly, over against Ezra–Nehemiah, a more positive tone marks the Chronicler's work. The writer affirms that the time of Israel's punishment is past (2 Chron. 36.21; contrast Ezra 9.7-8; Neh. 9.36-37) and encourages his community to hope in a yet greater fulfilment of the ancient promises which the temple mediates.

Finally, as Japhet (1989) and Williamson (1977a) have demonstrated, the Chronicler has an altogether more comprehensive definition of 'Israel' than the exclusive understanding of the community reflected in Ezra–Nehemiah. The appeal of Chronicles is to embrace within the Restoration community all who have a rightful claim to belong to 'Israel', and the popular temple cult especially is the focus of such a gathering.

45. At the linguistic level we may note the use of מעל in Ezra 9.2, 4; 10.2, 6, 10; Neh. 13.27, although in these passages it narrowly denotes intermarriage with foreigners, which is not an issue in Chronicles (contrast Neh. 1.8). Cf. Chapter 3 above on the tradition-historical background to the Chronicler's use of מעל.

5. Conclusion

The Chronicler sets forth in his work a conscious reinterpretation and development of the earlier scriptural traditions of Israel, according to his own distinctive perspectives and his reflection on the meaning of the Return as the resumption of Yahweh's saving history with his people. Themes in Samuel–Kings are recast to emphasize Yahweh's mercy and restorative purposes, rather than the reality of judgment. By the same token, although Ezra–Nehemiah showed that the initial Return appeared to have failed to obtain its bright objectives of a renewed and faithful community (this seems the likeliest way of reading the rather dismaying conclusion in Nehemiah 13, in which the sin of intermarriage persists[46]), the Chronicler nevertheless affirms that earlier work of restoration as a decisive and positive stage in 'building Yahweh's house', and he puts it in the context of God's irrefrangible promise to David.

46. Cf. Williamson 1985: 402; McConville 1986b: 211-13.

Chapter 10

CONCLUSIONS

The renewed attention that Chronicles has enjoyed in recent years has led to a reappraisal of much of the consensus about the work that prevailed in earlier generations of research. Older assumptions about the extent, *Tendenzen* and historical setting of Chronicles have been effectively challenged from several quarters. While it would be too early to speak of a new consensus, it is evident that the work is being considered, at least in Anglo-American circles, in a very different light from the relative neglect (not to mention disdain) which it has faced for most of the modern period.[1]

This study stands consciously in that line of reconstruction and reinterpretation. By undertaking a detailed investigation of two of the principal theological concerns of the work, it has sought to penetrate more closely to the nature of the Chronicler's outlook and purpose. A number of steps and approaches have been involved in this process.

First, by distinguishing Chronicles from Ezra–Nehemiah and placing it chronologically *after* that work, we are able to consider Chronicles separately, on its own terms, as well as in comparison with Ezra–Nehemiah. Such an approach, I believe, best expresses the real continuities which commentators have long observed between these works, as well as their striking *dis*continuities.[2]

---

1. See Strübind (1991: 1-4 and especially n. 17) on the continuing reception (or rejection) of Chronicles in German-language circles, much of which can still be attributed to Wellhausen's (1878) exposition of its *Grundgedanken*. The survey above (Chapter 2) of the history of interpretation of retribution in Chronicles has confirmed the decisive influence of Wellhausen's views even up to Japhet. Further, the 'anti-' or 'realized' eschatological interpretation of recent years must now appear a wrong turning, the more closely the structure of the Chronicler's thought is examined.

2. For different configurations of these works, see most recently Clines 1990: 85-105 and Ackroyd 1991: 344-59.

Secondly, some of the older critical assumptions relating more generally to the history and ideology of the exilic/post-exilic period have been questioned or rejected, at least in their classical form. A number of these views provided the ideological frame within which Chronicles has often been interpreted, and as they are modified or rejected, the Chronicler's message needs to be considered afresh.[3]

Thirdly, this study has emphasized the literary achievement of the Chronicler and the carefully wrought form of his work as a fundamental element in interpretation. Of particular importance here are the writer's special recurrent theological vocabulary, and the narrative structure of the book, which makes implicit as well as explicit comment on the nature of Yahweh's involvement with his people.

Fourthly, in attempting to reconstruct something of the life and thought of this period, we have made some use of analogous sociological models for interpreting the function of the genealogies. Here a caveat is in order: while the use of such models is certain to grow in importance, nevertheless it raises critical questions of methodology and fact, about which there must always be a large degree of provisionality.[4] As Wilson reminds us (1984: 82), 'Explorations of the social dimensions of the Old Testament world are most useful when employed in conjunction with more traditional interpretative tools'.

It must be recalled, of course, that the texts themselves are the most

3. Such as the notion of 'corporate personality' and developing concepts of individual responsibility, or Chronicles being fundamentally about theodicy (von Rad, North), or reflecting the (supposedly) 'anti-eschatological' viewpoint of the Priestly Writing (Plöger). Differences in outlook between English-language and German scholarship are also reflected in the ascription by Rudolph and Plöger (following Noth) to Chronicles of an anti-Samaritan *Tendenz*; cf. Becker 1988; Oeming 1990; contrast Coggins 1975: 68-72 and Williamson 1977; 1982 on 2 Chron. 13, who finds nothing in Chronicles relating to the Samaritan controversy.

4. Hanson (1975; 1986) is explicitly indebted to sociological models that derive from Troeltsch, Weber and Mannheim in reconstructing what he believes were the different 'parties' and groups of the post-exilic period and their supposed ideologies, but we have found little *textual* evidence for his proposals, and a good deal in Chronicles that contradicts it. The contrast which Plöger drew between 'theocracy' and 'eschatology' is equally questionable. For examples of sociologically based approaches to the post-exilic period, see most recently the essays in Davies 1991, although these discussions do not engage much with Chronicles. Richard Horsley's 'Response' in this collection (pp. 163-74) makes some salutary remarks on the practical limitations to applying modern sociological models to ancient Near Eastern imperial society.

234

important witnesses for a historical period about which there are still (and will most probably remain) large gaps in knowledge. In using largely 'traditional interpretative tools' and applying them to the writer's retributive and eschatological thought, we are led to a number of conclusions about Chronicles and its period that differ in significant respects from some prevalent and long-standing opinions. The following points summarize the ways in which I believe this study has contributed to a more accurate interpretation of the work.

First, it is clear that in both its retributive and eschatological doctrine the Chronicler's thought is fundamentally *positive and forward-looking*.

1. The Chronicler's theology of retribution, so far from being a sclerotic dogmatism about cause and effect or a species of 'divine pragmatism', as it has been generally depicted, is in fact a reflex of the writer's convictions about *divine grace*, an emphasis concerned above all to highlight Yahweh's mercy and restorative activity toward his people. Similarly, the writer's eschatological outlook, though difficult to characterize clearly in the full extent of its expectation, does not express satisfaction with the status quo as the fulfilment of the Restoration community's expectations, as some more recent writers have urged, but in every respect reflects a hopeful 'openness' to the future. These points have been established in this study through a consideration of a wider body of evidence than earlier studies have afforded, including the 'tendency' or direction of the themes and motifs of the work, and its narrative structure. The Chronicler's thought is not an idiosyncratic, ideological *cul de sac* but belongs rather within the mainstream of Old Testament theology in its emphasis on restoration and fulfilment, and in looking hopefully to God to accomplish a new work of salvation for the sake of his covenant people.[5] Indeed, the author seems to have

5.   Rather than being, for example, 'at the edge of the canon' in its supposed anti-eschatological outlook (Rudolph 1955: xxiii), or diverging radically from the wider biblical tradition in depicting Israel's history as the 'absolutization of divine justice' in its retributive thought, as Japhet (1989: 153-54) claims. The extremism of this latter opinion is clear. On the Davidic covenant in Chronicles (quite neglected by Japhet), already von Rad (1930: 136) affirmed: 'Chronicles is a single great appeal to Yahweh's promise' ('*Die Chronik ist ein einziger großer Rekurs auf Jahwes Verheißung*', emphasis original); while Childs (1979: 643-44) states concisely: '[The Chronicler's] purpose in writing seems entirely straightforward. The author was attempting to interpret to the restored community in Jerusalem the history of Israel as an eternal covenant between God and David which demanded an obedient response to the divine law. On the basis of past history he sought repeatedly to draw the lesson

understood his own work as an authoritative summation and (to some extent) a development of the earlier scriptural traditions of his people, in which he testifies to the resumption in his own time of the flow of salvation history, of Yahweh's renewed saving activity among his chastened and forgiven people.

2. We may now appreciate more clearly the integral relationship between retribution and eschatology in the Chronicler's work. They are related first as dimensions of the Davidic covenant, which for the Chronicler is eternally valid and continues to mediate Yahweh's promises for the Davidic line, the people and the land, and defines the meaning of the temple as a symbol of the covenant and the place of restoration.[6] However, a closer relationship between these doctrines arises from the fact that retribution in Chronicles has itself *a forward-looking or eschatological character*: as the doctrine is described above, it is basically a call to repentance and hope in Yahweh's restoration. This is in marked contrast to the usual 'pragmatic' understanding of the doctrine, which is non-eschatological and orientated to the present (cf. 'immediate retribution'). The older view notwithstanding, the real function of the Chronicler's retributive doctrine is to hold up before the community the possibilities of its *future* existence; in an important sense, the community's future is actually dependent on its response to the offer of restoration and the summons to repentance, faith and reform which this doctrine embraces (hence the pervasive paraenetic tone of the work).

Thus, the Chronicler's theology, as it is expressed through his doctrine of retribution and his eschatology, possesses an underlying coherence and unity. This fact is derived ultimately from the writer's perception of Yahweh's character: the God of Israel is presented as a forward-looking and merciful God committed to the restoration of his people, and the Chronicler's interpretation of the Davidic covenant duly reflects this understanding.[7]

that Israel prospered when obedient, but courted God's wrath and the destruction of the nation through disobedience. In spite of continual warnings from the prophets, Israel abandoned God's law and suffered the consequences (2 Chron. 36.15-16). However, after the judgment, God once again restored his people who continue to stand under the same divine imperatives.' This approach is developed independently and most extensively by Selman (1994a: 45-65).

6.   Cf. 1 Chron. 17.4-14; 2 Chron. 7.12-22.
7.   Cf. 1 Chron. 17.9-10, 20-21; 2 Chron. 36.22-23.

A further conclusion of this study concerns the writer's historical method. As far as we can judge from the special Chronistic material relating to reward and punishment in 2 Chronicles 10–36, it appears that the Chronicler set about his task of re-presenting the past to his community in a historically responsible way and was not cavalier in the invention of the facts to suit his case. While the question of the Chronicler's extrabiblical sources may never be satisfactorily resolved, it appears that the author made extensive use of such materials and worked within their constraints. Neither the older representations of Chronicles as a tendentious falsification of the past (de Wette) nor the recent, more positive suggestions that it is edifying fiction (Welten), an extended piece of typology (Mosis), or 'aggadic exegesis' (Fishbane), do proper justice to the character of the work. Of course, the writer's *purpose* in his *Sondergut* is evident enough: it is to demonstrate from Judah's history the consequences of obedience and disobedience and to elicit the appropriate response of repentance and faith. No doubt the degree of evident moralizing in the Chronicler's work has raised suspicions about the traditions he purports to draw on. However, it is salutary to recall that *every* narrative history (as opposed to annalistic 'chronicle') is to some extent an aesthetic and moral construct. The philosopher of history Hayden White has well remarked that that no story can be told without asserting connections between events, and it is these which lend moral direction to the story as a whole. While this is true for fact or fiction, history exerts a much greater persuasive force upon its readers, as White recognizes (1981: 20): 'We can comprehend the appeal of historical (narrative) discourse by recognizing the extent to which it makes the real desirable, makes the real into an object of desire, and does so by its imposition, upon events that are represented as real, of the formal coherency that stories possess.'

In the Chronicler's hands the narrative possesses its persuasive force precisely because it is based in the history of the people to whom it is addressed. The point is well expressed by Patrick and Scult, who observe in their study of the rhetoric of the biblical histories (1990: 48) that 'a narrative which makes a claim to historicity takes a much more aggressive and direct stand in relationship to the audience. The events portrayed in a historical narrative happened in the real world and so have a forward movement that carries directly into the world of the reader'. It is clear from passages such as 1 Chron. 9.2-3 and 28.8 that the Chronicler understands his community as living in unbroken continuity with pre-exilic Israel and inheriting its promises and obligations. These concerns notwithstanding, there is substantial evidence that the Chronicler depended upon extrabiblical sources for his retributive motifs in 2 Chron. 10–36, a fact which should caution us from accepting the sharp distinction often drawn between theology and history in the Chronicler's work.

Moving more tentatively from the text to its situation, we may consider now what light the Chronicler's treatment of retribution and eschatology cast on the *Sitz im Leben* of the work. Two interests in particular are suggested by the rhetorical character of the book.

First, Chronicles appears as a *genuinely populist work*: it repeatedly depicts the consultation, encouragement, and collective activity of the leadership and people of Israel and Judah around one constant focus, the foundation, support and reform of the Jerusalem cult. The work tirelessly reiterates the point that support of the cult leads to the community's benefit, but neglect and apostasy lead to its detriment. It may be fairly inferred from so prominent a Chronistic theme that the writer was concerned to foster popular support for the cult of his own day. Such evidence as we have from the middle Persian period (Mal. 3.8-10; Neh. 12.44-47; 13.10-13) certainly suggests that at different times tithe support for the Levites was by no means assured or forthcoming, and against this the Chronicler no doubt set the ideal portrayed in passages such as 2 Chron. 31.4-19 as a positive counterpoise. In connecting such support for the temple and clergy with the prosperity of the community, the Chronicler reflects a typical theme of post-exilic temple circles.[8]

However, the writer has wider concerns in his religious programme than the immediate question of material support for the cult and its officers. The Chronicler's broad appeal to the community at large, his markedly positive depiction of the people, and the frequent descriptions of their festive joy all indicate that the writer is interested in the revival and transformation of his community through its participation in temple worship and prayer; for it is precisely there that Israel may recognize its identity and hope as being established in the ancient covenant promises to which the temple testifies.

Related to this emphasis is the Chronicler's *concern for unity,* which others have rightly found reflected for example in his 'pan-Israelitism'. Recently Talmon has sketched the internal diversification of Judaism in the early Hellenistic period, which he believes must be understood

8. Cf. Mason 1990: 182-83, 253.

against the backdrop of the Babylonian Exile and the Return (1991: 16-43, esp. 20-30). Talmon cogently argues that the loss of those political and religious 'centres' which accorded homogeneity and uniformity to the pre-exilic kingdom of Judah (in particular monarchy, statehood and temple) was a factor in the rise of considerable heterogeneity and diversity within post-exilic Judaism. While this question cannot be examined here, we may well see a reflex of that development in the way in which the Chronicler presents the Davidic-Solomonic dynasty and temple as the foci of unity for 'all Israel', against the likely centrifugal social and religious tendencies of his day.[9]

We cannot say with any certainty how the message of Chronicles was immediately appropriated or what impact it exercised in its day. Light on this question would certainly aid the correct interpretation of the work, but the relative paucity of information about the middle and later Persian period does not permit us to assign too precise a date or *Sitz im Leben* to the book. Nevertheless, while the early *Wirkungsgeschichte* of this work is unknown, it is certainly true as a general principle that the received scriptures of a community exercise a continuing influence in their history and thought, and it is surely not without significance that Chronicles came to mark the conclusion, in its canonical form, of the Hebrew Bible.[10] Japhet (1989: 507) unhesitatingly sees Chronicles as a bridge to 'post-biblical thought', especially in its retributive doctrine, which she characterizes as the germ of the rabbinical understanding of divine justice and strict recompense (pp. 184-85), and its futurist outlook, which she claims is 'non-eschatological', neither setting any store by the Davidic covenant (pp. 453-67) nor expecting any divine intervention that would significantly alter the essentially stable circumstances of that community's life. However, as I have argued at length above, these interpretations are ill-founded, as is Japhet's more general attempt to read Chronicles as a progenitor of a kind of later rationalistic Judaism. I certainly endorse Japhet's strictures against the ways in which the 'Davidism' of Chronicles has been understood by many Christian inter-

---

9.   Cf. Braun 1976; Williamson 1991; cf. also Williamson 1977a: 132-40 on the related question of the definition of 'Israel' in the post-exilic period.

10.   That this arrangement was well established by the first century CE is evidently reflected in Mt. 23.35; Lk. 11.51; cf. 2 Chron. 24.20-21. See Johnstone's articles (esp. 1983) for some suggestive reflections on the place of Chronicles in the canonical arrangement of the Hebrew Bible.

preters,[11] but would suggest (however tentatively) that there are broader—and deeper—lines of continuity connecting the Chronicler's concern with the Davidic covenant (and its implicit messianism) with the subsequent historical period. This suggestion derives from the central theological insistence of Chronicles, that the covenant constituted Israel as the earthly manifestation of the kingdom of God, in a reality manifested by the temple, appointed for atonement and prayer, and the Davidic line, the personal expression of God's rule. Thus, as the Hebrew Bible in its canonical form concludes by reaffirming the perdurance of this promise (2 Chron. 36.23), it issues an invitation to respond (ויעל), and in doing so it opens up trajectories that may take us into the centre of New Testament faith.

---

11. Riley (1993: 196-98), makes an analogous point independently in his discussion of 2 Chron. 6.42 (= Isa. 55.3b), which he denies has any reference to the Davidic line.

APPENDIX: RETRIBUTIVE MOTIFS IN 2 CHRONICLES 10–36

Reign	Motifs of Blessing and Reward								
	Building	Progeny	Wealth, Fame	Gifts, Tribute	Cult Reform	Army	Military Success	'Fear of YHWH' upon enemy	'Rest' for the land
Rehoboam	11.5-12	11.19-21							
Abijah		13.21				13.3	13.15-16		
Asa	14.5-6				14.2-4, 8-16				13.23; 14.4-6, 15, 19
Jehoshaphat	17.12-13		18.1	17.5,11	17.6; 19.4-5	17.2, 13-19	20.22-23	17.10; 20.29	17.10; 20.30
Jehoram									
Ahaziah									
Joash		24.3			23.16-17				23.21
Amaziah						25.5	25.11-12		
Uzziah	26.2, 6, 9-10		26.15	26.8			26.6-7		
Jotham	27.3-4			27.6			27.5		
Ahaz									
Hezekiah	32.5		32.23, 27-29	32.23	29.3-4; 30.14; 31.1-2	32.6	32.21		
Manasseh	33.14				33.15	33.14			
Amon									
Josiah					34.3-4, 29-30				
Jehoahaz									
Jehoiakim									
Jehoiachin									
Zedekiah									

	Motifs of Punishment and Restoration							Assessment
Apostasy	Prophetic Word	Military Defeat	Exile	Repentance	Restoration	Sickness or Death as Punishment	Burial Notice	
12.1	12.5	12.4		12.6	12.7		12.16	negative
							13.23	?
	15.1; 16.7					?16.12	16.14	positive
18.1; 20.35	18.2, 16-17; 19.2-3; 20.14-17, 37			18.31 [19.4-5]	18.32		21.1	positive.
21.4-5, 11	21.12-15	21.8-10, 16-17				21.17-19	21.20	negative
22.3-5						22.6, 9	22.9	negative
24.17-18	24.19-22	24.23-24.				24.25	24.25	negative
(?25.6) 25.14	25.7-9, 15	25.22-24		(25.10		25.27	25.28	negative
26.16	26.18					26.19	26.23	?negative
							27.9	positive
28.2-4, 16, 22-25		28.5, 17-20	28.5, 8				28.27	negative
32.25				32.26	32.26	32.24	32.33	positive
33.2-3 33.22-23	33.10	33.11	33.11	33.12	33.13		33.20	negative
						33.24	–	negative
	34.23-24 (35.22)			34.29-30		(?35.23-24)	35.24	positive
			36.4				–	?
36.8			36.6				–	negative
36.9			36.10				–	negative
36.12-13	36.12-13	36.17	36.20				–	negative

BIBLIOGRAPHY

Ackroyd, P.R.
    1970   *Israel under Babylon and Persia* (Oxford: Oxford University Press).
    1973   *I and II Chronicles, Ezra, Nehemiah* (Torch Bible Commentaries; London: SCM Press).
    1987   *Studies in the Religious Tradition of the Old Testament* (London: SCM Press).
    1991   *The Chronicler in his Age* (JSOTSup, 101; Sheffield: JSOT Press).
Aharoni, Y.
    1979   *The Land of the Bible: A Historical Geography* (London: SCM Press, 2nd edn [1967]).
Albright, W.F.
    1924   'Egypt and the Early History of the Negev', *JPOS* 4: 146-47.
Allen, L.C.
    1974   *The Greek Chronicles: The Relation of the Septuagint of I and II Chronicles to the Massoretic Text. Part 1. The Translator's Craft. Part 2. Textual Criticism* (VTSup, 25, 27; Leiden: Brill).
    1988   'Kerygmatic Units in 1 and 2 Chronicles', *JSOT* 41: 21-36.
Alonso Schökel, L.
    1988   *A Manual of Hebrew Poetics* (AnBib; Rome: Pontifical Biblical Institute).
Auld, A.G.
    1994   *Kings without Privilege: David and Moses in the Story of the Bible's Kings* (Edinburgh: T. & T. Clark).
Bahat, D.
    1981   'The Wall of Manasseh in Jerusalem', *IEJ* 31: 235-36.
Barag, D.
    1966   'The Effects of the Tennes Rebellion on Palestine', *BASOR* 183: 6-12.
Barr, J.
    1961   *The Semantics of Biblical Language* (Oxford: Oxford University Press).
    1982   'Hebrew ʿd, especially at Job i. 18 and Neh. vii. 3', *JSS* 27: 177-88.
Bartlett, J.R.
    1969   'The use of the word ראש as a title in the Old Testament', *VT* 19: 205-24.
    1989   *Edom and the Edomites* (JSOTSup, 77; Sheffield: JSOT Press).
Becker, J.
    1980   *Messianic Expectation in the Old Testament* (ET; Philadelphia: Westminster Press [1977]).

1986   *1 Chronik* (Die Neue Echter Bibel; Würzburg: Echter Verlag).
1988   *2 Chronik* (Die Neue Echter Bibel; Würzburg: Echter Verlag).
Beentjes, P.C.
1993   'Tradition and Transformation. Aspects of Innerbiblical Interpretation in 2 Chronicles 20', *Bib* 74: 258-68.
Begg, C.T.
1982   ' "Seeking Yahweh" and the Purpose of Chronicles', *Louvain Studies* 9: 128-42.
1986   'The Significance of Jehoiachin's Release: A New Proposal', *JSOT* 36: 49-59.
1987a   'The Death of Josiah in Chronicles: Another View', *VT* 37: 1-8.
1987b   'The Fate of Judah's Four Last Kings in the Book of Chronicles', *OLP* 18: 79-85.
1989   'Constructing a Monster: the Chronicler's *Sondergut* in 2 Chronicles 21', *ABR* 37: 35-51.
Bendavid, A.
1972   *Parallels in the Bible* (Jerusalem: Carta).
Berg, S.B.
1980   'After the Exile: God and History in the Books of Chronicles and Esther', in J. Crenshaw and S. Sandmel (eds.), *The Divine Helmsman* (New York: Ktav).
Bickerman, E.
1966   *From Ezra to the Last of the Maccabees* (New York: Schocken Books [1947]).
Blenkinsopp, J.
1989   *Ezra–Nehemiah* (OTL; London: SCM Press).
Boström, L.
1990   *The God of the Sages* (ConBOT, 29; Stockholm: Almqvist & Wiksell).
Botterweck, G.J.
1956   'Zur Eigenart der chronistischen Davidgeschichte', *TQ* 136: 402-35.
Braun, R.L.
1971   'The Message of Chronicles: "Rally 'Round the Temple" ', *CTM* 42: 502-14.
1973   'Solomonic Apologetic in Chronicles', *JBL* 92: 503-16.
1976   'Solomon, the Chosen Temple Builder: the Significance of 1 Chronicles 22, 28, and 29 for the Theology of Chronicles', *JBL* 95: 581-90.
1977   'A Reconsideration of the Chronicler's Attitude toward the North', *JBL* 96: 59-62.
1979   'Chronicles, Ezra and Nehemiah: Theology and Literary History', in J. Emerton (ed.), *Studies in the Historical Books of the Old Testament* (VTSup, 30; Leiden: Brill): 52-64.
1986   *1 Chronicles* (WBC; Waco, TX: Word Books).
Brett, M.G.
1991a   'Motive and Intention in Genesis 1', *JTS* 42: 1-16.
1991b   *Biblical Criticism in Crisis? The Impact of the Canonical Approach on Old Testament Studies* (Cambridge: Cambridge University Press).

Bright, J.
  1977   *Covenant and Promise* (London: SCM Press).
Broshi, M.
  1974   'The Expansion of Jerusalem in the Reigns of Hezekiah and Manasseh', *IEJ* 24: 21-26.
Brueggemann, W.
  1985   *David's Truth in Israel's Imagination and Memory* (Philadelphia: Fortress Press).
Brunet, A.-M.
  1959   'La théologie du Chroniste: théocratie et messianisme', *Sacra Pagina* 1: 384-97.
Butler, T.C.
  1978   'A Forgotten Passage from a Forgotten Era (1 Chr xvi. 8–36)', *VT* 28: 142-50.
Caquot, A.
  1965   'Les "grâces de David". A propos d'Isaie 55/3b', *Semitica* 15: 45-59.
  1966   'Peut-on parler de messianisme dans l'oeuvre du Chroniste?', *RTP* 16: 110-20.
Carlson, R.A.
  1964   *David the Chosen King: A Traditio-historical Approach to the Second Book of Samuel* (Stockholm: Almqvist & Wiksell).
Childs, B.S.
  1967   *Isaiah and the Assyrian Crisis* (SBT, 2.3; London: SCM Press).
  1983   *Introduction to the Old Testament as Scripture* (Philadelphia: Fortress Press [1979]).
Christ, H.
  1977   *Blutvergießen im Alten Testament: Der gewaltsame Tod des Menschens untersucht am hebräischen Wort dam* (Basel).
Clines, D.J.A.
  1978   *The Theme of the Pentateuch* (JSOTSup, 10; Sheffield: JSOT Press).
  1990   *What Does Eve Do to Help? And Other Readerly Questions to the Old Testament* (JSOTSup, 94; Sheffield: JSOT Press).
Cody, A.
  1969   *A History of the Old Testament Priesthood* (AnBib, 35; Rome: Pontifical Biblical Institute).
Coggins, R.J.
  1975   *Samaritans and Jews: The Origins of Samaritanism Reconsidered* (Oxford: Oxford University Press).
  1976   *The First and Second Books of the Chronicles* (CBC; Cambridge: Cambridge University Press).
Coggins, R.J., and M.A. Knibb
  1979   *The First and Second Books of Esdras* (Cambridge: Cambridge University Press).
Cook, J.M.
  1983   *The Persian Empire* (London: Dent).
Cotterell, P., and M. Turner
  1989   *Linguistics and Biblical Interpretation* (London: SPCK).

Cross, F.M.
1958   *The Ancient Library of Qumran* (New Haven: Yale University Press).
1973   *Canaanite Myth and Hebrew Epic* (Cambridge, MA; Harvard University Press).
1975   'A Reconstruction of the Judean Restoration', *JBL* 94: 4-18.
Curtis, E.L., and A.A. Madsen
1910   *The Books of Chronicles* (ICC; New York: Charles Scribner's Sons).
Davies, P.R.
1990   'Marching as to War: 2 Chronicles 20', paper presented to SBL Seminar.
Davies, P.R. (ed.)
1991   *Second Temple Studies. 1. Persian Period* (JSOTSup, 117; Sheffield: JSOT Press).
1992   *In Search of 'Ancient Israel'* (JSOTSup, 148; Sheffield: JSOT Press).
Davies, W.D., and L. Finkelstein (eds.)
1984   *The Cambridge History of Judaism. I. Introduction; The Persian Period* (Cambridge: Cambridge University Press).
Day, P.L.
1988   *An Adversary in Heaven: Satan in the Hebrew Bible* (Atlanta: Scholars Press).
De Vries, S.J.
1986   'The Land's Sabbaths in 2 Chronicles 36.21', *PEGLMBS* 6: 96-103.
1987   'The Schema of Dynastic Endangerment in Chronicles', *PEGLMBS* 7: 59-77.
1988   'Moses and David as Cult Founders in Chronicles', *JBL* 107: 619-39.
1989   *1 and 2 Chronicles* (FOTL, 11; Grand Rapids: Eerdmans).
Deboys, D.G.
1990   'History and Theology in the Chronicler's Portrayal of Abijah', *Bib* 70: 48-62.
Dietrich, W.
1972   *Prophetie und Geschichte: eine redaktionsgeschichtliche Untersuchung zum deuteronomistischen Geschichtswerk* (FRLANT, 108; Göttingen; Vandenhoeck & Ruprecht).
Dillard, R.B.
1980   'The Reign of Asa (2 Chronicles 14–16): An Example of the Chronicler's Theological Method', *JETS* 23: 207-18.
1984   'Reward and Punishment in Chronicles: The Theology of Immediate Retribution', *WTJ* 46: 164-72.
1984   'The Literary Structure of the Chronicler's Solomon Narrative', *JSOT* 30: 85-93.
1987   *2 Chronicles* (WBC; Waco, TX: Word Books).
Dion, P.-E.
1985   'The Angel with the Drawn Sword (II [sic] Chr 21.16): An Exercise in Restoring the Balance of Text Criticism *and* Attention to Context', *ZAW* 97: 114-17.
Dorsey, D.A.
1991   *The Roads and Highways of Ancient Israel* (Baltimore, MD: Johns Hopkins University Press).

Driver, S.R.
1913   *An Introduction to the Literature of the Old Testament* (Edinburgh: T. & T. Clark).

Duke, R.K.
1990   *The Persuasive Appeal of the Chronicler: A Rhetorical Analysis* (JSOTSup, 88; Sheffield: JSOT Press).

Eichrodt, W.
1961   *Theology of the Old Testament*, II (ET; Philadelphia: Fortress Press).

Eissfeldt, O.
1965   *The Old Testament: An Introduction* (Oxford: Oxford University Press).

Elmslie, W.
1916   *The Book of Chronicles* (Cambridge: Cambridge University Press).

Eph'al, I.
1988   'Syria–Palestine under Achaemenid Rule', in *The Cambridge Ancient History* (Cambridge: Cambridge University Press, 2nd edn).

Eskenazi, T.C.
1986   'The Chronicler and the Composition of 1 Esdras', *CBQ* 48: 39-61.
1988   *In an Age of Prose: A Literary Approach to Ezra–Nehemiah* (Atlanta: Scholars Press).

Estes, D.J.
1991   'Metaphorical Sojourning in 1 Chronicles 29.15', *CBQ* 53: 45-49.

Even-Shoshan, A.
1989   *A New Concordance of the Old Testament* (Jerusalem: Kiryat Sefer).

Fishbane, M.
1985   *Biblical Interpretation in Ancient Israel* (Oxford: Oxford University Press).

Fohrer, G.
1970   *Introduction to the Old Testament* (ET; London: SPCK [1965]).

Freedman, D.N.
1961   'The Chronicler's Purpose', *CBQ* 23: 436-42.

Frye, R.N.
1984   *The History of Ancient Iran* (Munich: C.H. Beck).

Gabriel, I.
1990   *Friede über Israel. Eine Untersuchung zur Friedenstheologie in Chronik I, 10–II, 36* (Österreichische Biblische Studien, 10; Klosterneuburg: Österreichisches Katholisches Bibelwerk).

Galling, K.
1954   *Die Bücher der Chronik, Esra, Nehemia* (ATD: Göttingen: Vandenhoeck & Ruprecht).

Gammie, J.G.
1970   'The Theology of Retribution in the Book of Deuteronomy', *CBQ* 32: 1-12.

Garfinkel, Y.
1988   '2 Chr 11.5-10 Fortified Cities List and the *lmlk* Stamps—Reply to Nadav Na'aman', *BASOR* 271: 69-73.

Gershevitch, I. (ed.)
  1985   *The Cambridge History of Iran* (Cambridge: Cambridge University
          Press).
Goettsberger, J.
  1939   *Die Bücher der Chronik oder Paralipomenon* (HSAT, 4.1: Bonn:
          Hanstein).
Goldingay, J.
  1975   'The Chronicler as Theologian', *BTB* 5: 99-126.
Good, R.M.
  1985   'The Just War in Ancient Israel', *JBL* 104: 385-400.
Gordon, R.P.
  1986   *1 and 2 Samuel* (Exeter: Paternoster Press).
Graham, M.P.
  1985   'A Connection Proposed Between II Chr 24, 26 and Ezra 9–10', *ZAW*
          97: 256-58.
  1990   *The Utilization of 1 and 2 Chronicles in the Reconstruction of Israelite
          History in the Nineteenth Century* (Atlanta: Scholars Press).
Gray, J.
  1964   *I & II Kings* (London: SCM Press).
Greenspoon, L.J.
  1981   'The Origin of the Idea of Resurrection', in B. Halpern and
          J.D. Levenson (eds.), *Traditions in Transformation* (Winona Lake, IN:
          Eisenbrauns): 247-34.
Gunn, D.
  1989   in J.C. Exum (ed.), *Signs and Wonders: Biblical Texts in Literary
          Focus* (Scholars Press: Atlanta): 147.
Gunneweg, A.
  1981   'Zur Interpretation der Bücher Esra–Nehemia', in J.A. Emerton (ed.),
          Congress Volume, Vienna 1980 (VTSup, 32; Leiden: Brill): 146-61.
Hals, R.M.
  1989   *Ezekiel* (FOTL, 19; Grand Rapids: Eerdmans).
Hanson, P.D.
  1975   *The Dawn of Apocalyptic* (Philadelphia: Fortress Press).
  1986   *The People Called: The Growth of Community in the Bible* (San
          Francisco).
Haran, M.
  1978   *Temples and Temple Service in Ancient Israel: An Inquiry into the
          Character of Cult Phenomena and the Historical Setting of the Priestly
          School* (Oxford: Oxford University Press).
  1985   'Book-Size and the Device of Catch-Lines in the Biblical Canon', *JJS*
          36: 1-11.
  1986   'Explaining the Identical Lines at the End of Chronicles and the
          Beginning of Ezra', *Bible Review* 2: 18-20.
Hill, A.E.
  1983   'Patchwork Poetry or Reasoned Verse? Connective Structure in
          1 Chronicles xvi', *VT* 33: 97-101.
Hobbs, T.R.
  1985   *2 Kings* (WBC; Waco, TX: Word Books, 1985).

Hoffmann, H.-D.
 1980   *Reform und Reformen: Untersuchungen zu einem Grundthema der deuteronomistischen Geschichtschreibung* (Zürich: Theologischer Verlag).

Holladay, W.L.
 1958   *The Root sûbh in the Old Testament* (Leiden: Brill).

Hurvitz, A.
 1974   'The Evidence of Language in Dating the Priestly Code', *RB* 81: 24-56.

Im, T.S.
 1985   *Das Davidbild in den Chronikbüchern: David als Idealbild des theokratischen Messianismus für den Chronisten* (Frankfurt: Peter Lang).

Janowski, B.
 1982   *Sühne als Heilsgeschehen: Studien zur Sühnetheologie der Priesterschrift und zur Wurzel KPR im Alten Orient und im Alten Testament* (Neukirchen–Vluyn: Neukirchener Verlag).

Japhet, S.
 1968   'The Supposed Common Authorship of Chronicles and Ezra–Nehemiah Investigated Anew', *VT* 18: 330-71.
 1979   'Conquest and Settlement in Chronicles', *JBL* 98: 205-18.
 1982/83   'Sheshbazzar and Zerubbabel—Against the Background of the Religious and Historical Tendencies of Ezra–Nehemiah', *ZAW* 94: 66-98; 95: 218-29.
 1985   'The Historical Reliability of Chronicles. The History of the Problem and its Place in Biblical Research', *JSOT* 33: 83-107.
 1989   *The Ideology of the Book of Chronicles and its Place in Biblical Thought* (BEATAJ, 9; Frankfurt: Peter Lang [1977]).
 1991   'The Relationship between Chronicles and Ezra–Nehemiah', in J.A. Emerton (ed.), *Congress Volume: Leuven, 1989* (VTSup, 43; Leiden: Brill): 298-313.
 1993   *I & II Chronicles: A Commentary* (OTL; Louisville: Westminster/John Knox).

Johnson, M.D.
 1988   *The Purpose of the Biblical Genealogies* (Cambridge: Cambridge University Press, 2nd edn [1969]).

Johnstone, W.
 1983   'Chronicles, Canons and Contexts', *AUR* 50: 1-18.
 1986   'Guilt and Atonement: the Theme of 1 and 2 Chronicles', in J.D. Martin and P.R. Davies (eds.), *A Word in Season. Essays in Honour of William McKane* (JSOT Sup, 42; Sheffield: JSOT Press): 113-38.
 1987   'Reactivating the Chronicles Analogy in Pentateuchal Studies, with Special Reference to the Sinai Pericope in Exodus', *ZAW* 99: 16-37.

Jones, G.H.
 1993   *1 & 2 Chronicles* (OTG; Sheffield: JSOT Press).

Joyce, P.M.
1979   'Individual Responsibility in Ezekiel 18?', in E.A. Livingstone (ed.),
        Studia Biblica 1978. I. *Papers on Old Testament and Related Themes*
        (JSOTSup, 11; Sheffield: JSOT Press): 185-96.

Junge, E.
1937   *Der Wiederaufbau des Heerwesens des Reiches unter Josia* (Stuttgart:
        Kohlhammer).

Kaiser, O.
1975   *Introduction to the Old Testament* (ET; Oxford: Basil Blackwell
        [1973]): 186.

Kaiser, W.C.
1989   'The Unfailing Kindnesses Promised to David: Isaiah 55.3', *JSOT* 45:
        91-98.

Kartveit, M.
1989   *Motive und Schichten der Landtheologie in 1 Chronik 1–9* (ConBOT,
        29; Stockholm: Almqvist & Wiksell).

Kaufmann, Y.
1969   *The Religion of Israel* (New York: Schocken Books).

Keil, C.F.
1966   *The Books of the Kings* (ET; repr.; Grand Rapids: Eerdmans [1872]).
1988   *The Books of the Chronicles* (ET; repr.; Grand Rapids: Eerdmans
        [1870]).

Kenyon, K.
1974   *Digging Up Jerusalem* (London: Benn)

Kitchen, K.A.
1986   *The Third Intermediate Period in Egypt* (Warminster: Aris & Phillips,
        2nd edn [1973]).

Kittel, R.
1902   *Die Bücher der Chronik* (Göttingen: Vandenhoeck & Ruprecht).
1987   *The Purification Offering in the Priestly Literature* (JSOTSup, 56;
        Sheffield: JSOT Press, 1987).

Klein, R.W.
1966   'Studies in the Greek Texts of the Chronicler' (ThD dissertation,
        Harvard University).
1969   'Old Readings in 1 Esdras: The List of Returnees from Babylon [Ezra
        2//Nehemiah 7]', *HTR* 62: 99-107.
1983   'Abijah's Campaign against the North (II Chr 13)—What Were the
        Chronicler's Sources?', *ZAW* 95: 210-17.

Kleinig, J.
1993   *The Lord's Song: The Basis, Function and Significance of Choral
        Music in Chronicles* (JSOTSup, 156; Sheffield: JSOT Press).

Knoppers, G.N.
1990   'Rehoboam in Chronicles: Villain or Victim?', *JBL* 109: 423-40.
1991   'Reform and Regression: The Chronicler's Presentation of
        Jehoshaphat', *Bib* 72: 500-24.

Koch, K.
1955   'Gibt es ein Vergeltungsdogma im Alten Testament?', *ZTK* 52: 1-42.

Kooij, A. van der
    1991a   'Zur Frage des Anfangs des 1. Esrabuches', *ZAW* 103: 239-52.
    1991b   'On the Ending of the Book of 1 Esdras', in C.E. Cox (ed.), *VII Congress of the International Organization for Septuagint and Cognate Studies, Leiden 1989* (Atlanta: Scholars Press): 37-49.
Le Déaut, R., and J. Robert
    1971   *Targum des Chroniques* (2 vols.; AnBib; Rome: Pontifical Biblical Institute).
Lemke, W.E.
    1965   'The Synoptic Problem in the Chronicler's History', *HTR* 58: 349-63.
Levenson, J.D.
    1981   'From Temple to Synagogue: 1 Kings 8', in B. Halpern and J.D. Levenson (eds.), *Traditions in Transformation* (Winona Lake, IN: Eisenbrauns): 143-66.
    1984   'The Last Four Verses in Kings', *JBL* 103: 353-61.
Lohfink, N.
    1978   'Die Priesterschrift und die Geschichte', in W. Zimmerli *et al.* (eds.), *Congress Volume: Göttingen 1977* (Leiden: Brill): 189-224.
Long, B.O.
    1984   *1 Kings; with an Introduction to Historical Literature* (FOTL, 9; Grand Rapids: Eerdmans).
    1991   *2 Kings* (FOTL, 10; Grand Rapids: Eerdmans).
Lowery, R.H.
    1990   *The Reforming Kings: Cult and Society in First Temple Judah* (JSOTSup, 120; Sheffield: JSOT Press).
Martin-Achard, R.
    1992   'Resurrection', in D.N. Freedman *et al.* (eds.), *Anchor Bible Dictionary* (New York: Doubleday): V, 680-84.
Mason, R.
    1990   *Preaching the Tradition: Homily and Hermeneutics after the Exile* (Cambridge: Cambridge University Press).
Matthias, D.
    1984   ' "Levitische Predigt" und Deuteronomismus', *ZAW* 96: 23-49.
Mayes, A.
    1989   *The Old Testament in Sociological Perspective* (London: SCM Press).
McCarthy, D.J.
    1972   *Old Testament Covenant: A Survey of Current Opinions* (Oxford: Oxford University Press).
    1982   'Covenant and Law in Chronicles–Nehemiah', *CBQ* 44: 25-44.
McConville, J.G.
    1986a   '1 Chronicles 28.9—Yahweh "seeks out" Solomon', *JTS* 37: 105-108.
    1986b   'Ezra–Nehemiah and the Fulfilment of Prophecy', *VT* 36: 205-24.
    1989   'Narrative and Meaning in the Book of Kings', *Bib* 70: 31-49.
    1992   '1 Kings viii 46-53 and the Deuteronomic Hope', *VT* 52: 67-79.
McKenzie, S.L.
    1985   *The Chronicler's Use of the Deuteronomistic History* (HSM, 33; Atlanta: Scholars Press).

1991   *The Trouble With Kings: The Composition of the Book of Kings in the
            Deuteronomistic History* (Leiden: Brill).

Michaeli, F.
1967   *Les livres des Chroniques, d'Esdras et de Néhémie* (Neuchâtel:
            Delachaux & Niestlé).

Milgrom, J.
1976a   *Cult and Conscience* (Leiden: Brill).
1976b   'The Concept of ma'al in the Bible and the ANE', *JAOS* 96: 236-47.
1983   *Studies in Cultic Theology and Terminology* (Leiden: Brill).

Miller, J.M.
1987   'Rehoboam's Cities of Defense and the Levitical City List', in
            L.G. Perdue *et al.* (eds.), *Archaeology and Biblical Interpretation*
            (Atlanta: Scholars Press): 273-86.

Miller, J.M., and J.H. Hayes
1986   *A History of Ancient Israel and Judah* (London: SCM Press).

Moriarty, F.L.
1965   'The Chronicler's Account of Hezekiah's Reform', *CBQ* 27: 399-
            406.

Mosis, R.
1973   *Untersuchungen zur Theologie des chronistischen Geschichtswerkes*
            (Freiburger theologische Studien; Freiburg: Herder).

Mowinckel, S.
1958   *He That Cometh* (Oxford: Oxford University Press).

Myers, J.M.
1965   *I Chronicles and II Chronicles* (AB, 12; Garden City, NY: Doubleday).
1966   'The Kerygma of the Chronicler', *Int* 20: 259-73.

Na'aman, N.
1986   'Hezekiah's Fortified Cities and the LMLK Stamp', *BASOR* 261: 5-
            24.

Nelson, R.D.
1981   *The Double Redaction of the Deuteronomistic History* (JSOTSup, 18;
            Sheffield, JSOT Press).

Newsome, J.D.
1975   'Toward a New Understanding of the Chronicler and his Purposes',
            JBL 94: 201-17.

Noordtzij, A.
1940   'Les intentions du Chroniste', *RB* 49: 161-68.

North, R.
1963   'Theology of the Chronicler', *JBL* 82: 369-81.
1974   'Does Archeology Prove Chronicles' Sources?', in H.N. Bream *et al.*
            (eds.), *A Light Unto My Path: Old Testament Studies in Honor of
            Jacob M. Myers* (Philadelphia: Temple University Press): 375-401.

Noth, M.
1945   'Eine palästinische Lokalüberlieferung in 2 Chr 20', *ZDPV* 67: 45-77.
1967   *Überlieferungsgeschichtliche Studien: Die sammelnden und
            bearbeitenden Geschichtswerk im Alten Testament* (repr.; Darmstadt:
            Wissenschaftliche Buchgesellschaft [1943]).

Oeming, M.
1990   *Das wahre Israel: Die genealogische 'Vorhalle' 1 Chronik 1–9* (Stuttgart: Kohlhammer).
Patrick, D., and A. Scult
1990   *Rhetoric and Biblical Interpretation* (JSOTSup, 82; Sheffield: JSOT Press).
Petersen, D.L.
1977   *Late Israelite Prophecy: Studies in Deutero-Prophetic Literature and in Chronicles* (SBLMS, 23; Missoula, MT: Scholars Press).
Pfeiffer, R.H.
1952   *Introduction to the Old Testament* (New York: Harper [1948]).
Plöger, O.
1968   *Theocracy and Eschatology* (ET; Oxford: Basil Blackwell [1957]).
Pohlmann, K.-F.
1970   *Studien zum dritten Esra. Ein Beitrag zur Frage nach dem ursprünglichen Schluß des chronistischen Geschichtswerkes* (Göttingen: Vandenhoeck & Ruprecht).
1991   'Zur Frage von Korrespondenzen und Divergenzen zwischen den Chronikbüchern und dem Esra/Nehemia-Buch', in J.A. Emerton (ed.), *Congress Volume: Leuven, 1989* (VTSup, 43; Leiden: Brill): 313-30.
Polzin, R.
1976   *Late Biblical Hebrew: Toward an Historical Typology of Biblical Hebrew Prose* (HSM, 12; Missoula, MT: Scholars Press).
Porton, G.
1981   'Defining Midrash', in J. Neusner (ed.), *The Study of Ancient Judaism* (New York: Ktav): 55-92.
Provan, I.W.
1988   *Hezekiah and the Books of Kings: A Contribution to the Debate about the Composition of the Deuteronomistic History* (Berlin: de Gruyter).
Rad, G. von
1930   *Das Geschichtsbild des chronistischen Werkes* (BWANT, 4.3; Stuttgart: Kohlhammer).
1951   *Der heilige Krieg im alten Israel* (Göttingen: Vandenhoeck & Ruprecht).
1953   *Studies in Deuteronomy* (ET; London: SCM Press [1948]).
1962   *Old Testament Theology*, I (London: SCM Press [1957]).
1966   *The Problem of the Hexateuch and Other Essays* (Edinburgh and London: Oliver & Boyd).
Rainey, A.F.
1988   'A Date for the Samaria Ostraca', *BASOR* 272: 69-74.
Riley, W.
1993   *King and Cultus in Chronicles: Worship and the Reinterpretation of History* (JSOTSup, 160; Sheffield: JSOT Press).
Rogerson, J.W.
1970   'The Hebrew Conception of Corporate Personality', *JTS* 21: 1-16.
1981   'Corporate Personality', in D.N. Freedman *et al.* (eds.), *Anchor Bible Dictionary* (Winona Lake, IN: Eisenbrauns): II, 1156-57.

1992   W.M.L. de Wette, Founder of Modern Biblical Criticism: An
            Intellectual Biography (JSOTSup, 126; Sheffield: JSOT Press).

Rooker, M.F.
1990   Biblical Hebrew in Transition: The Language of the Book of Ezekiel
            (JSOTSup, 90; Sheffield: JSOT Press).

Rothstein, J.W., and J. Hänel
1927   Das erste Buch der Chronik (KAT, 18.2; Leipzig: Reichart).

Rudolph, W.
1952   'Der Aufbau der Asa-Geschichte', VT 2: 367-71.
1954   'Problems in the Book of Chronicles', VT 4: 401-409.
1955   Chronikbücher (HAT, 21; Tübingen: Mohr).

Saebø, M.
1980   'Messianism in Chronicles? Some Remarks to the Old Testament
            Background of the New Testament Christology', HBT 2: 85-109.

Sailhamer, J.
1989   '1 Chronicles 21.1—A Study in Inner-Biblical Interpretation', Trinity
            Journal 10: 33-48.

Schenker, A.
1982   Der Mächtige im Schmelzofen des Mitleids: Eine Interpretation von
            2 Sam 24 (Göttingen: Vandenhoeck & Ruprecht).

Schmidt, L.
1983   'Deuteronomistisches Geschichtswerk', in H.-J. Boecker et al. (eds.),
            Altes Testament (Neukirchen–Vluyn: Neukirchener Verlag): 112-19.

Schniedewind, W.M.
1991   'The Source Citations of Manasseh: King Manasseh in History and
            Homily', VT 51: 450-61.

Seeligmann, I.
1953   'Voraussetzungen der Midraschexegese', in G.W. Anderson et al.
            (eds.), Congress Volume: Copenhagen 1953 (VTSup, 1; Leiden: Brill):
            150-81.
1979–80   'The Beginnings of Midrash in the Book of Chronicles', Tarbiz 49:
            14-32.

Segal, J.B.
1963   The Hebrew Passover: From the Earliest Times to A.D. 70 (London
            Oriental Series, 12; New York: Oxford University Press).

Selman, M.J.
1989   'The Kingdom of God in the Old Testament', TynBul 40.2: 161-83.
1994a   1 Chronicles (TOTC; Leicester: IVP).
1994b   2 Chronicles (TOTC; Leicester: IVP).

Shaver, J.R.
1989   Torah and the Chronicler's History Work (Missoula, MT: Scholars
            Press).

Shiloh, Y.
1984   'Excavations at the City of David, I, 1978–82', Qedem 19 (Jerusalem).

Shinan, A., and Y. Zakovitch
1986   'Midrash on Scripture and Midrash within Scripture', in S. Japhet
            (ed.), Studies in Bible (Scripta Hierosolymitana, 31 Jerusalem: Kiryat
            Sefer): 257-77.

Ska, J.L.
1990   *'Our Fathers Have Told Us.' Introduction to and Analysis of Hebrew Narrative* (AnBib; Rome: Pontifical Biblical Institute).
Smith, M.
1984   'Jewish Religious Life in the Persian Period', in W.D. Davies and L. Finkelstein (eds.), *The Cambridge History of Judaism*. I. *Introduction: The Persian Period* (Cambridge: Cambridge University Press): 221-48
Soggin, J.A.
1981   *Judges* (London: SCM Press): 80-81.
Steck, O.H.
1968   'Das Problem theologischer Strömungen in nachexilischer Zeit', *EvT* 28: 445-58.
Stern, E.
1982   *The Material Culture of the Land of the Bible 538–332 BC* (Warminster: Aris & Phillips)
Stinespring, W.F.
1961   'Eschatology in Chronicles', *JBL* 80: 209-19.
Strübind, K.
1991   *Tradition als Interpretation in der Chronik: König Josaphat als Paradigma chronistischer Hermeneutik und Theologie* (Berlin: de Gruyter).
Talmon, S.
1991   'The Internal Diversification of Judaism in the Early Second Temple Period', in S. Talmon (ed), *Jewish Civilization in the Hellenistic-Roman Period* (JSPSup, 10; Sheffield: JSOT Press).
Talshir, D.
1988   'A Reinvestigation of the Linguistic Relationship between Chronicles and Ezra–Nehemiah', *VT* 38: 165-93.
Tangberg, K.A.
1987   *Die prophetische Mahnrede: Form- und traditionsgeschichtliche Studien zum prophetischen Umkehrruf* (Göttingen: Vandenhoeck & Ruprecht).
Thiele, E.R.
1985   *The Mysterious Numbers of the Hebrew Kings* (Grand Rapids: Zondervan, 3rd edn).
Thompson, J.A.
1979   'Israel's Haters', *VT* 29: 200-205.
Thompson, M.E.W.
1982   *Situation and Theology: Old Testament Interpretations of the Syro-Ephraimite War* (Sheffield: Almond Press).
Throntveit, M.A.
1982   'Linguistic Analysis and the Question of Authorship in Chronicles, Ezra and Nehemiah', *VT* 32: 201-16.
1987   *When Kings Speak: Royal Speech and Royal Prayer in Chronicles* (SBLDS, 93; Atlanta: Scholars Press).
1988   'Hezekiah in the Books of Chronicles', in D.J. Lull (ed.), *SBL Seminar Papers 27* (Atlanta: Scholars Press).

Torrey, C.C.
1954   *The Chronicler's History of Israel: Chronicles-Ezra-Nehemiah Restored to its Original Form* (New Haven, CT: Yale University Press).

Ulrich, E.C.
1978   *The Qumran Text of Samuel and Josephus* (HSM, 19; Missoula, MT: Scholars Press).

Van Seters, J.
1983   *In Search of History: Historiography in the Ancient World and the Origins of Biblical History* (New Haven, CT: Yale University Press).

Vaux, R. de
1961   *Ancient Israel: Its Life and Institutions* (ET; New York: McGraw–Hill; [1958]).
1964   *Studies on Old Testament Sacrifice* (Cardiff: University of Wales Press).

Veijola, T.
1975   *Die ewige Dynastie: David und die Entstehung seiner Dynastie nach der deuteronomistischen Darstellung* (Helsinki: Soumalainen Tiedeakatemia).

Wagner, S.
1978   דרש, *TDOT*, III: 293-307.

Walters, S.D.
1991   'Saul of Gibeon', *JSOT* 52: 61-76.

Waltke, B.K., and M. O'Connor
1990   *An Introduction to Biblical Hebrew Syntax* (Winona Lake, IN: Eisenbrauns).

Webb, B.G.
1987   *The Book of the Judges: An Integrated Reading* (JSOTSup, 43; Sheffield: JSOT Press).

Weinberg, J.P.
1979   'Das Eigengut in den Chronikbüchern', *OLP* 10: 161-81.
1985   'Krieg und Frieden im Weltbild des Chronisten', *OLP* 16: 11-129.

Weiser, A.
1961   *Introduction to the Old Testament* (ET; London: Darton, Longman & Todd [1948]).

Welch, A.C.
1935   *Post-Exilic Judaism* (Edinburgh and London: Blackwood).
1939   *The Work of the Chronicler: Its Purpose and its Date* (London: British Academy).

Wellhausen, J.
1885   *Prolegomena to the History of Israel* (Edinburgh: T. & T. Clark [1878]).

Welten, P.
1973   *Geschichte und Geschichtsdarstellung in den Chronikbüchern* (Neukirchen–Vluyn: Neukirchener Verlag).
1979   'Lade–Tempel–Jerusalem: zur Theologie der Chronikbücher', in A.H.J. Gunneweg and O. Kaiser (eds.), *Textgemäß: Aufsätze und Beiträge zur Hermeneutik des Alten Testaments* (Göttingen; Vandenhoeck & Ruprecht): 169-83.

Wenham, G.
 1979   *The Book of Leviticus* (Grand Rapids: Eerdmans): 332.
 1987   *Genesis 1–15* (Waco, TX: Word Books).
Westermann, C.
 1969   *Handbook to the Old Testament* (ET; London: SPCK [1962]).
 1969   *Isaiah 40–66* (ET; OTL; London: SCM Press [1966]).
Wette, W.M.L. de
 1806   *Beiträge zur Einleitung in das Alte Testament,* I (Halle: Schimmelpfenning).
White, H.
 1981   'The Value of Narrativity in the Representation of Reality', in W.T.J. Mitchell (ed.), *On Narrative* (Chicago: University of Chicago Press): 1-23.
Whitelam, K.W.
 1979   *The Just King: Monarchical Judicial Authority in Ancient Israel* (JSOTSup, 12; Sheffield: JSOT Press).
Wilda, G.
 1959   *Das Königsbild des chronistischen Geschichtswerkes* (Bonn: Rheinische Friedrich-Wilhelms-Universität).
Willi, T.
 1972   *Die Chronik als Auslegung. Untersuchungen zur literarischen Gestaltung der historischen Überlieferung Israels* (FRLANT, 106; Göttingen: Vandenhoeck & Ruprecht).
 1991   *1 Chronik* (BKAT; Neukirchen–Vluyn: Neukirchener Verlag).
Williams, R.J.
 1976   *Hebrew Syntax: An Outline* (Toronto: University of Toronto, 2nd edn).
Williamson, H.G.M.
 1973   'A Note on 1 Chronicles vii. 12', *VT* 23: 375-79.
 1976   'The Accession of Solomon in the Books of Chronicles', *VT* 26: 351-61.
 1977a   *Israel in the Books of Chronicles* (Cambridge: Cambridge University Press).
 1977b   'Eschatology in Chronicles', *TynBul* 28: 115-54.
 1978   ' "The Sure Mercies of David": Subjective or Objective Genitive?', *JSS* 23: 68-90.
 1979a   'Sources and Redaction in the Chronicler's Genealogy of Judah', *JBL* 98: 351-59.
 1979b   'The Origins of the Twenty-Four Priestly Courses: A Study of 1 Chronicles 23–27', in J.A. Emerton (ed.), *Studies in the Historical Books of the Old Testament* (VTSup, 30; Leiden: Brill): 251-68.
 1981   ' "We are yours, O David." The Setting and Purpose of 1 Chronicles 12.1-23', *OTS* 21: 164-76.
 1982   'The Death of Josiah and the Continuing Development of the Deuteronomistic History', *VT* 32: 242-48.
 1982   *1 and 2 Chronicles* (NCB; London: Marshall, Morgan & Scott).

1983a	'The Dynastic Oracle in the Books of Chronicles', in A. Rofé and Y. Zakovitch (eds.), *Essays on the Bible and the Ancient World. Festschrift I.L. Seeligmann* (Jerusalem: Rubinstein), III: 305-18.
1983b	'The Composition of Ezra i-vi', *JTS* 34: 1-30.
1985	*Ezra, Nehemiah* (WBC; Waco, TX: Word Books).
1987a	'Reliving the Death of Josiah: A Reply to C.T. Begg', *VT* 37: 9-15.
1987b	'Did the Author of Chronicles also Write the Books of Ezra and Nehemiah?', *Bible Review* 3: 56-59.
1988	'History', in D.A. Carson and H.G.M. Williamson (eds.), *It is Written: Scripture Citing Scripture: Essays in Honour of Barnabas Lindars* (Cambridge: Cambridge University Press): 25-38.
1991	'The Temple in the Books of Chronicles', in W. Horbury (ed.), *Templum Amicitiae: Essays on the Second Temple Presented to Ernst Bammel* (JSNTSup, 48; Sheffield: JSOT Press): 15-31.

Wilson, R.R.

1975	'The Old Testament Genealogies in Recent Research', *JBL* 94: 169-89.
1977	*Genealogy and History in the Biblical World* (New Haven, CT: Yale University Press).
1979	'Between "Azel" and "Azel": Interpreting Biblical Genealogies', *BA* 42: 11-22.
1984	*Sociological Approaches to the Old Testament* (Philadelphia: Fortress Press).

Wolff, H.W.

1961	'Das Kerygma des deuteronomistischen Geschichtswerks', *ZAW* 73: 171-86.
1977	*Joel and Amos* (Philadelphia: Fortress Press).

Wright, J.W.

1989	'The Origin and Function of 1 Chronicles 23–27' (PhD dissertation, University of Notre Dame).
1990	'Guarding the Gates. 1 Chronicles 26.1-19 and the Roles of Gatekeepers in Chronicles', *JSOT* 48: 69-81.
1991	'The Legacy of David in Chronicles. The Narrative Function of 1 Chronicles 23–27', *JBL* 110: 229-42.

Würthwein, E.

1984	*Die Bücher der Könige. 1 Kön 17–2 Kön 25* (Göttingen: Vandenhoeck & Ruprecht): 481-84.

Yadin, Y.

1963	*The Art of Warfare in Biblical Lands* (London: Weidenfeld & Nicolson, 1963).

Younger, K.L.

1990	*Ancient Conquest Accounts: A Study in Ancient Near Eastern and Biblical History Writing* (JSOTSup, 98; Sheffield: JSOT Press).

Zalewski, S.

1989	'The Purpose of the Story of the Death of Saul in 1 Chronicles x', *VT* 39: 449-67.

Zimmerli, W.

 1968 *Der Mensch und seine Hoffnung im Alten Testament* (Göttingen: Vandenhoeck & Ruprecht).

Zunz, L.

 1966 *Die gottesdienstlichen Vorträge der Juden historisch entwickelt* (repr.; Darmstadt: Wissenschaftliche Buchgesellschaft [1832]).

INDEXES

INDEX OF REFERENCES

OLD TESTAMENT

Reference	Pages
16.35	173-75, 185
16.36	171, 175
16.37-38	199
16.37	170, 171
16.38	78
16.39-42	170
16.40-41	168, 170, 171
16.40	169
16.43	152
17–20	157
17.3-15	70
17.4-14	59, 159, 168, 237
17.4-5	197
17.5	181
17.9-10	47, 237
17.9	184
17.10-14	92, 147, 148, 230
17.10	151, 157, 162, 197
17.11-12	231
17.11	148, 154, 159
17.12	23, 83, 92, 157, 159, 162
17.13-14	161
17.13	69, 83, 161
17.14	67, 157, 185, 211, 212
17.16-27	54
17.23	161
17.27	189
18–20	80, 197
18.1-3	191
18.5	207
18.6	191
18.11	126
18.12-13	126
18.13	81
21–29	157
21–22	107
21	72, 75, 80, 108
21.1–22.1	79, 83
21.1	79, 80
21.2-6	79
21.2	81, 181
21.3	81, 82
21.5	81
21.6	79, 82
21.7	79, 81, 82
21.8-14	79
21.8	81
21.9-14	82
21.9-13	81
21.12	79, 81, 82
21.13	35, 82
21.14	81, 82, 85
21.15-27	82
21.15	81, 82
21.16	79, 81
21.17-26	79
21.17	81, 82, 107
21.18-27	82
21.18	92
21.22-25	181
21.26–22.1	79
21.26	83, 162, 168
21.27	79, 81
21.29-30	82
21.30	51, 52, 79, 81
22–29	80, 83
22	72, 75, 83, 199
22.1	79, 82, 87, 92
22.2-5	83
22.2-4	27
22.2-3	83
22.3	83
22.6-19	188
22.6-13	147
22.6	231
22.7-19	231
22.7	173
22.8	84, 85
22.9-10	159
22.9	83, 198
22.10	83, 92, 231
22.11-13	83, 85
22.11	152
22.12	36, 147
22.13	53, 83, 152, 161, 170
22.18-19	231
22.18	197
22.19	51-53, 188
22.22	152
22.24	152
22.26	152
23–27	26, 27, 83
23.2-6	170
23.2-5	169
23.3	147
23.25-32	169, 170
23.28-31	170
23.30-31	170
25.1-31	169
25.1-6	170, 171
25.1-2	199
26.1-4	78
26.4-6	78
26.5	78
26.28	69
28	72, 83
28.1–29.9	199
28.1	184
28.2-10	147, 188, 231
28.2	83, 142, 198
28.3	84, 85
28.4-5	165
28.5-7	159
28.5-6	92
28.5	185, 211, 212
28.6-7	160
28.6	83, 157, 231
28.7	83, 160, 161
28.8-9	85, 86
28.8	83, 86, 181, 188, 196, 238
28.9-10	53, 83, 86
28.9	51, 52, 57
28.10–29.30	83
28.10	152, 160
28.11	23
28.12	23, 152

OTHER ANCIENT REFERENCES

JOURNAL FOR THE STUDY OF THE OLD TESTAMENT

Supplement Series